THE ROOSEVELT
REVOLUTION

A Da Capo Press Reprint Series

FRANKLIN D. ROOSEVELT
AND THE ERA OF THE NEW DEAL

GENERAL EDITOR: FRANK FREIDEL
Harvard University

THE ROOSEVELT REVOLUTION

First Phase

by Ernest K. Lindley

DA CAPO PRESS • NEW YORK • 1974

Library of Congress Cataloging in Publication Data

Lindley, Ernest Kidder, 1899-
  The Roosevelt revolution: first phase.

  (Franklin D. Roosevelt and the era of the New Deal)
  Reprint of the ed. published by Viking Press, New
York.
  1. United States—Politics and government—1933-
1945. 2. Roosevelt, Franklin Delano, Pres. U. S., 1882
-1945. 3. United States—Economic policy—1933-1945.
I. Title. II. Series.
E806.L56   1974   320.9'73'0917   74-637
ISBN 0-306-70651-2

This Da Capo Press edition of *The Roosevelt Revolution*
is an unabridged republication of the first edition
published in 1933 in New York. It is reprinted with the
permission of the author.

Published by Da Capo Press, Inc.
A Subsidiary of Plenum Publishing Corporation
227 West 17th Street, New York, N.Y. 10011

The
Roosevelt Revolution

·

FIRST PHASE

·

The Roosevelt Revolution

✧

FIRST PHASE

✧

By ERNEST K. LINDLEY

NEW YORK
THE VIKING PRESS
1933

DISTRIBUTED IN CANADA BY
THE MACMILLAN COMPANY OF CANADA, LTD.
PRINTED IN U. S. A.

THIS BOOK IS DEDICATED TO

B.G.L.

WHO DOESN'T THINK THE ROOSEVELT REVOLUTION
IS A REAL REVOLUTION YET. (AND SHE MAY BE RIGHT.)

Preface

THE primary purpose of this book is to bring order out of confusion—insofar as there has been order instead of confusion. To a large extent I have used a chronological framework. Much that may have seemed bewildering since March 4, 1933, explains itself when it is correlated with its background and with contemporary events. The vast social experiment now under way in the United States is moving too rapidly to admit firm conclusions. It is easier and, to me, more enlightening to look at what has happened and to examine why it happened than to try to capture a fluid state of affairs in a hard analytical mold. On the whole, I have adhered to the main line of action. However, I have followed my own inclination in slighting aspects which unquestionably are worthy of more detailed treatment and in devoting attention to two or three minor matters which seem to me to have current interest.

The book is tentative. I reserve the right to amend it and enlarge it as errors or new facts come to my attention. I have written primarily from my own knowledge, accumulated as a newspaperman who has observed Franklin D. Roosevelt at close range since he became Governor of New York in 1929. In refreshing my recollection I have used the files of the *New York Herald Tribune* and of various periodicals. I found particularly useful the excellent summaries in *News-Week* and some of the articles in the *Literary Digest* during the recent months that it has been edited by Arthur Draper.

I have tried to throw light on a few dark spots with information which, so far as I know, has not been published heretofore. For most of this information I am indebted to individuals who because of their official positions must remain anonymous. I wish to acknowledge also courtesies and assistance of various kinds from several of my newspaper colleagues, especially Theodore C. Wallen, chief of the Washington Bureau of the *New York Herald Tribune,* and J. Fred Essary, chief of the Washington Bureau of the *Baltimore Sun.* I cannot list all the other people to whom I owe thanks for assistance, but among them are: Eileen Douglas, Virginia Grimes, Amy and Hyman Schroeder, and Irene and Louis Stern. Most of all I am indebted to Betty Grimes Lindley. The passage about Mrs. Roosevelt is chiefly hers, and at several other points she stated my ideas so much better than I could state them that I calmly plagiarized her language.

ERNEST K. LINDLEY.

Contents

The
Roosevelt Revolution

·

FIRST PHASE

·

I

Roots of the Revolution

ONCE during his campaign for the Presidency in 1932 Franklin D. Roosevelt used the word "revolution." It was in a very short impromptu speech to a group of Democratic party workers in Indianapolis on October 20. In his informal manner, Mr. Roosevelt expressed the hope that Election Day would bring not just a victory or a landslide, "but a revolution—the right kind, the only kind of revolution this nation can stand for—a revolution at the ballot box." A few newspapermen who thought they knew the full implications of Mr. Roosevelt's program made the most of that sentence, but it received only passing comment.

Certainly there was nothing of the revolutionary in the manner or language of this charming, cultured aristocrat with his factual speeches and leaven of gay humor. He promised no utopia; he calmly asserted that he knew no patent remedies and did not believe in them; he used no fervid oratory; he had no glowing battle cries to inflame the emotions of the electorate. In fact, he seemed deliberately to shrink from the tempting political advantage in fanning the smoldering discontent throughout the country.

Mr. Roosevelt was no great popular idol during the presidential campaign of 1932. Vast crowds came out to look at him eagerly, hopefully. They liked him but they went away still skeptical. The terrific pre-convention at-

tack on Mr. Roosevelt, keyed to Walter Lippmann's un-
forgettable description of him as a pleasant gentleman
who had no important qualifications for the Presidency,
had left its effect. The country yearned for a Messiah,
Mr. Roosevelt did not look or sound like a Messiah. He
was not even a Bryan. But he was the one sure means of
rebuking the party in power. The depression had become
unbearable to great masses of the electorate. They wanted
a change, and the vote on November 8 showed that they
wanted a change more than they had ever wanted it
before.

Within sixty of those breath-taking days that followed
March 4, the arrival of a revolution had been proclaimed
by several discerning periodicals, and the curiosity of the
world focused on the American Experiment. It was a
bloodless revolution, to be sure. In fact, a completely
peaceful revolution accomplished without an ounce of
armed force, or the threat of its use, without a black
shirt, a brown shirt, an underground organization. On
the contrary, it was effected with the most scrupulous ob-
servance of the recognized processes of law-making and
meticulous regard for the historic rights of free speech and
free assemblage. Yet the word "revolution" sprang naturally to the lips. No other word seems strong enough to
describe a change so swift and so fundamental. The United
States had embarked on an experiment in new economic
relationships of revolutionary audacity and magnitude.
As an incident to this, President Roosevelt had been endowed with greater power than any American had possessed in peace-time since the adoption of the Constitution. Probably never before had a change so abrupt and
far-reaching been wrought peaceably within the framework of democratic institutions. It was a revolution

shaped by one man yet certainly impelled by mass forces. Although there were increasing cries of pain or fright from the old régime as a few hallowed economic shrines sank from view, it was, in its initial stages, almost a co-operative revolution.

The revolution was thoroughly saturated with cherished American ideals. Its objectives were security, happiness, self-respect, a decent standard of living for the ordinary man, the idea of generally distributed well-being expressed in the Declaration of Independence, or in any other summary of the aspiration of a democratic or socialistic state. In Professor Tugwell's words: "What we are doing is simply, in the light of modern realities, to seek trails toward the oldest aspirations of the race."

Herbert Hoover could subscribe to the avowed objective of the revolution. Yet Mr. Hoover solemnly (and correctly) warned the country that the campaign of 1932 was more than a contest between two men and two parties, that it was a contest "between two philosophies of government." To that much Mr. Roosevelt heartily agreed. Mr. Hoover went on to assert that the "inchoate new deal" propounded by Mr. Roosevelt would "undermine and destroy the American system" and "crack the timbers of the Constitution." From that Mr. Roosevelt stoutly dissented. He very naturally defended his own philosophy as the true embodiment of the American ideal. And, as he later demonstrated, he considered the Constitution too flexible to crack. The timbers which he heard cracking were those of the American economic structure, as it gradually broke beneath the weight of the greatest depression in the country's history.

The words "conservative" and "liberal" conveniently serve to describe the philosophies of government which joined in the contest of 1932. But an eighteenth- or nineteenth-century definition of liberalism will not suffice to denote Franklin D. Roosevelt's political philosophy— as many observers who had placidly considered themselves liberals these many years found to their dismay when the Revolution of 1933 swiftly unfolded. Although it had older roots, the Revolution of 1933 was the culmination or fulfillment of economic forces that began to manifest themselves in political dissent in the United States during the last quarter of the nineteenth century. In that period forceful evidence began to appear that the method of unbridled exploitation by which the country had been developed since the first settlers landed was no longer giving complete satisfaction. Free land, the historic outlet for the rugged individualism of the man at the bottom, was almost gone. As the American economy was elaborated by the growth of industry and finance, the farmer, a rugged individualist, found that the fruits of his enterprise were being wrested from him by other more powerful individualists and by the operations of economic forces which he could not control. The small business man began to suffer this same experience. The demand went up for control of the railroads and of the trusts. The protests manifested in the Granger and Populist movements broadened and sharpened as the American economic machine grew. When times were relatively good, the protests subsided. When times were bad, they became formidable and won or were appeased with concessions.

There is no need to trace the economic and political development of the United States in the twentieth century. But it is pertinent to inquire into Mr. Roosevelt's political philosophy. The wide publicity given the brilliant college professors who came to be known as his brains trust may have given the impression that they provided him with a political philosophy. It would be reasonable to assume, also, that, skillful politician that he undoubtedly is, he merely adopted a political philosophy and program designed to make the economic depression of 1929–33 his springboard to the Presidency. As a matter of fact—as his speeches and career demonstrated—Mr. Roosevelt had developed his political philosophy long before the depression began and long before he met any member of his brains trust. The brilliant gentlemen in that group were among those who helped to apply Mr. Roosevelt's philosophy to the specific conditions of 1932–33. Mr. Roosevelt did not recruit his professorial advisers to provide him with a point of view; he drew them to him because their point of view was akin to his own.

What are the main roots of Mr. Roosevelt's political philosophy? Some of them are obvious: Jeffersonian Democracy, the Progressivism of Theodore Roosevelt, the New Freedom of Woodrow Wilson. Mr. Roosevelt is not only firmly imbedded by his antecedents in the American tradition; he is exceptionally well versed in American history, particularly that of the later colonial period and early years of the Republic. Go back through his speeches and you will find that he has paid his share of tribute to the Founding Fathers. But it is significant that he has not quoted them as the authors of doctrine to be observed reverently for all time to come. He has had the habit, rather, of extolling them for their boldness and intelligence in handling the practical situations with which they were confronted. Of that group of men, Jefferson has always been his idol. The bond is much stronger than that of the ordinary born-and-bred Democrat for the founder of his party. Possibly it is the affinity of one country squire of democratic beliefs for another. As conditions have changed, it is useless to look for a literal expression of Jeffersonian political philosophy in the Roosevelt Revolution. The association is to be found rather in Mr. Roosevelt's belief in the good sense and rights of the average man and elevation of the "larger good" above privilege. More specifically it appears in Mr. Roosevelt's leaning toward decentralization of industry and his strong emotional attachment to an economic system based on the small individual farmer.

Theodore Roosevelt was at the height of his career during Franklin D. Roosevelt's youth and young manhood, and perhaps family ties, drawn closer by marriage, heightened the younger Roosevelt's admiration for the dynamic champion of the Square Deal. Among Theodore Roosevelt's contributions to the elements of the Roosevelt Revolution may be noted: a stanch nationalism, a conception of a broader nationalist interest rising above class and sectional cleavages, the belated movement for conservation of national resources.

Woodrow Wilson was Franklin D. Roosevelt's next political mentor. As the first decade of the century closed, Mr. Wilson perceived the fundamental ways in which the closing of the frontier and the growth of the corporation had changed the conditions of life in the United States. Despite the anti-trust laws, the corporation had developed into "a little economic state," as Mr. Wilson termed it in one of his addresses. The scope of free initiative had narrowed; the life of the ordinary man was more and more at the mercy of economic powers, personal and institutional, over which he had no control. Mr. Wilson said: "We are facing the necessity of fitting a new social organization to the happiness and prosperity of the great body of citizens, for we are conscious that the new order of society has not been made to fit and provide the convenience or prosperity of the average man." Mr. Wilson's beginning toward the remodeling of the American social system was tragically interrupted by the World War venture.

During the next twenty years the factors noted by Mr. Wilson were tremendously accentuated, particularly by the rapid industrial and financial growth of the United States during the World War and in the third decade of the century. Mr. Wilson's little economic states grew into an amorphous empire controlled by a comparatively small number of financiers. These twenty years embraced Mr. Roosevelt's public career up to the time he emerged as an active candidate for the Presidency. The influences of Jefferson, Theodore Roosevelt, and Wilson merged with Mr. Roosevelt's own experience and observation of the contemporary world to form his own political or economic philosophy.

In 1928 when laissez-faire was holy and "less government in business" was a favored watchword of conservative thought in both parties, Mr. Roosevelt chose to incorporate in a small official sketch of himself this dissenting summary of his own viewpoint: "The phrase 'the best government is the least government' is a sound phrase, but it applies only to the simplification of governmental machinery and to the prevention of improper interference with the legitimate activities of the citizens. But the nation or state which is unwilling by governmental action to tackle new problems caused by the immense increase of population and the astounding strides of modern science is headed for a decline and ultimate death from inaction."

In his speeches, over a period of many years, Mr. Roosevelt repeatedly stressed this note: "What I emphasize, what I plead recognition for, is the fact that in the thirty years of the twentieth century more vital changes in the whole structure of civilization have taken place than in the three hundred years which went before."

Mr. Roosevelt called himself a "liberal" or a "progressive," preferring the latter description no doubt because it was better suited to the practical political objective which he sought. His consistent ambition for many years prior to his election to the Presidency was to form a new liberal party by attaching the Republican Progressives and miscellaneous liberals to the Democratic party, thus effecting a new political alignment which had meaning. The Democrats began angling for the Progressives of the Republican party as soon as Theodore Roosevelt abruptly ended the Bull Moose movement by supporting Charles E. Hughes for the Presidency in 1916. In that year Woodrow Wilson got enough help from the Progressives to sweep the West and win re-election by a hair, despite his loss of the East. There was no important economic issue in the post-war election of 1920. In 1924 both major parties nominated conservatives and the Progressives rallied behind LaFollette. In 1928 Alfred E. Smith made an earnest bid for the support of the dissident Republicans of the West, but was frustrated by other issues. Franklin D. Roosevelt, a progressive Democrat, bearing the surname most intimately associated with progressive Republicanism, endowed with many other political qualifications, and lacking marked political liabilities, was the ideal man to effect the new political alignment. That, at any rate, was the rôle he had cut out for himself long before the country started sliding into the depression of 1929.

Mr. Roosevelt's program as Governor of New York was in complete accord with his political philosophy and ultimate objectives in the national political arena. His programs for the relief of agriculture, reforestation, redistribution of population through better utilization of the land, public development of water power, more rigid control of public utilities, old age pensions, unemployment insurance, and unemployment relief marked his dissent from the creed of laissez-faire. Long before the presidential campaign of 1932 Mr. Roosevelt had emerged as the leading Democratic exponent of a modern liberalism of which the kernel was readiness to use the power of political government to redress the balance of the economic world. He advocated few startling innovations, but his work at Albany was a steadily expanding application of this twentieth-century liberalism.

To all of that must be added the depression. Like the rest of the world, Mr. Roosevelt had to look at the senseless paradox of deepening poverty and economic and social disintegration in the midst of the means to produce plenty. Neither Theodore Roosevelt nor Woodrow Wilson had that experience at a comparable stage in the economic growth of the nation or of the world. As the depression wore on, Mr. Roosevelt revealed in his speeches and conversation that he understood the distributing mechanism of the capitalistic system. He clearly got a good grip on the fact that capitalism distributes only when it is expanding. He put that together with the observation that the field for expansion had rapidly narrowed. The rapid industrialization of one nation after another had reduced the areas of the world left for exploitation. The productive plant of the United States itself was highly developed. Additional capital could be used for replacements; new inventions would lead to investments in new enterprises. But the obvious fact remained that the United States already could produce a sufficiency to provide a generous living for every citizen if a workable system of distribution could be created.

A vague awareness of the nature of the capitalistic mechanism for distribution crept into the thought of business men during the nineteen-twenties. It manifested itself in the acceptance of the necessity for high wages. Real wages rose during that decade, but they did not rise enough. Too large a proportion of the product of industry was skimmed off in profits.

Franklin D. Roosevelt was, I believe, the first American with any practical chances of reaching the Presidency to grasp the essentials of the distributing mechanism of capitalism and at the same time to see that the processes which had begun with the industrial revolution had at last brought the United States to the point where it was doubtful that this distributing mechanism could automatically operate. He had already challenged the laissez-faire system because it had concentrated dangerous economic powers in the hands of a comparatively few men and made it impossible for millions of other men to rise above poverty or, at best, to attain security by their own endeavors. He could now challenge it because it was at least doubtful whether it could operate at all; and it was certainly clear that the chief exploiters could not operate it.[1]

As the depression ran its relentless course, as the millions of unemployed grew steadily, as the price level continued to fall, and the debt structure ominously cracked, the chances of the American system's escaping complete collapse or forcible overthrow were much discussed in Mr. Roosevelt's circle, as in other groups throughout the land. Among his friends the discussion was perhaps as intense as it was anywhere because of their hope that he would become President. There were men in this group

---

[1] The expression "laissez-faire" is used with full consciousness that the American system was far from being a freely functioning capitalism. Over a long period of years many interferences had been set up. Some, like the tariff, established favored groups in the American economy. In the nineteen-twenties, as the United States became able to export industrial products and capital on a large scale, industry and finance, which previously had been almost united in favor of the tariff, began to divide on the issue. During the same decade the American farmer moved in the reverse direction. His old quest for equality with industry had expressed itself predominantly in demand for a lower tariff to reduce the cost of the manufactured articles which he bought. In the post-war period he wanted not only equality, but equality at a higher price. The high tariff system was intrenched. The wartime land speculation had left the farmers saddled with an overhead of fixed debt for which mere equality with industry was no relief. Hence, the search for a device that would give the farmer a benefit equivalent to the tariff. McNary-Haugenism beat its head in vain against the imperturbable Mr. Coolidge. From Mr. Hoover, the farmer got the Farm Board and open market purchases of basic agricultural commodities. Like unemployment insurance, that was nothing more than a buffer or purported stabilizer. It ignored the fundamental readjustments necessary in American agriculture. Neither did it suppose a world-wide depression; and it, of course, collapsed. Other interferences with free functioning capitalism, such as regulation of public utilities, had been vitiated by constitutional interpretation and often by falling under the direct control of the vested interests that were supposed to be regulated. Others, such as the anti-trust laws, had been circumvented while at the same time they created obstacles that retarded natural growth and perhaps prevented financial and industrial leaders from operating the system a little better than they did operate it. Still others, such as regulation of working hours, workmen's compensation, and similar reforms, had come to be accepted as desirable by many employers as well as by employees in some states. Nevertheless, laissez-faire is a suitable expression to describe the economics of those who did not want fundamental changes made in the American system as it existed in 1932, or who wanted only such changes made as would give finance more, instead of less, freedom.

as firmly wedded as Mr. Hoover or any orthodox economist to the belief that this was just another depression—
or perhaps an unusual coincidence of several depressions.
Their recipe was to be stoical while waiting for the bottom to be reached and the chance event or the self-
restorative powers supposedly inherent in capitalism to
start another upward cycle. There were others as firmly
of the belief that, unless radically and swiftly altered,
the American economic system—and that of the whole
capitalistic world—was riding surely toward its doom.
They saw that the imported revolutionary doctrines had
not made much headway against the self-conscious nationalism of the average American. But they saw, too,
that the conditions of life in the United States were rapidly becoming unbearable to such large numbers of people that mass uprising might occur at any time.

In May 1932, one of Mr. Roosevelt's friends summarized his own opinion in this way: "If Hoover is re-
elected, the chances are at least one in three that next
winter will bring widespread disorders which will grow
into a revolution or be repressed by armed force. If a
conservative Democrat is nominated and elected, the
eruption will be postponed. Hope will sustain the country
from Election Day until some months after March 4,
until it has become clear that conservative Democracy is
no more capable than conservative Republicanism of
meeting the crisis. If Roosevelt is nominated and elected,
the chances are five to one we will pull through without
a revolution. He is the only man in sight with any chance
of election to the Presidency who has the understanding,
daring, and the flexibility to save us."

How Mr. Roosevelt assessed the situation cannot be
stated. He has the type of mind to which little is impos-

sible and nothing is inevitable. Blind faith in the self-restorative powers of capitalism, the certainty of its doom —both are alien to his way of thinking. He has never been a doctrinaire. Reared in a self-confident tradition, his observations of the world had never driven him to refuge in a creed. With a sense of continual movement that comes from the study of history and from practical experience in politics, Mr. Roosevelt was fully aware that the "iron laws" of successive schools of orthodox economists, no less than the patent remedies of successive schools of visionaries, have been ground to bits by the interplay of changing forces. He could no more trust the cyclical theory than the tenets of communism.

It may be recalled that as the depression progressed the Republican party officially dropped the prophecy that prosperity was just around the corner and warmly embraced the theory of the international banker that the difficulties were international in origin. The public was told that the depression was a heritage of the World War. The deduction implied, and usually stated, was that the only remedies for the situation were international. The eyes of the country were directed towards Europe. When a big bank failed abroad, it was an unfortunate occurrence which prevented the United States from starting the upward turn towards prosperity. War debts, maldistribution of the world gold supply, and related questions were debated publicly pro and con. In that period, the spring of 1932, Sir Arthur Salter was hailed by our leading publicists as the great oracle. Mr. Hoover could not control Congress, and neither Congress nor Mr. Hoover had a domestic program worthy of mention. Wall Street vented its dismay and trepidation in attacks on Congress, and big business men began to talk guard-edly of the need of a dictatorship. The West and South prepared to rebuke Mr. Hoover. The whole country felt, and was encouraged to feel, that it was in the grip of terrible cosmic forces beyond the power of democratic institutions or of any man to understand or control.

Mr. Roosevelt could not reverentially accept the depression as the periodic penance that the nation must undergo in return for the bounteousness of capitalism in its good moments. The unliquidated heritage of the World War in Europe probably was a contributing cause of the depression. The successive collapses of the capitalist credit structure abroad, each accentuating the general decline, did have their effect on this country. But that did not forbid a purely national effort at recovery. To a country lacking in natural resources or with an economy elaborately interwoven with the economies of other nations, an independent effort at recovery probably was difficult, if not impossible. At the same time, the explanations of the international financiers ignored the defects common to all capitalistic nations, or peculiar to each. (This is not an indirect way of praising communist Russia. The problems there are so different that they are not comparable.)

The United States had an abundance of natural resources and an industrial plant capable of yielding a sufficiency for every citizen who was willing to work. For it to deny its ability to direct its own destiny was farcical. Mr. Roosevelt expressed his reaction to such a denial in a speech in May 1932, prior to his nomination to the Presidency. He asserted that drastic changes, including a more equitable distribution of the national income, were necessary to make the American system function. More important, he proposed a method of achieving the objective: "bold, persistent experimentation." As he put it: "It is common sense to take a method and try it; if it fails, admit it frankly and try another. But above all, try something." The Eastern opposition was at that time so intent on establishing the thesis that Mr. Roosevelt had no program that it overlooked the fact that he had proposed an intelligent method of action, probably the only alternative to complete collapse and revolution. The experimental attitude forbids adherence to any hard-and-fast program. It does, or did in Mr. Roosevelt, suppose an objective. It is important to note that Mr. Roosevelt advocated experimental tactics as a means not only for climbing out of the depression but for achieving a better and more stable economic order.

Mr. Roosevelt's campaign for the presidential nomination was fought on the basic economic issue. The underlying conflict was obscured to some extent by the hangover of the religious issue of 1924 and 1928, the personalities of individual candidates, and other political cross currents. But the watershed which separated Mr. Roosevelt from the opposing coalition at Chicago was the rough dividing line between economic liberalism and laissez-faire. Alfred E. Smith, a liberal in some respects in 1928, had taken his stand in 1932 on the platform of international finance with one important modification, a large public works program. It may be recalled that John J. Raskob, his chairman of the Democratic National Committee, still averred in the summer of 1932 that repeal of the Eighteenth Amendment was one of the most important "economic" issues of the day.

The Democratic platform, adopted in June 1932, did not fully reflect Mr. Roosevelt. In the first place it was a party document in which had to be fitted together conflicting viewpoints ranging from the extreme right to the left wing. In the second place, it was a platform of specific pledges, intended to be performed. It was, therefore, a minimum program based on conditions as they were in June 1932. Mr. Roosevelt and the other leaders of the party were of one mind on the desirability of a platform which would break traditions by being short, specific, and performable. It was much needed if faith in democratic institutions and party government were to be restored.

The platform promised many long-range reforms. Some of them were designed to prevent a recurrence of the speculative excesses of the extraordinary boom which preceded an extraordinary deflation. In this category fell reform of the banking system and regulation of the stock and commodity exchanges.

In meeting the economic dislocations resulting from the depression the Democratic party had the broad choice between an inflationary and a deflationary policy. The diminished volume of business at a drastically lower price level could not support the overhead weight of debt and taxation built up at a higher price level. The rigid deflationists would have brought the overhead of debt and taxation down to the lower price level. Their program assumed that the price level would stay where it was instead of falling lower as the overhead was cut down. The extreme inflationists would have pushed the price level up high enough to support the highest levels of the old debt structure. Their program ignored the fact that the top level was no longer a plateau but a series of peaks with deep valleys in between, and that full reliance on inflation would cause a second uncomfortable dislocation to those portions of the economic system which already had become adjusted to lower positions.

The platform struck a compromise. Mr. Hoover had

preserved some of the peaks of the debt structure by using federal credit, through the R.F.C., and had done nothing effective to raise commodity prices. The Democratic platform proposed the corrective course: an orderly reduction of the peaks of debt and taxation and the raising of commodity prices until debts and prices were again in a workable relationship to each other.

The most extremely deflationary pledge on the Democratic platform was to balance the budget with the help of a 25% reduction in the cost of the Federal government. That met with a vengeance the demands of the budget-balancing school of recovery. (It was very doubtful whether many of those who had howled for a reduction in Federal expenditures thought a 25% cut really could be made.) The platform also pledged "a sound currency to be preserved at all hazards," coupling with it a cautious word of encouragement to the silver advocates. It did not promise adherence to the gold standard. To the orthodox a "sound currency" meant nothing else than the gold standard. The Democratic convention was at heart in favor of currency inflation. The party still had a good many free-silverites and the "farm dollar" idea had spread through the conservative South as well as the West. A severe open conflict on the currency issue was curbed by the hope of victory through a united party. The politicians of all monetary faiths were anxious to avoid a repetition of the defeat of 1896. But the inflationists were strong enough to keep the word gold out of the Democratic monetary pledge.

On the constructive side of the problem of coping with the depression the Democratic platform offered both international and national remedies. The international remedy proposed was the restoration of international trade through a competitive tariff for revenue, reciprocal tariff agreements, and an international economic conference. The salient domestic remedies were the spreading of employment by reduction in the hours of labor, the use of federal credit for unemployment relief, expansion of the federal program of necessary and useful construction, and the restoration of agriculture. Taken as a whole, the Democratic platform was a reasonably conservative document which swung hardly farther to the left than Alfred E. Smith's program in 1928.

In his campaign speeches, Mr. Roosevelt expanded the platform and gave it more definite form. It is here that the work of that group of men who became celebrated as the brains trust began to be important.

There is no novelty in the employment of college professors for expert services. Many of our better governors and mayors have used them. The late National Electric Light Association found them useful in educating the public, through school children and the press, on the magnanimity and essential virtue of the electrical utilities. And it found no dearth of professors willing to serve on the financial terms offered. Other trade associations, industries, and subsidized survey groups have employed academic talent with profit to all concerned. President Hoover used college professors on many of his commissions and appointed a university president to his cabinet. The advice of such economists as Walter W. Stewart of Amherst, O.W.M. Sprague of Harvard, and Edwin Kemmerer of Princeton have been sought by foreign governments and central banks. Although a college professorship has not been the usual route to public life in this country, we have had the academic world represented in elective offices by such men as President Woodrow Wilson, Governors Wilbur L. Cross and John G. Pollard, and Senators Hiram Bingham and Simeon D. Fess.

As Governor of New York, Mr. Roosevelt drew heavily on academic talent. From Columbia he took Professor James C. Bonbright for a public utility investigation and for appointment to the state Power Authority and Robert Murray Haig for duty on a temporary power commission and as expert to a committee to revise the state's system of taxation. Professors from Syracuse and Cornell helped to work out his broad state program for relief of agriculture, reforestation, and better land utilization. Through Frances Perkins, his Commissioner of Labor, he had the advice of the best talent available in the drafting of his programs for unemployment, old age insurance, and emergency unemployment relief. College professors were among the men who helped to develop his penal reform program and a twenty-year public health plan. Mr. Roosevelt valued highly the disinterestedness and thoroughness of trained experts from the universities. He wanted what he liked to call "complete pictures," drawn with an eye to the larger public interest. If politics or practical administration required modifications, he could make them himself. On the whole, however, his administration was notable for the frequency with which he took a complete plan for a particular purpose drafted by experts and fought for it. Yet no one had heard of a brains trust.

The little group that came to be labeled the brains trust was formed early in 1932 when Mr. Roosevelt began to need data on national problems for his presidential campaign. Louis McHenry Howe, who liked to take a hand in the preparation of Mr. Roosevelt's speeches on national subjects, was completely engrossed in getting Mr. Roosevelt nominated. Samuel I. Rosenman, counsel to the Governor (now a New York State Supreme Court Justice), was Mr. Roosevelt's chief assistant in the preparation of speeches and messages on state problems. Rosenman had no more than an intelligent layman's knowledge of national problems and his ambition lay toward the state bench rather than toward Washington. He suggested to Mr. Roosevelt that a competent man be selected to take full charge of gathering and assimilating material for Mr. Roosevelt's campaign. With Mr. Roosevelt's assent, he asked Raymond Moley, Professor of Public Law at Columbia, to undertake the job. Rosenman explained later that Moley was the only one of the few college professors he knew who struck him as having a level head.

Professor Moley was not an economist. He had a national reputation as an authority on the causes of organized crime and the failure of the law enforcement authorities to cope with it. Before Mr. Roosevelt's nomination to the Governorship in 1928, Mr. Moley had been retained by the New York State Crime Commission as an expert.

In 1928 Mr. Moley, then working for Alfred E. Smith at Democratic National Headquarters, was introduced to Mr. Roosevelt by Louis McHenry Howe, who in his years as Secretary of the National Crime Commission had become acquainted with most of the experts on crime and penology in the country. Professor Moley's first service for Mr. Roosevelt was two years later as a member of a committee which drafted a plan for a model state parole system. Mr. Roosevelt earmarked him for membership on a commission to revise the administration of justice, but a deadlock with the Republican legislature delayed the survey for a year. Meanwhile, he was employed as an ex-

pert to assist Samuel Seabury, as representative of the
Governor, in the hearing of charges of inefficiency against
T.C.T. Crain, Tammany District Attorney.

At the end of 1931 Mr. Moley was still a minor figure
on the fringe of Mr. Roosevelt's circle. When I wrote a
biography of Mr. Roosevelt at that time I did not even
mention him. He was getting a little closer to the center,
however. In February 1932, he helped to prepare a
speech for Mr. Roosevelt on reforming the state administration of justice. He was asked to lend a hand in drafting the definition of public policy which Mr. Roosevelt issued in removing Sheriff Thomas M. Farley of New York
County—a definition which established a new standard
for the judgment of public officials and foredoomed
Mayor James J. Walker.

When Mr. Roosevelt approved the choice of Professor
Moley to supervise the preparation of material for the
national campaign, he was in search of no theorist; a college professor harboring dogma was the last person he
wanted. He wanted a high-grade research assistant and
literary secretary, an intelligent reliable man who knew
where to get facts and ideas, and how to analyze them
and put them in usable form.

Professor Moley met with Mr. Rosenman and Basil
O'Connor, Mr. Roosevelt's former law partner, who had
made himself a general handyman, and they drew a tentative list of topics on which data were needed. He then
began scouting among his friends at Columbia University
to find willing and qualified assistants. To the next meeting he brought his next-door neighbor, Rexford G. Tugwell, Professor of Economics at Columbia. He then introduced Frederic Mills, also a professor of economics at
Columbia. Mills soon dropped out. His view on currency

inflation did not conform to the program Mr. Roosevelt
had in mind. For both political and economic reasons Mr.
Roosevelt had determined long before the Chicago Convention not to advocate tinkering with the money system.
He had had close contacts with the Cornell group of commodity dollar enthusiasts: George F. Warren, Frank A.
Pearson, and William I. Myers. More than a year later
he revealed that he believed the preservation of a dollar
of stable purchasing power to be both necessary and feasible. However, he did not accept the doctrine that the
primary causes of the depression lay in the money system
and that inflation and subsequent currency management
were cure-alls. (That was trying to explain too much with
one idea. But the rejection of extreme claims of the commodity dollar advocates did not forbid the use of inflation
and currency management as rough instruments for bringing prices and debts into more workable relationship to
each other.) As his program proved, Mr. Roosevelt
thought a great many fundamental readjustments had to
be made if the American economic machine were to be
revived and preserved. One of these was the reduction of
the output of basic agricultural crops to a restricted
market. Dr. Tugwell's perception of one of the main
causes of the depression in the failure of the industrial
system to distribute the surplus piled up by the astonish-
ing growth of efficiency in the nineteen-twenties harmo-
nized with Mr. Roosevelt's own observations.

The next recruit for the brains trust was Adolf A.
Berle, Jr., Professor of Law at Columbia. Like many liberal intellectuals, he did not at that time favor Mr. Roosevelt for the Presidency. However, he had available the
services of a number of statisticians. He submitted an excellent memorandum on federal finances, met Mr. Roose-

velt, and found, as many other of his type did later, that Roosevelt was the man in public life for whom he had long been in search. Charles Roberts, a friend of Mr. O'Connor's, threw in a plan for taxing corporation surpluses. Professors Moley and Tugwell canvassed several of their academic friends, especially those at Columbia, since they were more accessible. One by one most of them were eliminated, either because they were immersed in doctrines developed out of their own particular specialties, or because they could not simplify and generalize their ideas for the uses of Mr. Roosevelt and his campaign. The group quickly simmered down to Moley, Tugwell, and Berle. After a few preliminary meetings with Rosenman and O'Connor they moved on to Albany. They would catch an afternoon train from New York, take tea with Mr. Roosevelt on the porch of the Executive Mansion, and the discussion would continue through the dinner hour and late into the night. There were several of these sessions before Mr. Roosevelt went to Warm Springs at the end of April for a month's vacation. The conversation roamed over the whole field of economics: the causes of the depression, the methods of relieving it, the main points of attack. The three professors learned the main trends of Mr. Roosevelt's thought and the kind of information he wanted. He enlarged and co-ordinated his knowledge of economics. The professors modified some of their own ideas. Dr. Tugwell has often acknowledged to his friends that his conception of a neatly planned society imposed by an economic council was shattered by Mr. Roosevelt's insistence on the need of fluidity. (The first sentence of the first chapter in Dr. Tugwell's book, *The Industrial Discipline*,[1] published a year

---

[1] The Columbia University Press, 1933.

later, is: "The fluidity of change in society has always been the despair of theorists.") When Mr. Roosevelt returned from Warm Springs at the beginning of June, the meetings were resumed. From a research group, the brains trust developed into a board of economic strategy for the campaign.[1]

Mr. Moley's first service in his new capacity as chief of the brains trust was during the preparation of a short but memorable speech. Mr. Roosevelt was dictating while Moley and Rosenman made comments and suggestions. At an appropriate point Moley reached down into his large store of apt literary allusions and pulled out William Graham Sumner's phrase, "the forgotten man." Mr. Roosevelt seized it instantly. That speech evoked strident attacks from the conservatives of both parties. Alfred E. Smith made it the opening for his denunciation of demagogy, which proclaimed to all who did not already know that a famous friendship and political alliance had been disrupted. But "the forgotten man" seized the imagination of the country. With the possible exception of "the new deal," it became the most telling catchphrase of the presidential campaign.

The "new deal" also grew out of a triangular speech-writing conference of Mr. Roosevelt and Messrs. Moley and Rosenman. The weight of evidence favors Mr. Rosen-

---

[1] The phrase "brains trust" was invented in the late summer of 1932 by James M. Kieran of the *New York Times*, who was "covering" Mr. Roosevelt at the time. A convenient appellation to distinguish this group of men from Mr. Roosevelt's political advisers was badly needed. Mr. Kieran at first tried "brains department." He then shortened it to "brains trust." Most of Mr. Kieran's colleagues resisted the expression, but the press associations finally began to use it, Mr. Roosevelt adopted it, and it slowly made its way into the public vocabulary. It was "brains trust," and so remained in Mr. Roosevelt's circle despite the later mass rebellion of newspaper and magazine copy readers against the plural form of "brain."

man as the author. But no great significance was attached
to the phrase at the time. Mr. Roosevelt closed his acceptance speech with the promise of "a new deal." As Mr.
Roosevelt put the address in final form during his airplane ride from Albany to Chicago, no advance copies
were available to the press. Newspapermen writing frantically to catch the early editions of the Sunday morning
papers found the proffer of "a new deal" the easiest point
at which to take hold of the speech. It was within headline
length and accordingly struck the public eye the next
morning. Mr. Roosevelt made several more speeches before he used the phrase again. It was Herbert Bayard
Swope, with his acute appraisal of public psychology, who
saw its potentialities and urged that it be hammered home.
Mr. Roosevelt began using it and gradually "a new deal"
became "The New Deal." It was several weeks after
Chicago before anyone in the Roosevelt entourage realized that "The New Deal" was a happy union of "The
Square Deal" of Theodore Roosevelt's Progressivism and
"The New Freedom" of Wilsonian Democracy.[1]

Dr. Tugwell took over the problems of agriculture,
which seemed to him to be among the most interesting
and fundamental of the day. The various contrivances,
such as the equalization fee and the export debenture plan,
which had been proposed in order to put the farmer on
an equality with tariff-protected industry, appealed to him
as examples of social invention. In 1927 he had made a
survey of the American agricultural problem for Alfred
E. Smith's campaign for the Presidency. Mr. Roosevelt
was familiar with the equalization fee and the export
debenture plans. During one of the earlier sessions of the

---

[1] Of the other phrases of the campaign: "industrial cannon fodder" was Professor Berle's and "half boom, half broke" was Mr. Roosevelt's.

brains trust, Dr. Tugwell spoke of the work that was then being done by a group of agricultural economists financed by a grant from the Laura Spelman Rockefeller Fund.

"I don't know exactly what they've got," said Dr. Tugwell, "but I understand it is something better than the old schemes."

About ten days before the national convention there was to be a meeting of agricultural economists at Chicago, at which the new scheme was to be discussed. Dr. Tugwell was assigned to attend the meeting, explore the plan, and determine if it met with general approval. He went. He telephoned to Mr. Roosevelt from Chicago, and explained the voluntary domestic allotment plan in a conversation which lasted nearly an hour.

A few minutes later, Mr. Roosevelt called back. "I don't understand it yet," he said. "Put it in a telegram."

Mr. Roosevelt was then working on his acceptance speech. He put into that speech a brief statement concerning surplus crops which forecast the main lines of his Topeka speech and of the new agricultural experiment launched a year later.

After the convention Dr. Tugwell brought to Albany Professor M. L. Wilson of Montana State Agricultural College, one of the chief authors of the domestic allotment idea. They went over the plan with Mr. Roosevelt, and were commissioned to prepare a detailed formula. While they were working in New York, Henry A. Wallace, the Iowa farm journal publisher, came through on his way to see Mr. Roosevelt. He favored the plan, and Mr. Wilson later went to Iowa and obtained Mr. Wallace's final approval of the finished draft of the speech.

After Mr. Roosevelt's nomination, the brains trust grew. The most active addition was Hugh S. Johnson, a

retired brigadier-general. For several years General Johnson had been a close associate of Bernard M. Baruch.
Mr. Baruch's attitude toward Mr. Roosevelt's nomination had been one of hostile neutrality. But after the
nomination he at once proffered his active services, and
put General Johnson at Mr. Roosevelt's disposal. A year
later, when Mr. Roosevelt made General Johnson administrator of the National Recovery Act, he was grate-
fully applauded for choosing a "practical" man instead
of a "theorist" from his brains trust. There is no doubt
about General Johnson's practicality, but among his versatile abilities are a sound grounding in economics, an inventive mind, a huge capacity for careful research, and a
talent for pungent phrases. Although he did not see a
great deal of Mr. Roosevelt during the presidential campaign, General Johnson was in fact the most important
member of the brains trust outside the original trio.
Through Mr. Moley, his data and ideas went to develop
such diverse parts of the Roosevelt program as federal
finances, the tariff, and railroad rehabilitation. Felix
Frankfurter, Professor of Law at Harvard, was another
important contributor, though he worked more or less
independently. Mr. Roosevelt had known him for many
years and frequently had sought his advice while Governor of New York.

Professor Tugwell and Henry Morgenthau, Jr., chairman of Mr. Roosevelt's agricultural advisory committee
for four years, developed a large brains trust for agriculture which included professors, economists, and leaders
of farm organizations from all over the country. Through
Mr. Moley many other persons furnished data for the
campaign. Among them was Ralph West Robey, financial
editor of the *New York Evening Post*. Mr. Robey broke

with the Roosevelt Administration on the money question in 1933 and became one of its most persistent critics. Through Mr. Robey came material from several of the economists of the financial district, including Alexander Sachs, the brilliant statistical economist and entertaining conversationalist, who later became chief economist of the NRA. Among other recruits were Professor John Dalton of the Harvard School of Business and Charles W. Taussig, President of the American Molasses Company.

Mr. Taussig was a warm personal friend of Professor Berle's but he made his contact with Mr. Roosevelt independently. Like many other people, Mr. Taussig and his friends spent a great deal of time discussing the parlous state of the nation and exchanging ideas for improving it. Early in the spring of 1932, before the brains trust was formed, Mr. Taussig startled his companions at a luncheon table—among them, Professor Berle—by proposing that they try to find men of influence in the political world to espouse some of their ideas. One of Mr. Taussig's ideas was to curb speculators and financial sharpshooters by requiring the fullest publicity concerning operations on the securities and commodities exchanges and making security selling houses responsible for full information concerning their issues. He went to Washington and talked to several Senators and stirred their interest in the idea. Meanwhile Professor Berle undertook to draft a bill. Business kept Mr. Taussig in the South during the several weeks in which the brains trust was formed. While riding North from New Orleans at the end of May he noticed that there were large crowds at every station. He made inquiry and discovered that Mr. Roosevelt was on the train, returning from Warm

Springs. Mr. Taussig went back to Mr. Roosevelt's drawing room and sent in his card. He was admitted and he promptly unfolded his scheme. Later Mr. Roosevelt invited him to come to Albany for further discussion, and asked him to join the brains trust, where his friendship with Professor Berle helped him to feel at home. A nephew of the well-known Harvard economist, Mr. Taussig did not have even one college degree. Yet he cheerfully undertook to master such abstruse subjects as the tariff and made various scattered contributions to the New Deal. An expert on the sugar business and on Cuba, he helped to formulate the Administration's program for the liberation and economic restoration of Cuba.

As the candidate of discontent and advocate of change, Mr. Roosevelt became the magnet for all of the million and one plans for recovery sired by three and one-half years of depression. Mr. Moley was the main funnel through which the worthy residue from this unending flow of suggestions reached Mr. Roosevelt. Moley has always taken pains to give credit for much of the work of culling this material to two of his young assistants, Celeste Jedel, his secretary, and Robert K. Straus, son of Jesse I. Straus, the present Ambassador to France.

Although none of the gentlemen classifiable as members of the brains trust had anything to do with the political management of the presidential campaign, several of the leading Democratic politicians had a good deal to do with some of Mr. Roosevelt's speeches. Professor Moley accompanied Mr. Roosevelt throughout the campaign. The data and ideas of Mr. Roosevelt and his brains trust were continually enlarged and modified by a revolving group of Senators and other leaders. Senator Thomas J. Walsh of Montana, who was with Mr. Roosevelt during

most of his swing through the Far West, Senator Key
Pittman of Nevada, monetary expert and silver enthusi-
ast, and Senator James F. Byrnes of South Carolina were
probably the men in this category who had the most influence. But no sharp line can be drawn. Mr. Roosevelt is
probably the most indefatigable gatherer of ideas and
impressions who has entered American public life since
the early days of the Republic. He had first-hand knowledge of almost every state in the Union long before he
became a presidential candidate—partly as a result of his
record-breaking vice-presidential tour in 1920. For years
he had carried on an extraordinarily large personal correspondence, not only with political leaders, but with men
in all walks of life. His correspondence was notable for
the fact that even the most obscure person who wrote to
him received a special answer, instead of a form letter.
Mr. Roosevelt habitually supplemented his correspondence with personal contacts. At Warm Springs, he welcomed to his cottage farmers from the countryside, store-
keepers, railway workers, editors of small-town papers,
and other assorted individuals. And so wherever he went,
he made himself accessible. He made friends; but, no less
important, he obtained information. During his campaign
travels in 1932, Mr. Roosevelt continually reiterated that
his primary purpose was to obtain information. There
were, of course, other reasons for the persistent touring
which carried him through thirty-eight of the forty-
eight states. One was to refute the whispered propaganda that he was physically unfit for the strain of the
Presidency. In the West he sought by personal contact
to precipitate the "bolt" of the Progressive leaders from
the Republican party. But Mr. Roosevelt's travels, which
carried him into the Solid Democratic South and other

states which were surely his without a speech or a visit, went far beyond the uses of the campaign. In fact, many of his advisers thought that he was taking unnecessary risks by speaking too often when the tide was running his way. Without question, at least two of Mr. Roosevelt's motives were related to the prodigious task that lay ahead of him if he were elected rather than to getting elected. He sought to spread a feeling of good cheer and national self-confidence and lay the base for that democratic direct contact with the electorate which he expected to maintain by radio from the White House. But Mr. Roosevelt's conduct proved beyond refutation that one of his major purposes really was to obtain information about local conditions. From before breakfast until late at night, wherever he went, Mr. Roosevelt was talking to men in every type of activity: cattle men, sheep men, wheat raisers, corn and hog farmers, miners and mine owners, mill workers, railroad executives and railroad workers, big industrialists and small-town shopkeepers, city bankers and village bankers, unemployed men, obscure county politicians, as well as United States Senators and Governors. By that direct method, Mr. Roosevelt freshened his already remarkable knowledge of the condition and temper of people in every section of the country. But he also got ideas. Mr. Roosevelt has an extraordinary capacity for putting men at ease and making them talk frankly. A rancher or a small-town business man with ideas would find himself detained for a long audience when a prominent politician or industrial leader with nothing new to contribute would be passed off with a friendly greeting and handshake. In fact, Mr. Roosevelt put on the shoulders of James A. Farley, national chairman, Edward J. Flynn, and other of his political advisers most of the incessant work of conferring with political leaders. If traced back, some of the novel ideas carried into action during the Roosevelt Revolution undoubtedly would be found to have had their origin in the grass roots and in the corner grocery stores instead of in the minds of the gentlemen of the brains trust. During the eleven months that preceded his inauguration, Mr. Roosevelt traveled approximately 27,000 miles and visited all but seven of the states.[1] These seven he skirted and through delegations of various types he received the kind of first-hand knowledge concerning them that he obtained in the other forty-one states. It is safe to assert that no previous President since the nation spread across the continent has entered the White House with the detailed physical acquaintance with the country and the intimate knowledge of the habits and psychology of different sections and different economic groups that Mr. Roosevelt made it his business to acquire.

It is unquestionably true that Mr. Roosevelt's campaign speeches did not prepare the public for the shock of the first months of the New Deal. Yet, with one exception, every important venture of the New Deal was forecast in Mr. Roosevelt's campaign. In his acceptance speech and on two other occasions he proposed to put large numbers of men to work in the forests. At Topeka he presented a detailed formula for the revolutionary experiment in controlling crop surpluses. At Salt Lake City he projected the main lines of a complete rationalization of the nation's transportation system. Mortgage relief for farm and home owners, direct federal unemployment re-

---

[1] In addition to the thirty-eight states through which he traveled in his campaign proper, Mr. Roosevelt visited three others during the eleven months preceding March 4, 1933.

lief aid, a public works program, the control of speculation, reform of the banking system and of the security
selling business, beer, repeal of the Eighteenth Amendment, shorter working hours—most of these were pledged
in the Democratic platform and proposals for all of them
were outlined by Mr. Roosevelt in his speeches. Mr.
Roosevelt's attitude toward organized labor had been
well established over a long period beginning in his
days as Assistant Secretary of the Navy and continuing
through his years as Governor of New York. In a eulogis-
tic public tribute to Mr. Roosevelt's leadership at his
second year in Albany, William Green, President of the
American Federation of Labor, wrote: "Labor has very
seldom secured the enactment of so many measures which
so favorably affect its economic, social, and industrial welfare during a single session of a legislative body."

Before the Commonwealth Club in San Francisco in
September Mr. Roosevelt made probably the fullest of
his presentations of his economic philosophy. It was there
that he declared the development of "an economic constitutional order" by business men in partnership with
the government to be "the minimum requirement of a
more permanently safe order of things." The Commonwealth Club speech was the most significant utterance
made by any major candidate for the Presidency in a generation, if not in a much longer period; and, if the American experiment succeeds, will be generally recognized as
such. Mr. Roosevelt's definition of "the greater social
contract" in that speech was perhaps the nearest thing to
the manifesto of the Roosevelt Revolution:

"Every man has a right to life; and this means that
he has also a right to make a comfortable living. He may
by sloth or crime decline to exercise that right; but it may

not be denied him. We have no actual famine or dearth; our industrial and agricultural mechanism can produce enough and to spare. Our government, formal and informal, political and economic, owes to everyone an avenue to possess himself of a portion of that plenty sufficient for his needs, through his own work.

"Every man has a right to his own property; which means a right to be assured, to the fullest extent attainable, in the safety of his savings. By no other means can men carry the burdens of those parts of life which, in the nature of things, afford no chance of labor: childhood, sickness, old age. In all thought of property, this right is paramount; all other property rights must yield to it. If, in accord with this principle, we must restrict the operations of the speculator, the manipulator, even the financier, I believe we must accept the restriction as needful, not to hamper individualism but to protect it."

The desirability of a more specific speech on the "economic constitutional order" was discussed by Mr. Roosevelt and his brains trust. At that time they had not chosen from among the many plans proposed or formulated a plan of their own. For the purposes of the campaign, the development of a specific plan was superfluous; in fact, it was not to Mr. Roosevelt's political advantage to disturb his comparatively smooth course toward victory by raising a contentious issue to prominence with too much emphasis and detail. Likewise, he did not unfold his full plan for the great experiment in regional planning in the Tennessee Valley, although it had long been full-fledged in his own mind.

In spite of the warnings of President Hoover and Secretary of the Treasury Ogden L. Mills, the public as a whole undoubtedly failed to see anything very revolution-

ary in Mr. Roosevelt's program. Mr. Roosevelt spread
his ideas by gentle persuasion rather than by shock. As in
the Commonwealth Club speech, his most far-reaching
conceptions were clothed in general statements of principles. The conservatives could pass them off as the mean-
ingless rhetoric of a political campaigner, and the liberal
intellectuals could doubt that he really understood their
implications or intended to apply them in specific action.
That was all to Mr. Roosevelt's political advantage. He
had long been adept at winning popular approval for
really radical reforms by eschewing radical language. The
doctrine of the good neighbor, the common law concerning nuisances, the Declaration of Independence, the Constitution, the Boy Scout Manual, the pioneering spirit of
America, a common-sense analysis of the requirements of
a specific situation—with these as his authorities and raw
materials and his own family tradition to embellish the
whole, Mr. Roosevelt was able to express some pretty
radical thoughts without frightening the conservatism of
many of those who merely wanted a change in Administration. The points on which Mr. Roosevelt specifically
strove to reassure conservatives were the balancing of
the budget by drastic governmental economies and the
preservation of sound money. Yet, adhering to the pattern of the Democratic platform, Mr. Roosevelt at no
time said that by sound money he meant the existing gold
standard or the existing gold content of the dollar. He
heartily lauded the scathing attack of Senator Glass on
the Republican Administration's financial record and on
Mr. Hoover's assertion that the United States had been
within two weeks of being forced off the gold standard in
the late spring of 1932. Mr. Roosevelt tied up sound
money with a balanced budget. He vigorously criticized

Mr. Hoover for violating the precepts of sound finance by permitting a dangerous, uncontrolled inflation through an unbalanced budget. He thus set himself against uncontrolled printing press inflation, but beyond that he did not define sound money. The conservatives naturally assumed he meant a dollar of the existing gold content, and Mr. Roosevelt undoubtedly was glad to have them think so without completely quashing the hopes of the inflationists of various schools. In retrospect the loopholes which Mr. Roosevelt left for himself in handling the money issue become significant. They indicate at least a mental reservation concerning the possibility or desirability of maintaining the existing gold standard.

From the beginning until the end of his campaign Mr. Roosevelt stressed the national character of his program. He did not close the door against international measures for recovery, but he definitely subordinated them. He relentlessly assailed the Republican policy of lending money to foreign nations to enable them to buy the increasing American surplus. The key to his own program was the restoration of the "forgotten market" in the agricultural regions of the United States.

In his Atlanta speech on October 24, Mr. Roosevelt summarized succinctly "the fundamental issue in this campaign."

"Mr. Hoover," he said, "believes that farmers and workers must wait for general recovery, until some miracle occurs by which the factory wheels revolve again. No one knows the formula for this miracle. I, on the other hand, am saying over and over that I believe that we can restore prosperity here in this country by re-establishing the purchasing power of half the people of the country, that when this gigantic market of fifty million people is able to purchase goods, industry will start to turn, and the millions of men and women now walking the streets will be employed.

"I am, moreover, enough of an American to believe that such a restoration of prosperity in this country will do more to effectuate world recovery than all of the promotional schemes of lending money to backward and crippled countries [1] could do in generations. In this respect, I am for America first.

"This doctrine I set forth when my campaign really began back in April. I said in a speech then that we had forgotten this potential market of the agricultural population, and that the true interest of this country was to return to this forgotten market. We have, as in the old story of the Holy Grail, looked beyond the seas for the riches that were lying unnoticed at our very feet."

When Mr. Roosevelt sought to correlate his national program with the traditional Democratic low tariff doctrine he ran into difficulties. In 1928 Alfred E. Smith had renounced the low tariff in favor of a protective tariff—but a protective tariff to be maintained "scientifically" instead of by log-rolling. Since then had come the Hawley-Smoot Act. Mr. Roosevelt was attacking it as one of the causes of the depression. Meanwhile, most of the rest of the world, including Great Britain, had adopted protection as a policy. Mr. Roosevelt's difficulties were brought out during the preparation of his main tariff address. Mr. Taussig had prepared a comprehensive tariff memorandum, including a proposal for a ten percent horizontal reduction, and at Mr. Roosevelt's request he submitted it to various party leaders for comment and suggestion.

---

[1] A paraphrase of one of Mr. Hoover's utterances of some years earlier.

Senator Cordell Hull of Tennessee, the Democratic
party's leading low tariff advocate, heartily approved it.
Other individuals whose interests ran primarily in the direction of the restoration of international trade approved
it. But most of Mr. Roosevelt's economic and political
advisers were critical of it. General Johnson wrote an entirely separate tariff memorandum which represented the
high tariff views of Mr. Baruch and himself. The Sioux
City speech and Mr. Roosevelt's other references to the
tariff were a hodgepodge of these two conflicting conceptions, but the main line of argument was furnished by
Messrs. Baruch, Johnson, and Moley and Senators Walsh
and Pittman, all of whom either opposed the low tariff
thesis on economic grounds or shrank from it for political
reasons. The net result was that the tariff reduction program which Mr. Roosevelt advocated was based primarily
on reciprocal agreements to be achieved by "old-fashioned
Yankee horse-trading." That was the natural supplement
to the restoration of a sound national economy. Foreign
outlets for the most oppressive domestic surpluses were
to be assured in return for slots cut in our own tariff wall
to admit those products which would least disturb the
domestic system. That implied departure from the old
Democratic low tariff policy and from the unconditional-
most-favored-nation principle to which the Republican
party was also bound. (In practice the unconditional-
most-favored-nation principle is susceptible to such refine-
ment that the principle is emasculated, so that this point
may be academic.) Nevertheless, enough of the shreds of
general low tariff doctrine remained in Mr. Roosevelt's
earlier tariff utterances to alarm his supporters in the industrial regions, and he subsequently gave assurances that

American industry and labor standards would be adequately protected.

While it contained a few troublesome spare parts for which no place could be found, the program of the New Deal, as originally conceived, as developed in Mr. Roosevelt's speeches, and as carried into action in 1933, was essentially national. It was predicated on the feasibility of independent economic recovery by the United States, and its long-range objective was the reshaping of the American economic system. In his inaugural speech on March 4, Mr. Roosevelt flatly restated this point when he said: "Our international trade relations, though vastly important, are in point of time and necessity secondary to the establishment of a sound national economy."

II

The Interregnum

THE election of November 8, 1932, gave a new lease of hope to the great majority of citizens who were suffering most acutely from the depression. Hope was only a sedative. How long it would soothe the intensifying pains of the country no one could say. Perhaps for a year—if the pains grew no worse. Probably there was no realistic observer in November 1932 who thought the existing social system could survive a second winter unless substantial recovery set in.

As a matter of fact, the state of the nation was rapidly growing worse. The rise in commodity and security prices during July and August 1932 had proved to be a false harbinger of recovery. As the autumn wore on, commodities sank, the volume of business shrank, and unemployment increased. Yet four precious months had to elapse before Franklin D. Roosevelt could assume the position which the electorate had entrusted to him by a most decisive verdict. Almost to a man, I believe, the country would have been delighted to see him step into the Presidency at once. Many who had voted against him were glad that, since he had won, it had been with a tremendous majority and that he had been given a Democratic Congress. Others bowed to the inevitable and, since the change had been decreed, would rather have seen it become effective at once than risk the dangers of a four months' interregnum.[1] Delicate foreign problems—the war debt controversy, the Sino-Japanese problem, Cuba—sharpened the stark reminder that the American Constitution had not been drafted with foresight of such a crisis as that in which the nation found itself at the end of 1932.

From several quarters sprang the idea that Mr. Roosevelt be elevated to the Presidency through the resignation of Secretary of State Stimson, the appointment of Mr. Roosevelt to the Secretaryship of State, and the resignation of President Hoover and Vice-President Curtis. Earlier in 1932 Colonel Edward M. House recalled in the presence of a newspaperman that in 1916 President Wilson had intended, if defeated for re-election, to follow that procedure and surrender the Presidency immediately to Charles E. Hughes. In view of Colonel House's record as a diplomatist and political manipulator, one is entitled to suspect that it was not by pure chance that his recollection brought forth that particular incident. The story lost some of its effect because of the recollection of others that, when Mr. Wilson had had a chance to surrender the Presidency after the 1920 election, he had not taken it.

Even had Messrs. Hoover, Curtis, and Stimson been willing, Mr. Roosevelt probably could not have been persuaded to assent. He needed time to organize his Cabinet and his program. Most important, there was no way of substituting the new Congress for the unmanageable collection of lame ducks who still had four months of constitutional life.

However, the interregnum brought contacts of unprecedented frequency between an outgoing President

---

[1] A word was needed to express the thought that the nation had no effective government between November 7 and March 4. Somebody tried "interregnum," and it became widely used.

and a President-elect of opposite political faiths. Mr. Hoover's congratulatory message to Mr. Roosevelt on election night hinted a readiness to co-operate. Twice during the interregnum—once in late November and once in mid-January—Mr. Roosevelt was invited, and went, to the White House to confer with Mr. Hoover. Between these conferences they were in almost continual communication through intermediaries and personal correspondence. In January Mr. Roosevelt and Secretary Stimson had a long talk and thereafter were in frequent direct touch by telephone. Beginning with the dramatic flight of the British Ambassador to Warm Springs in late January, Mr. Roosevelt practically took over the direction of American foreign policy, with Mr. Stimson's co-operation.

These contacts, up to the last two weeks before Mr. Roosevelt's inauguration, when the banking convulsion introduced a new element, were concerned chiefly with foreign affairs. Mr. Hoover's desire to see Mr. Roosevelt arose from the war debt problem and the related preparations for the World Economic Conference. It developed that Mr. Hoover's desire was less to co-operate in putting Mr. Roosevelt's policies into effect than to persuade Mr. Roosevelt to support Mr. Hoover's policies.

Co-operation in domestic affairs was another matter. Mr. Hoover could not have recommended to Congress or even affixed his signature to most of the important measures in Mr. Roosevelt's program without repudiating his political principles and swallowing some of his most earnest campaign utterances.

Until January 1, Mr. Roosevelt was still Governor of New York, with several important problems, including a financial crisis in New York City, to handle. From

January 1, until March 4, he was technically a private citizen. He publicly assumed the broad position that for him to attempt to assert the prerogatives of a President before March 4 would violate the fundamental principle of responsibility fixed by the Constitution and indispensable to orderly government. The theoretical importance of that doctrine is evident. But behind it lay a number of extremely practical reasons why Mr. Roosevelt could not afford to assume responsibility without power. In the field of foreign relations, where Mr. Hoover besought Mr. Roosevelt's co-operation, sympathetic and effective application of a policy is vital, and between Mr. Hoover's and Mr. Roosevelt's views on the economic aspects of the international situation there was a wide gulf. At home, the leadership of Congress by the President, even under the most favorable conditions, requires day-by-day management—a luncheon conversation with this committee chairman, a telephone communication to that Senator, perhaps several conferences daily, the driving of a patronage bargain or the threat to use the big stick. Only a President actually in the White House, endowed with all the prestige and power of his office, can effectively direct Congress. And it was doubtful how far the lame duck Congress could be managed, even with all the powers of the Presidency in the hands of a man so skilled in their use as Mr. Roosevelt. The Democrats had a bare majority in the House. The Senate was nominally Republican by one vote but actually at the mercy of a majority of Democrats and Progressive Republicans, whose political views ranged from Toryism to the moderate left. Many of them were individualists beyond the control of any man.

It was extremely important to Mr. Roosevelt to have

that Congress pass certain legislation. He could ask the
co-operation of the Congressional leaders of his own
party and of the Republican Progressives who had supported him in the election in getting that legislation
enacted. But so far as possible he used his influence quietly
and tactfully. He could not afford to make enemies pre-
maturely among men whose aid he would need later
when he could more effectively demand it. Above all, he
could not afford to risk the impairment of his prestige in
the eyes of the country. The country looked to him to
shatter the terrifying wall of governmental inaction, in-
decision, and futility. Only faith or hope that he could do
that held the nation together.

Mr. Roosevelt knew he faced a tremendously difficult
situation which he had to overcome before the winter of
1933–34. He knew that if he were to have any chance of
success he had to strike a succession of sledge-hammer
blows with all the force that he could summon. He did
not dare fritter away his prestige and the country's hope
by inviting rebuke from an insubordinate, dying Congress
or risk close collaboration with an Administration which
the nation had overwhelmingly rebuked and with which
he had little in common. The wisdom of his decision was
proved by the public reaction to his most overt violation
of it. The squabble in his own party over new taxes compelled him to deny that he favored the sales tax. That in
turn led him to summon Congressional leaders to New
York in early January to agree on a tax program which
they then promptly abandoned. The press reaction in all
parts of the country to the incident was perceptibly damaging to Mr. Roosevelt's prestige. Protests from the
floor of the Senate against Mr. Roosevelt's announced
plan to handle war debt discussions himself further

evinced the Congressional sense of independence of the President-elect. Confidence in him was clearly waning until a chance event on February 15—the attempt at his assassination—suddenly rallied the entire nation behind him. His superb personal conduct and the shudder of the country at the thought of the debacle which would have ensued if the attempt had succeeded buried all doubts and quibbling. The nation seemed to realize what it had only vaguely felt, that, whatever his weaknesses and strength, he was democracy's last hope.

Although he did not assume publicly the reponsibilities of leadership, Mr. Roosevelt determined even before the election to get as much as possible of his program through the lame-duck Congress which convened in December for its last short session. He had at most one year in which to defeat the depression. The new legislation which he needed was more than Congress, at its habitual pace, could enact in three years. He also wished to avoid calling a special session of the new Congress until he had had at least five or six weeks after his inauguration to install his administration and get a firm hold on the government. Publicly he announced that he hoped to avoid the necessity for any special session, and so obtain nine months' freedom from Congress at the outset. But that presupposed that the short session would do the impossible by giving him all the new authority which he needed. By ordinary criteria all that could be expected of the short session was the passage of appropriation bills.

In his conference with Democratic leaders in November at Washington and in December at Warm Springs, Mr. Roosevelt urged that the special session act on the following major items in the Democratic program: repeal of the Eighteenth Amendment, legalization of beer, the domestic allotment plan, mortgage relief for farmers, a bill to expedite bankruptcy proceedings, and the balancing of the federal budget.

Prompt repeal of the Eighteenth Amendment and modification of the Volstead Act had been pledged. Mr. Roosevelt's overwhelming election on a platform containing these pledges furnished an impeccable excuse for Senators and Congressmen from the allegedly dry states to switch their votes to the wet side. Prompt submission of a repeal resolution would permit the regular 1933 sessions of the state legislatures to provide for the election of the special state conventions, through which, by the pledges of both parties, repeal was to be acted upon. Repeal lost in the first test in the House. It was then brought up in the Senate, surrounded by dry qualifications. In his early January conference with Democratic leaders in New York City, Mr. Roosevelt squashed the Senate's repeal resolution in one sentence: "It doesn't conform to the platform." A resolution conforming to the platform passed the short session in its closing days. The legalization of beer was blocked, ostensibly by the disagreement between the House and the Senate as to whether 3.2 or 3.05 alcoholic content was the line of demarcation between an intoxicant and a non-intoxicant.

Legislation to relieve insolvent debtors of legal delays and the huge tolls of lawyers and bankers was a necessity on which President Hoover and President-elect Roosevelt agreed. The Bankruptcy Law passed in the closing days of the short session established mechanisms by which railroads could reorganize without going through bankruptcies and by which individual debtors could have their debts pared down by conference with their creditors under the ægis of the federal courts or, in the case of farmers, through conciliation commissioners.

Congress was overflowing with bills for the supplementary purpose of extending federal credit to reduce the burden of farm mortgages, but agreement could not be reached on the extent of the obligation which the government was to assume; and no bill passed.

Preparations for balancing the federal budget required, first, new taxes, and second, the creation of a method by which the current expenses of government could be drastically reduced. For temporary purposes Mr. Roosevelt accepted the Treasury Department's official income estimates for the current year (which were obviously too high) and he endeavored to get the Democratic leadership to pass enough taxes to bring the budget into theoretical balance. For the far more difficult objective to which Mr. Roosevelt was pledged—the reorganization of the federal government and the reduction of its cost of operation by 25 percent—a special mechanism had to be sought.

It was in this connection that the practical advantage of the delegation by Congress of extraordinary powers to the Executive was first discussed. A growing number of people were asserting that the exigencies of the depression required that the President be vested with wartime powers. The idea originated in the East, home of the vested interests which distrusted Congress and of the school of thought which held economy in government to be the first essential to recovery. But the idea spread. In a magazine article early in 1932 Mr. Roosevelt had said that the depression should be fought with wartime methods—and he was not thinking primarily of balancing the federal budget. But, nevertheless, it was particularly for the purpose of reducing the cost of government that the idea first became popular, even among Congressmen. It was an oft-spoken axiom that economy was popular in principle but unpopular in detail. Congress had demonstrated beyond dispute that it would or could not effectively economize. The feat had to be accomplished, if it were done at all, by an executive who could defy the loose coalition of job holders and pensioners which terrified a great majority of the members of Congress. Many Senators and Representatives who thought that tremendous economies had to be made were only too willing to transfer to the Executive the perilous duty of deciding who should suffer. In the rider to the Treasury-Post Office Appropriations bill passed at the end of the short session Mr. Roosevelt got a portion of the authority that he needed. He could combine and abolish commissions, bureaus, and divisions of the government (except departments), subject to a veto by a majority of both houses of Congress within sixty days. He was denied the power to reduce salaries and to trifle with that fortress of expense —payments to veterans.

Legislative authorization by the lame-duck Congress for the experiment in lifting the price of agricultural staples seemed imperative. The prices of farm products had to be raised during the summer of 1933 or the whole credit structure was sure to collapse. It was important to have the new machinery established and working before the spring planting season.

The voluntary domestic allotment plan, as originally conceived, seemed to have several superiorities. The bounty which was to be paid to the farmer for reducing his production was to come from a processing tax, so that there would be no drain on the federal treasury. The plan was theoretically self-enforcing, since each farmer would watch his neighbor. Most important, it faced squarely the fact that the output of farm staples had to be reduced to the needs of the domestic market plus a severely contracted foreign market.

For the first time, too, all the leading farm organizations had been brought to agreement on one plan. Mr. Roosevelt had promised them that he would adopt any workable scheme on which they would all agree. The assurance that they were at last to have their chance after a decade of frustration tended to rally them behind the domestic allotment plan. In conferences between Mr. Roosevelt and farm leaders in November and December 1932, it was decided to experiment with the price-lifting of four major crops—cotton, wheat, tobacco, and corn (the latter in the form of hogs).

From the proposed agricultural experiment arose the realization of the desirability of a second great enlargement of the power of the Executive. The administration of the plan was impossible unless the Executive was to have power to fix yearly quotas, to levy and readjust processing taxes, and to bring about agreements among processors. In addition, a difference of opinion cropped up again immediately after election on the practicability of the domestic allotment plan for use in controlling certain products, such as hogs. For hogs, the export debenture plan seemed better devised. Thus in the Warm Springs conversations various farm leaders proposed that to avoid a deadlock the Executive be given authority to choose between two or three different plans.

The effort to get the farm bill through the lame-duck Congress was a ludicrous failure. For the first time in history the representatives of the leading farm organizations declared their support of the same bill. By the time the House Committee on Agriculture had finished tinkering with the bill it was hardly recognizable as the expression of Mr. Roosevelt's announced policy. The safeguards stipulated by Mr. Roosevelt were gone. Peanuts, flax, rice, and dairy products were added to the original four crops. The bill received short shrift from the Senate, less, perhaps because of its weaknesses, than because Senator Ellison D. Smith, the ranking member of the Senate Committee on Agriculture, did not like it and had his own plan for reducing cotton acreage. If the bill had not died, Mr. Hoover, one assumes, would have vetoed it. He did pocket-veto Senator Smith's cotton control plan.

While prompting the old Congress to action as best he could behind the scenes, Mr. Roosevelt went ahead with the preparation of his own program. He enlisted the help of Swagar Sherley, wartime chairman of the House Appropriations Committee, Daniel C. Roper, and Representative Louis W. Douglas in a survey of the federal government with a view to its complete and most economical reorganization. His objectives were not only to abolish useless commissions and jobs, but to eliminate every function of government which could be spared in a time of emergency, and to put as many as possible of those services which were needed on a self-sustaining basis.

Similarly, Mr. Roosevelt carried forward his study of the railroad problem to the development of a complete plan for reorganization of the nation's transportation system under control of a single agency. He also prepared his other plans, including one for the development of the Tennessee Valley, which gave the public its first view of the full sweep of his imagination, and one for federal relief for the unemployed.

Mr. Roosevelt's other important task during the interregnum was to form a Cabinet. The election returns had no sooner been reported than the East began clamoring for a Cabinet of "big" men. By "big" men these publicists meant usually the conservatives whom Mr. Roosevelt had defeated for the presidential nomination at Chicago. With rare exceptions they were either employees of the dominating financial interests of the country or were saturated with the point of view of the old order. Most of them were men of unusual personal ability. Without question, a great many individuals who thought Mr. Roosevelt was a weak and uninformed man or who had seen nothing at Chicago or during the campaign except conflicting personal ambitions, joined in the demand for a Cabinet of "big" men. Yet at its core the cry was the last effort of the financial powers which had been defeated at Chicago and on Election Day to retain control of the government. It was curious to observe how rarely the name of Senator Thomas J. Walsh, certainly one of the finest and ablest men produced by either party in a generation, was suggested by the advocates of a Cabinet of "big" men. When his name was uttered in Wall Street, it was with inquiry as to whether he would prosecute the financial buccaneers with the same relentless diligence with which he had investigated the oil scandals. Within six weeks after March 4 it was apparent to everyone why few, if any, of the "big" men would have been qualified to serve in Mr. Roosevelt's Cabinet.

The perilous state of the credit structure of the country did recommend, nevertheless, that reassurances be

given to the financial and banking worlds. It happened
that one of industry's big men, Owen D. Young, had the
personal confidence of Mr. Roosevelt. Indirectly he had
been of great assistance in bringing about Mr. Roosevelt's nomination by refusing to let his name be used as
a rallying point for the opposition. His speech in behalf
of a liberal government in the last week before the election had been one of the Democratic party's most powerful counter-attacks against the Republican campaign of
fear. He was one of the comparatively liberal men in the
inner circle of American financiers and industrialists, and
his experience with the financial aspects of the European problem marked him as a man qualified to be Secretary of State. However, Mr. Young had the same strong
personal reasons for wishing to remain in private life that
had led him to refuse to be a candidate for the presidential nomination. Moreover, when the Western Progressives heard that Mr. Roosevelt was considering the
appointment of Mr. Young to the Cabinet, they protested.
It was plain that Mr. Young could not be confirmed without a Senate fight at the very outset of the new Administration. Late in January Mr. Young wrote Mr. Roosevelt, asking that no consideration be given him for any
public office.

With the exception of Mr. Young, the older heads to
whom Mr. Roosevelt turned were in the Senate. His
readiness to strip the Senate was perhaps an only partly
recognized omen of the impending delegation of tremendous powers by Congress to the President. At one time it
seemed conceivable that he would draw on Senatorial
talent to fill four of his ten Cabinet posts: Carter Glass
for the Treasury; Cordell Hull for State or Commerce;

Thomas Walsh for Attorney General; and Hiram W.
Johnson or Bronson M. Cutting for the Interior. The
qualities deemed essential for the Secretary of the Treasury pointed directly toward Glass, who had held the
post for a time under President Wilson and was the
Democratic party's most generally accepted authority on
banking. He was independent of Wall Street and could
lash the buccaneering and speculation of the nineteen-
twenties, yet he was an immovable defender of sound
money. His mere appointment would give bankers what
they appeared to value above all else, "confidence," and
restrain panicky capitalists from running to the banks for
gold. Senator Glass was reluctant to enter the Cabinet
for two reasons: his ailing health and his uncertainty that
Mr. Roosevelt was at heart irrevocably committed to the
existing gold standard. Like many other people, he had
heard of the unorthodox views of Mr. Roosevelt's brains
trust. He sought assurances that under no circumstances
would there be resort to inflation. He failed to get them.
Although Mr. Roosevelt put tremendous pressure on Senator Glass to enter the Cabinet, he did not give the unqualified guarantees that Senator Glass sought. The last
discussion between the two men took place on the train
on February 17 during Mr. Roosevelt's northward journey from Miami. Three days later Senator Glass gave his
final "no." It was a fortunate decision both for him and
for Mr. Roosevelt. Within a few weeks he would have
had to renounce his dearest principles or disrupt the new
Cabinet at a critical moment in the history of the country. The Michigan moratorium was already several days
old and the paralysis of the banking system was creeping
into other states. The chief purpose which the appoint-

ment of Senator Glass would have served had already been frustrated. The final convulsion had begun and the existing gold standard was toppling.

With the elimination of Glass, Mr. Roosevelt drafted his personal friend, William H. Woodin, president of the American Car and Foundry Company. Mr. Woodin, a Republican who had deserted his party to support Alfred E. Smith in 1928, had wide business interests, was a New York bank director, and was esteemed in the highest quarters of Wall Street. But he had shown his independence of his brethren in the big business world by supporting Mr. Roosevelt before the Chicago Convention. He had been one of the three contributors of $10,000 each to the small original fund of the "Friends of Franklin D. Roosevelt," which was used in the pre-convention campaign, and had endeavored to reassure conservatives that Mr. Roosevelt's elevation to the Presidency would not ruin the country. His warm interest in the work of rehabilitating victims of infantile paralysis at Mr. Roosevelt's Georgia Warm Springs Foundation had created a peculiarly strong personal bond. In Mr. Woodin, Mr. Roosevelt had a man who relieved the qualms of the orthodox money people, but on whose personal loyalty he could rely.

In forming his Cabinet Mr. Roosevelt gave the customary attention to sectional and political distribution. More specifically he wanted to cement the alliance of Democrats and Progressive Republicans which had elected him into a new liberal party. Above all, he required a Cabinet that would be loyal to him even under the most trying circumstances. Anybody familiar with Mr. Roosevelt's personal associations and the development of his presidential campaign could have picked five

or six of the new Cabinet members with reasonable as-
surance before Election Day: James A. Farley, Miss
Frances Perkins, Henry A. Wallace, Governor George
H. Dern of Utah, Senators Walsh and Hull, and Senator
Claude A. Swanson of Virginia (if Senator Glass refused
the Treasury portfolio).

Mr. Farley had been Mr. Roosevelt's pre-convention
manager and was chairman of the Democratic National
Committee. He was the obvious man for the Postmaster-
Generalship. All the newspapermen had him planted in
his new job for almost two months, however, before Mr.
Roosevelt even mentioned the subject to his trusted lieutenant. His method of breaking the news was characteristic. A news item had just been printed about the new
automobile with a higher top which Postmaster General
Walter F. Brown had bought so that he could wear a
top-hat while riding. In the middle of a conversation with
Mr. Farley on patronage, Mr. Roosevelt said: "I see
your predecessor is having difficulty with his hat." Mr.
Farley hesitated a moment, but habitual alertness and
political experience told him to make the most of "your
predecessor."

"Thanks," he said, "I accept."

Senator Hull, an old-fashioned Democrat from Tennessee, had been Mr. Roosevelt's reserve candidate for
Secretary of State for many months. He had been one of
the directing minds of the pre-convention campaign, and
had been earmarked for another place in the Cabinet if
he did not receive the portfolio of State. Twelve years
out of power had left the Democratic party without anyone eminently qualified to handle the foreign relations of
the government. Throughout his career Senator Hull had
made the study of the tariff his specialty. He knew the

commerce of every nation, and he was one of the few men in the Senate who regularly read foreign periodicals. He was a conservative, but a low-tariff conservative, who regarded the tariff as the chief bulwark of special interests.

Senator Walsh, a moderate liberal whose rectitude and fearlessness had set him apart in a loose and cynical period in American public life, was the obvious man to become Attorney General. His death two days before Mr. Roosevelt's inauguration left a large gap in the incoming Cabinet. Mr. Roosevelt filled the place with Homer S. Cummings of Connecticut, who, like Senator Walsh, was a moderate liberal and had supported Mr. Roosevelt for the presidential nomination. Mr. Cummings had been designated previously for the Governor-Generalship of the Philippines. His services during the banking crisis made him a fixture in the Cabinet.

George H. Dern, whose long service as Governor of Utah expired in 1932, was another middle-of-the-road liberal with whom Mr. Roosevelt had struck up a friendship through the annual Governors' Conference. He had been one of Mr. Roosevelt's earliest supporters for the presidential nomination. Senator Swanson, a conservative party wheelhorse, had been a personal friend of Mr. Roosevelt's since the war days, when Mr. Roosevelt was Assistant Secretary of the Navy and Senator Swanson was chairman of the Naval Affairs Committee. He was the only Virginia leader who had favored Mr. Roosevelt's nomination. By taking Senator Swanson into the Cabinet, Mr. Roosevelt provided an outlet for former Governor Harry F. Byrd, who succeeded to Senator Swanson's seat. Miss Perkins, a liberal of Mr. Roosevelt's own stripe, had been his Commissioner of Labor in New

York. In selecting her, Mr. Roosevelt established two precedents: the appointment of a woman to the Cabinet and of a Secretary of Labor from outside the leadership of organized labor. Daniel C. Roper, the third Southern Democrat in the Cabinet, was an old lieutenant of William G. McAdoo's. He had joined the Roosevelt movement at an early date and had been helpful in effecting the switch of the Garner-McAdoo delegates that broke the deadlock at the Chicago convention. How far Mr. Roper's inclusion in the Cabinet was a recognition of Mr. McAdoo's services and how far of Mr. Roper's has never been definitely answered. The appointment of Mr. Roper brought into the Cabinet an exceptionally shrewd politician and an executive whose ability had been proved by his organization of the Internal Revenue Bureau under Mr. Wilson.

The portfolios of Agriculture and Interior were put aside for the Progressive Republicans. Henry A. Wallace, the young Iowa farm journal publisher, was the symbol of the agrarian revolt. His father had resigned the Secretaryship of Agriculture under President Coolidge to support McNary-Haugenism. The Secretaryship of the Interior was at the disposal of the Progressive Senators who left the Republican party to support Mr. Roosevelt: Hiram W. Johnson, George W. Norris, Robert M. La-Folette, Jr., and Bronson M. Cutting. None of them wished to leave the Senate. The process of elimination finally worked the list of potentialities down to Harold L. Ickes, the Progressive Republican "lone wolf" from Chicago, whom Senator Johnson had originally recommended for Chief of the Indian Bureau. Mr. Ickes had been speaking favorably of Mr. Roosevelt as the Progressive hope since 1930 and had taken an active part in

the post-convention campaign. However, Mr. Ickes was
not well known in the country at large and Mr. Roosevelt's acquaintance with him was very casual. Shortly before his inauguration, Mr. Roosevelt summoned Mr.
Ickes to New York, and immediately offered him the
Secretaryship of the Interior. "I liked the cut of his jib,"
Mr. Roosevelt explained at the time. Mr. Ickes was the
one real dark horse of the Cabinet. Within six months he
was known as its strongest man.

The completed Cabinet evoked little applause from
the defeated proponents of a Cabinet of "big" men, but
it was a neat piece of craftsmanship. Conservatism was
balanced with liberalism, elder statesmanship with youth,
and the main geographical sections of the country were
represented. Taken as a whole the Cabinet was an accurate physical embodiment of the Democratic platform,
with its range across a broad front and with its inherent
inconsistencies. Superficially it was a coalition that struck
a balance "slightly to the left of the center." But it was a
coalition bound by strong ties of loyalty to one man.
Eight of its ten members were tested personal friends of
Mr. Roosevelt's who had supported him from the beginning of his fight for the presidential nomination.

Mr. Roosevelt applied the same principles of balance
and loyalty in selecting other members of his official family before he went to Washington. He chose Henry Morgenthau, Jr., chairman of his agricultural advisory committee for four years at Albany, to be head of the Farm
Board, which soon became the centerpiece of the new
Farm Credit Administration. He selected one of his
closest friends in the Wilson Administration, William
Phillips, a career diplomat, to be Under Secretary of
State. He put the chief of his brains trust, Raymond

Moley, in the State Department as an Assistant Secretary, and Professor Rexford G. Tugwell under Mr. Wallace as Assistant Secretary of Agriculture. Professor Berle, the third member of the original brains trust, could have had a post of corresponding importance but he did not want it. For the extremely important post of Budget Director, Mr. Roosevelt selected Lewis W. Douglas, the young Democratic Representative from Arizona. Mr. Douglas had shown his mettle by his bold defiance of the veterans' lobby. His appointment reassured the East that Mr. Roosevelt seriously intended to make the drastic economies he had promised.

As chief of his secretariat, Mr. Roosevelt chose Louis McHenry Howe, who had been at his side as a secretary and general assistant for twenty years. As his assistant secretaries he chose Stephen T. Early and Marvin H. McIntyre, two former newspapermen who had been his loyal friends since war days and had traveled with him in his vice-presidential campaign in 1920.

"Slightly to the left of the center" is Mr. Roosevelt's own phrase. That is the direction in which he was consciously headed during the campaign and immediately afterward. But it was only a tentative direction. He saw events threatening that might enable him to swerve sharply to the left. With that in view he chose a Cabinet mobile and cohesive enough to follow him in the dashes and sharp turns of the ensuing months.

No remarkable perception was required at the beginning of 1933 to see that the badly weakened and distorted economic structure was on the verge of complete collapse. The prices of wheat, corn, sugar, and other basic commodities hovered near the low levels of the preceding summer, which were the lowest ever recorded in terms of

the dollar. They were expected to support a burden of
debt beyond the imagination of the country when it had
struggled through its previous great depressions. Disre-
garding a mountain of supplementary debt, the farming
industry was saddled with between eight and nine billion
dollars in mortgages. Those mortgages had been incurred
when the general price level, on a rough average, was
twice as high as it was at the beginning of 1933, and when
the price of farm products was, on the average, four
times what it was at the end of 1932. In terms of power
to buy finished goods, the farm creditor had lent only
half what was owed him; in terms of farm crops, the
farmer owed four times as much as he had borrowed.
The farmers' share of the public debt and of the higher
cost of current operations of government, which he paid
through taxes, was from to two to four times its former
cost in terms of crops. As a matter of fact, some crops
were not worth on the market the cost of their fertilizer
and seed and expense of harvesting.

The railroad industry had a bonded indebtedness of
approximately eleven billion dollars. In 1932 the railroad
system as a whole had fallen far short of earning the
interest charges on this debt. During the preceding decade, governmental units, from the local sewer district to
many of the state governments, had run up tremendous
debts to finance public improvements. As the national income shrank, a larger and larger percentage of it had to
be drained off to meet the carrying charges on the public
debt. Many sources of taxation, particularly the tax on
real estate, had been exhausted. Municipalities dependent
on property taxes could no longer collect enough to remain solvent. Owners of farms and homes had been
compelled to defer payments until tax sales and mortgage

foreclosures on a wholesale scale were on the verge of occurring.

The disparity between what was left of the debit-credit level and contracting economic activity on a lower price level had to be corrected quickly. Yet the full downward readjustment of farm mortgages, railroad debt, and the obligations of public agencies and of the basic industries could not be made. They were the prime investments of savings banks, insurance companies, mortgage companies, trust companies, and, to an extent, of commercial banks.

Debt deflation meant practically the obliteration of the remaining credit structure. It was a grave question how long the credit structure would stand in mid-air. Nobody knew the exact condition of banks and insurance companies. Most of the savings banks were being kept legally solvent by the practice of giving their investments in many categories, especially railroad bonds, values considerably in excess of current prices. The same practice was followed with other banks; no one knew exactly to what extent because they were under forty-nine different supervisory authorities. Insurance companies, drawn on heavily for loans to policy-holders and suffering from the relinquishments of policies, were hard pressed for cash. They could not foreclose farm mortgages and resell the properties for more than a fraction of their old conservative first-mortgage value.

With the possible exception of Germany, no nation since the development of modern industry and finance had slid so far down the chute of deflation as the United States had between the end of 1929 and the beginning of 1933. Every nation that participated in the World War, except Great Britain and the United States, had lightened its load of debt by currency revaluation in the years immediately afterward. France and Italy had written off practically four-fifths of their internal debt. Germany and some of the lesser Central European countries had nearly obliterated theirs. As the world depression settled down and falling price levels and diminished economic activity made the burden of debt unbearable, one nation after another had cut loose from gold. Great Britain's departure from gold in the autumn of 1931 was quickly followed by other nations which had not accumulated the wartime excess of debt. The sterling bloc, as it was called, floated on the world price level, thus escaping the stress and pain of the last thirty percent of the decline which threatened the entire American financial structure. At the beginning of 1933, the United States, Holland, and Switzerland were the only nations on a gold basis which had not lightened their debt loads since the World War.

The demand from American producers of raw commodities for relief by currency inflation had grown steadily for two years. In January 1933 the ancient proposal for the free coinage of silver at a ratio of sixteen to one, received eighteen votes in the Senate. It was well known that many other Senators favored inflation, but by other methods. Careful analysis of the temper of the farm belt and of the make-up of the incoming Congress indicated that the demand for inflation would have a power that few men could stay.

Mr. Roosevelt, as we have seen, had at least a mental reservation as to the possibility or desirability of maintaining the gold standard. But he could not admit it or even hint at it except in the most intimate circle of tight-lipped friends. Only a hint that he contemplated departure from the gold standard or inflation and he would have instantly caused the catastrophe that everyone wished to avoid. So long as men were legally entitled to exchange currency for gold and to export capital in the form of gold, a collapse could be averted only by solemn reassurance that they would continue indefinitely to have these rights. Suspension of specie payments and an embargo of gold exports were indispensable prerequisites to the adoption of any overt form of inflation, unless the country was willing to lose all its gold. And an unstemmed demand for gold meant the quick disintegration of the banking system. As was subsequently shown, a large number of canny speculators and prudent business men had already, during the preceding year and a half, withdrawn and sequestered gold from fear or belief that the dollar sooner or later would be forced off gold.

Back of the precarious state of the financial structure of the country lay even more disturbing situations. Dwindling industrial activity had cast off between 12,000,000 and 15,000,000 workers. Counting children, between 30,000,000 and 35,000,000 persons in the world's once most prosperous country were dependent on private or public charity for their very existence. Perhaps another forty or fifty percent of the population of the country, including most of the farmers and village tradesmen were barely subsisting by their own efforts. Still other individuals were draining the dregs from their old savings. These are all estimates made by conservative people in the winter of 1932–33. There were no central agencies for gathering and analyzing accurate statistics. The financial and business leaders of the country had long before found it necessary or useful to have regular reports on such indices as brokers' loans, bank clearings, the state of the Federal Treasury and of the Federal Reserve banks, car loadings, steel tonnage, and the infinite assortment of statistics on everything from oysters in Samoa to burnooses in the Sahara, that the Department of Commerce was staffed to gather and publish. But such fundamental economic indices as the number of unemployed, the number of people on the dole, the unemployment relief expenditure, the weekly wage distribution were not considered necessary. In fact, they were very nearly taboo. When this field was reached, Mr. Hoover's own avidity for statistics turned into an aversion to letting anybody know them. Even the test figures on factory unemployment gathered by the Federal Department of Labor were wrong, as Miss Frances Perkins, then Commissioner of Labor for New York, so surely proved. Still further in the background stood more disquieting evidence of social disintegration. In many communities throughout the country lack of funds had compelled the closing of schools and the operation of others on part time. Poverty was forcing many young people to discontinue their education even though they could find nothing to do in the world outside. The transmission line of civilization was beginning to fray.

The vast and growing army of unemployed was kept pacified by the dole. In the early years of the depression a considerable amount of energy and propaganda had been expended by financial and business leaders and the Federal Administration in trying to keep the word "dole" out of the American language. We were even told that it was the "dole" which kept certain European nations from enjoying the heights of prosperity which the United States recently had experienced and would enjoy again if it could only escape the dole. The campaign probably served useful purposes. It helped to develop "made work" and promote experiments with other forms of aid than the pure dole (which, in fact, no European nation had, except to a limited extent). It also helped to shake large contributions for relief out of some of the people who could best afford them, since, by fortunate coincidence, they were the people who most feared the dole and were willing to take out insurance against it. (That was before Mr. J. P. Morgan was seized with such enthusiasm for the idea of having the unemployed supported by five, ten and, twenty-five cent weekly contributions from white collar workers and laborers still fortunate enough to be working that he overcame his aversion to addressing the public and made a radio speech in behalf of the block-aid campaign.)

But the fact that it was neither humane nor safe for the existing order to let large numbers of people starve was as irresistible in the United States as it had been in Europe. By the beginning of 1933 the nation which had exorcised the dole had more people on the dole, in its various forms, than any nation had ever before had in the history of the world. The dole had already eaten its way through diminishing private resources and vanishing funds and credit of municipalities. It had overrun state credit in many instances and arrived at the Federal Treasury. Even the stalwart foes of a federal dole were forced to relent to the extent of permitting the Reconstruction Finance Corporation to lend funds for public works and relief. And back of the R.F.C. and the Federal Treasury lay an unbalanced budget. The state of mind of the unemployed, compounded of blind despair, unquenchable hope, and imperviousness to radical agitators, was one of the wonders of the depression. (In only three of the cities visited by Mr. Roosevelt in his 1932 campaign could one sense that large groups of unemployed were moved by a determination to improve their condition. These cities were Seattle, where the Unemployed Citizens League had made

itself a controlling political force; Pittsburgh, where
Father Cox had given many of the unemployed a leadership which they could follow; and Detroit, another un-
usually distressed locality where, after comparatively generous treatment by the municipality under Mayor Frank
Murphy, the unemployed were feeling the pinch of con-
stricting relief as the city's credit became exhausted, and
where Father Coughlin was a man of influence.) Nevertheless, it was obvious that only the dole stood between
the country and chaotic disorder.

The first signs that the economic state of the country
had become unbearable came, not from the hordes of industrial offcasts, but from the richest section of the American farm belt. It was a property-owners' revolt. The spirit
of rugged individualism still lived in the state of Mr.
Hoover's birth. Since neither the law nor the "American
system" protected his home and farm, the Iowa farmer
decided to protect it himself with rifle, shotgun, and noose,
in the true frontier manner glorified in the American tradition. He banded together with his neighbors to frustrate
the legal processes of tax sales and foreclosures by in-
timidating bank and insurance company agents, sheriffs
and judges, bidding in property for a few cents or a few
dollars, and restoring it to the former owners.

As early as the spring of 1932 reports of these first
resorts to the revolutionary tactic of direct action had
begun to reach the Eastern newspapers. As the property-
owners' rebellion met with success, it spread rapidly. In
the late summer of 1932, under the militant leadership
of Milo Reno, Iowa farmers experimented with a second
method: the strike. The first Iowa milk strikes were sup-
pressed after some physical violence. The Farmers' Holiday movement, utilizing both devices, spread quickly and

haphazardly over the country. In the early winter of 1933, foreclosures were prevented by grim bands of farmers as far west as the Pacific Coast, as far south as Kentucky and Oklahoma, and as far east as the Delaware River. Revolting farmers marched to uncounted court houses and into the capitols of Wisconsin, Nebraska, Iowa, and other states in the farm belt. Late in January Governor Herring of Iowa appealed to all mortgage holders to withhold foreclosure proceedings until the State Legislature could act. Other states took action of one kind or another to allay the rebellion. At the end of January, the Senate Agriculture Committee heard a warning from Edward A. O'Neal, President of the American Farm Bureau Federation, which represented the more conservative farmers of the corn belt. Mr. O'Neal said: "Unless something is done for the American farmer, we'll have revolution in the countryside in less than twelve months."

At the beginning of February 1933, it was a nice question which would crack first: the twisted framework of the credit structure or human endurance. That was settled by the Detroit banking crisis and the bank moratorium in Michigan. From Michigan paralysis of the banking system spread, at first gradually, then at quickening pace, until it reached the two great financial centers, Chicago and New York, on the very eve of Mr. Roosevelt's inauguration. In all history there have been few such ironic coincidences as this collapse of an economic order in the last minutes of its zealous guardianship by the man who thought it fundamentally perfect. At 1:06 o'clock Saturday afternoon, March 4, Mr. Hoover presented the prostrate form of his American system to Mr. Roosevelt.

III

The Crisis

IN RETROSPECT the swift and kaleidoscopic movements of the first days of Mr. Roosevelt's Administration remain a series of impressions.

The frenzied conferences in every city and every capitol. The country's blind fright and sense of engulfment in chaos. The weary and heart-broken Mr. Hoover and the gay Mr. Roosevelt riding up Pennsylvania Avenue together to participate in the hard-won ceremony for the transfer of power under a constitutional democracy. Mr. Roosevelt's burning proclamation of the failure and abdication of the money changers, his resolute pledge to action and "action now"—as the entire nation and much of the world hung on his words. The instant confirmation of the new Cabinet and its swearing in at the unprecedented ceremony at the White House that night. The new President reviewing the five-hour inaugural parade, the death pageant of the old, or the prologue to a new, era—no one knew which. The summoning of the new Congress into special session on March 9. The first lightning stroke from the White House—closing every bank, embargoing gold, and making the hoarding of gold and currency a penal offense. The country's momentary release from terror in laughter at its predicament. Mr. Woodin moving through the turmoil of bankers and distraught "big minds" with the elfin happiness of a character from one of his own nursery ballads.

The emergency banking act finally hammered together in the early morning hours and jammed through a frightened Congress which knew little of its contents. The President's swift demand for authority to slash half a billion dollars from the federal budget, mostly from the heretofore impregnable veterans' appropriations. The suspense as the economy bill stuck in the House and then slithered through. Mr. Roosevelt's Sunday night radio speech, explaining the banking situation and what he had done about it with the informal simplicity of a man describing a vacation experience to his family. The reopening of the banks (some of them) and the rush to redeposit gold and currency. As the economy bill reached the Senate, beer tossed out from the White House like a stick of dynamite into a log jam.

These are among the imperishable impressions of the almost miraculous transition of the nation from panic to restored hope. These were the first strokes in the exciting and bewildering onflow of events which marked the Roosevelt Revolution in its first phase. They were all the more startling because the public could not see everything that was occurring backstage. The three weeks leading up to Mr. Roosevelt's inauguration were a period during which the average citizen knew little about the real economic state of the country except as he saw how his neighbors behaved and heard the fast spreading waves of rumor. A panic of that sort puts the press in an embarrassing position from which there is no wholly satisfactory escape. The press could not publish all that it knew without aggravating the panic; yet it could not ignore the situation without undermining public confidence in the press and perhaps giving wild rumor more leeway than it otherwise would have had. In the second place, the press experienced unusual difficulty in obtaining reliable information. The few men who had it were likewise trying to allay rather than accelerate the panic. In the third place, the best-informed men—in the banking centers and in Washington—were in reality meagerly informed. As in the thick of a battle on a broad front, infinite numbers of events were happening simultaneously, the lines of communication were uncertain, the reports from different points were colored by the emotional state of the men who made them. A complete picture of the rapidly changing situation could neither be assembled nor coolly judged. The more reputable newspapers adopted the sensible course of publishing the evidence of the progress of the panic as it was shown by moratoria, restrictions, and gold and currency withdrawals, without frightening headlines or doleful comment which would have whipped even higher the waves of fear. It is doubtful if the story of the banking crisis and Mr. Roosevelt's first week in office ever can be put together to the satisfaction of everyone. The main participants in the drama were too numerous and they emerged from long days and nights of tension with blurred and conflicting memories. However, it is now possible to supply some of the missing facts.

On February 14, when the failure to straighten out the tangled affairs of the $51,000,000 Union Guardian Trust Company of Detroit led Governor Comstock to declare an eight-day banking holiday in Michigan, Mr. Roosevelt was on Vincent Astor's yacht enjoying his last vacation before entering the White House. As he traveled northward from Miami three days later, Jesse H. Jones, a Democratic member of the Reconstruction Finance Corporation, boarded the special train in Georgia and put Mr. Roosevelt abreast of the situation. The markets were falling, money in circulation (partly an index of hoarding) was jumping, the dollar was wobbling on the foreign exchange as gold was flowing out. The country as a whole was not in a panic but the bankers were. There had been few months since the late fall of 1930 without the surge of a banking panic in some section of the country. Help from stronger banks and local capitalists and later prompt and generous aid from the R.F.C. had succeeded in localizing and stemming each panic. Nevertheless, Nevada had had a banking holiday late in 1932 and Louisiana, after several narrow escapes, had one only two weeks before the Detroit collapse. There had been two hard runs on gold: one in October 1931, after Great Britain's departure from the gold standard, and the other in May and June 1932. Both were attributed primarily to foreign withdrawals but undoubtedly were augmented by the flight of American capital.

When the eight-day Michigan moratorium expired and no way had been found to reopen the Detroit banks, even with the aid of immense loans from the R.F.C., the panic began in earnest. The bankers, following a well-worn pattern, blamed Congress. They denounced a Senate investigating committee's current exposé of the banking methods and ethics of Charles E. Mitchell, chairman of the board of the National City Bank. Their theory was that it created distrust in bankers and made the public rush for currency and gold. Persons better acquainted with the country knew that most of it had long ago made up its mind that Mr. Mitchell and most other New York bankers were brigands. The fact that Mr. Mitchell was still head of the country's second largest bank more than three years after the stock market crash of 1929 was confirmation of the average man's diagnosis of the Wall Street fraternity. The current exposé, while interesting in detail, merely confirmed his suspicions. Besides, it showed that Mr. Mitchell had been no less thorough in retreat than in advance: the National City Bank's liquidity at the end of 1932 was the envy of bankers throughout the country. Mr. Roosevelt, incidentally, spoke the word which led to Mr. Mitchell's resignation. On Saturday, February 25, important directors of the bank sought his advice through Mr. Woodin, who was one of them. Mr. Roosevelt said he thought Mr. Mitchell should resign at once. Mr. Mitchell and Hugh Baker, President of the affiliated National City Company, resigned over the week-end. That did not stem the panic.

From the moment of his return to New York on February 17, Mr. Roosevelt was in continual communication with the leading bankers of New York and with the Hoover Administration, directly and through Mr. Woodin and other intermediaries. The bankers looked to Mr. Roosevelt to save them, and they had definite ideas about the way he should do it. Their first plea was for a statement that would create confidence by promising that, come what might, there would never be any departure from the existing gold standard. Mr. Roosevelt firmly refused to make such a statement. The average citizen who was going to the bank to get currency cared nothing about the gold standard: he wanted money before the bank closed. The gold standard meant something to the financiers and corporations who were making large conversions into gold but most of them were intelligent enough to see that the suspension of specie payments probably would come soon, no matter what anybody might say. Mr. Hoover had helped to undermine his prestige by making optimistic statements which everybody knew were not supported by fact. The chances were overwhelming that the effect of a statement from Mr. Roosevelt would have been not to stop the demand for currency and gold, but to injure public confidence in him and destroy his chances of dealing effectively with the situation after March 4.

As the crisis deepened, some New York bankers turned to the idea, popular in Congress, of throwing the federal credit back of the banking system on a gigantic scale. Federal guarantee of bank deposits and huge loans from the R.F.C. were the main alternatives suggested by these proponents of "less government in business" and of the balance-the-budget school of recovery. (It was not surprising, as the operation of the R.F.C. had shown to everybody who had not realized it before, that the big bankers were most enthusiastic raiders of the public treasury when their own interest was served by it. That did not deter them from being the first to applaud when Mr. Roosevelt's Economy Bill went through Congress.)

When the New York bankers first proposed huge loans by the R.F.C., which had been making larger and larger loans for months, only four states had bank holidays or restrictions. But it was estimated then that a billion dollars was needed to take care of the banks already in distress. The R.F.C. had approximately one-tenth of that amount and could not get more until the Federal Government did new financing. In any event, it was an open question whether most localities would have been calmed or incited to swifter withdrawals by R.F.C. loans to their banks.

After one of his many telephone conversations with banking leaders in New York during this period Mr. Roosevelt turned to a person in his study. "These New York bankers haven't any more notion of public psychol-

ogy than a chicken," he remarked. Mr. Roosevelt was
working on his inaugural address at this time. It is safe to
assume that his daily contacts with the banking fraternity
did not dispose him to soften his reference to the money
changers in his inaugural speech.

Mr. Hoover would not act without the concurrence of
Mr. Roosevelt. Probably he could not have done anything
requiring Congressional approval without Mr. Roosevelt's open support. Mr. Roosevelt still refused to accept
responsibility without power, and could not see anything
sound in the proposals of the Wall Street guardians of
"soundness" in financial affairs. Undoubtedly, the feeling
arose among some of Mr. Roosevelt's friends that the
Hoover Administration's chief concern was to tide things
over until after March 4, so that the final crash would be
known as the "Roosevelt Panic." Undoubtedly, many of
Mr. Hoover's friends thought that Mr. Roosevelt was
non-co-operative because he wanted the final crash to come
before Mr. Hoover left office. The indications were, however, that the real obstacles were inability to agree on
what should be done and the fact that Mr. Roosevelt felt
he could not afford to take responsibility for any policy
over the execution of which he would not have full control.

Apart from a large number of intermediaries, Mr.
Hoover and Mr. Roosevelt were also in direct communication by personal correspondence. The contents of this
correspondence have never been disclosed. Late in December, Chief Moran of the Secret Service made a trip from
the White House to the Executive Mansion in Albany, and
it was rumored that he carried a long letter to Mr. Roosevelt written in Mr. Hoover's own hand. Whenever the
correspondence began, Mr. Hoover sent Mr. Roosevelt

several highly confidential letters on the state of the nation and the world, to which Mr. Roosevelt replied. Two of these exchanges occurred in February when the banking panic was spreading. A few days before he left office, Mr. Hoover was talking to a close friend in the White House. Presumably he had just received Mr. Roosevelt's last confidential reply.

"My God!" Mr. Hoover is reported to have said. "He's going off gold."

Whether Mr. Roosevelt definitely stated such an intention or whether Mr. Hoover deduced it from Mr. Roosevelt's rejection of Mr. Hoover's proposals remains undisclosed. Until a few days before the inauguration, the prevalent belief in Mr. Roosevelt's circle was that, if the panic did not naturally subside, it at least would not reach its crisis for another week or ten days. But, on Monday and Tuesday, February 27 and 28, the panic intensified. On Wednesday, March 1, fifteen states and the District of Columbia were in the area of suspended or restricted banking operations, and the Federal Reserve Bank of New York lost $36,000,000 in gold. On Thursday six more states declared holidays and the weekly statement of the Federal Reserve Board contained the following significant figures: a record-breaking increase of $732,000,-000 of currency in circulation and the loss of $226,310,-000 in gold.

Mr. Roosevelt and his entourage arrived in Washington Thursday night amid suspense and blind fear unprecedented in the peacetime history of the country. Mr. Roosevelt called the Congressional leaders of the party into conference in the Mayflower Hotel, and was put in touch with the White House and Treasury.

Mr. Roosevelt took with him to Washington several

alternative plans for dealing with the emergency, as soon
as he could act. One of them was a practically forgotten
statute of war days, the Trading with the Enemy Act.
Mr. Roosevelt's rediscovery of this act came out of a conversation he had in early January with René Léon, an
economist and retired banker who had served during the
previous year as an expert for the House Banking and
Currency Committee's investigation of the money problem. They were discussing the perilous discrepancy between the debt level and prices and the imminent danger
of a collapse. They agreed that it was imperative that the
President should have the power to put an embargo on
gold exports, suspend specie payments, and close the
banks.

"I wonder if any of the old wartime statutes are still
alive," Mr. Roosevelt said. Mr. Léon said he thought
they might be. A few days later he sent Mr. Roosevelt a
transcript of the Trading with the Enemy Act of 1917,
designed to prevent gold from reaching enemy nations.
Under this act President Wilson had embargoed gold exports during the war. The law had been amended several
times and it was questionable whether or not it had been
repealed in its entirety. Mr. Roosevelt had a check made
and sought several legal opinions. They were divided.
Senator Walsh, Attorney General designate, was doubtful
but promised that if the powers were needed in an emergency he would rule that they were valid. When Mr.
Roosevelt drafted Mr. Cummings on March 2, after Senator Walsh's death, he at once handed him the folder on
the Trading with the Enemy Act. Mr. Cummings studied
the question anew and decided that the requisite authority was still alive.

Ogden L. Mills, Secretary of the Treasury, also had

rediscovered the Trading with the Enemy Act, and urged Mr. Hoover to act under it. On the morning of March 3, it was proposed to Mr. Roosevelt that he join Mr. Hoover in proclaiming a nation-wide banking moratorium and embargo on gold exports. Mr. Roosevelt refused, for the same reasons that he had refused to take joint action before, plus the fact that he felt he could not make a decision until he had all the facts before him. At four o'clock that afternoon, he went to the White House to pay the customary courtesy call of the President-elect on the President. Within a few minutes the social amenities were disposed of. Mr. Hoover summoned Secretary Mills and Eugene Meyer, Governor of the Federal Reserve Board. Mr. Roosevelt sent for Professor Moley. The five men conferred for almost an hour. It was proposed that Mr. Hoover and Mr. Roosevelt issue a joint statement that there would be no inflation.

Mr. Roosevelt's refusal to sign his name to a joint proclamation left the way open for Mr. Hoover to act alone. Mr. Hoover felt deterred from employing the Trading with the Enemy Act. It was said that Attorney General William D. Mitchell had submitted an informal opinion that it was extremely doubtful that the act was still in force.

Meanwhile, the leading bankers of New York and Chicago gathered in the Federal Reserve Banks of the respective districts. A check-up showed, among other things, that during the day the record-breaking amount of $116,-349,600 in gold had been exported or earmarked for foreign account in New York. However, the half-day of business Saturday would be followed immediately by the change in administration and, possibly, a sharp change in public psychology could be expected before Monday.

Early Friday evening Thomas W. Lamont of J. P. Morgan & Co. telephoned to Mr. Roosevelt recommending on behalf of the New York group that no action be taken in Washington. Shortly afterward, Mr. Hoover telephoned Mr. Roosevelt to tell him that he had decided to take no action. Both gentlemen were very busy on the telephone and in conferences throughout the evening. About one o'clock Mr. Hoover telephoned to Mr. Roosevelt to tell him that there was not much new, and Mr. Roosevelt suggested that they both go to bed and get a night's sleep before a trying day.

Meanwhile, Secretary Mills and the Treasury and Federal Reserve Board Officials felt the urgent necessity for protecting the New York and Illinois banks against more runs on Saturday morning. Mr. Woodin and Professor Moley joined their deliberations. The New York banking leaders apparently still thought they could pull through another half-day. Governors Lehman of New York and Horner of Illinois were caught between conflicting opinions. Finally, after a conversation with Mr. Roosevelt, Governor Lehman declared a two-day banking holiday in New York and Governor Horner followed suit. Before morning all banking operations were suspended or heavily restricted in every state. The closing of all security and commodity exchanges except the Chicago Livestock Exchange was announced before ten o'clock.

As soon as Mr. Roosevelt had delivered his Inaugural Address, he began to act. At his request the Senate immediately confirmed his Cabinet without reference to committee. He had the Cabinet sworn in at the White House at six o'clock and instructed them to take over their respective departments at once. He then summoned Congressional leaders to confer with him on Sunday to fix the

date for an extraordinary session. Meanwhile he reviewed
the inaugural parade. In the anxious hours of Thursday
and Friday several people had urged that the trimmings
of the inauguration be curtailed. Mr. Roosevelt had insisted that they go on as if nothing had happened. That
was undoubtedly good psychology. But anyone who may
think that Mr. Roosevelt's devotion of five hours at the
most critical point in the nation's history since the Civil
War to the pleasure of reviewing the inaugural parade
was merely an act effectively performed to keep up the
public morale, does not know his man. Mr. Roosevelt
really wanted to see the parade. It was part of his own
inauguration, which he had planned in most active co-
operation with Rear Admiral Cary T. Grayson, chairman
of the Inaugural Committee. I have no doubt that while
he was watching the parade he enjoyed himself fully as
much as if it had been held at the heydey of American
prosperity. On Sunday, haggard bankers from Chicago
and New York poured into Washington. Mr. Woodin, a
stranger to public life, found himself at the head of a department in which he knew no one except a few higher
officials. He asked and promptly got the co-operation of
the Republicans in charge from Governor Meyer and Secretary Mills down. Mr. Roosevelt assembled his Cabinet
and told them what he proposed to do. When he had finished he turned to Attorney General Cummings and inquired: "How much time will you require to prepare an
opinion?" Mr. Cummings, who had missed most of the
inaugural parade in order to read the record of the pertinent debates in Congress and examine the law, promptly
replied: "Mr. President, I am ready to give my opinion
now." Mr. Roosevelt nodded to him to proceed. Mr.
Cummings said his opinion was that all the powers in the

Trading with the Enemy Act which the President wished to use were still alive.

Mr. Roosevelt then went over the situation with Congressional leaders and called a special session of the new Congress for Thursday, March 9. That gave four days to prepare emergency legislation. Invoking the powers of the Trading with the Enemy Act, he proclaimed:

1. A four-day bank holiday throughout the country.
2. An embargo on the withdrawal or transfer for export or domestic use of gold, or silver.
3. A maximum penalty of $10,000 fine or ten years' imprisonment for violation of the proclamation.
4. Power to the Secretary of the Treasury to make exceptions to the proclamation.

It is difficult to recall the remarkable effect which that proclamation had. The country as a whole perhaps little understood its implications, but it was action, like a streak of lightning out of a black sky. Men familiar with finance and law and accustomed to the old ways of individualism were incredulous before the threat of prison sentences and heavy fines for hoarding currency and gold. The citizen who had got currency at his bank or who had exchanged his currency for gold had merely been exercising his rights, had he not? The proclamation of the early morning of March 6 was the new régime's first application of the principle that the larger welfare stands above the individual right.

The Federal Reserve Bank officials who happened to be present in Washington were still dubious that the Federal Reserve Banks could be closed by the presidential proclamation. About two o'clock Monday morning, Secretary Woodin, former Secretary Mills, Governor Meyer of the Federal Reserve Board, and Professor Moley were discussing the question.

"Well," Professor Moley said at last, "if two Secretaries of the Treasury and the Governor of the Federal Reserve Board can't close the Federal Reserve Banks, who can?" Governor Meyer got up and left the room to call George L. Harrison, Governor of the Federal Reserve Bank of New York. A few minutes later he returned and said that all the Federal Reserve Banks would close.

The hours between Mr. Roosevelt's inauguration and the night of March 9 were among the maddest Washington has ever experienced. Conferences ran practically without interruption for four days and nights. To the casual observer, it seemed incredible that any workable scheme for reopening the nation's banks could come out of this confusion. There was neither order nor common understanding of objectives and methods. The situation was unprecedented, and most of the men who undertook to meet it were excited or unnerved by previous days and weeks of intense worry. Several, including one who had been the leading bankers' candidate for Secretary of the Treasury, went to pieces under the strain. The only calm persons in the madhouse appeared to be Mr. Roosevelt and the diminutive Mr. Woodin, who never lost an opportunity to smile and assure the country that he was "very happy."

The problems presented by the emergency fell into three parts: First, keeping the country fed and business operating so far as possible while the banks were closed. Second, salvaging as much of the banking system as possible. Third, giving assurance that those banks which were opened would remain open.

To meet the immediate problem the banking moratorium was relaxed. All banks were empowered to make
loans for the movement of food. Banks with cash on hand
were authorized to permit withdrawals to meet payrolls,
to enable individual depositors to buy food and medicine
and other vital necessities, day by day, and to make
change. The Postal Savings Banks were kept open. All
banks were authorized to cash checks drawn on the Treas-
urer of the United States. Orders were given to permit
free access to safety deposit boxes so that hoarded currency and gold could be taken out.

In addition, the President's proclamation authorized
the Secretary of the Treasury to direct local clearing
house associations to issue scrip. In the large cities the
printing of scrip on the order of bankers had begun early
Saturday morning. Governor Lehman of New York
swiftly put through the Legislature a bill providing for a
statewide scrip issue. Many of the banking leaders who
came to Washington were preoccupied with methods of
issuing scrip. Talk of a nationwide scrip issue was prevalent for at least forty-eight hours. The more farflung
schemes for the use of scrip sprang primarily from the
bankers' habit of relying on precedent instead of on common sense. In the banking panic of 1907, there had been a
great scrip issue. That was before the creation of the
Federal Reserve System, which provided new facilities for
the conversion of bank loans and investments into currency. Scrip haunted the minds of the big bankers assembled at Washington like a mania. On Tuesday night Mr.
Woodin quietly but abruptly put an end to the argument
over a national scrip issue. The plan that he outlined for
dealing with the emergency had two main points: the
printing of all the currency necessary, to be issued against

the sound assets of banks, and the assumption by the government of a large measure of control of the banking system without a guarantee of deposits.

The preparations made for the issue of local scrip were prompted by other considerations. In many localities it was questionable whether the banks had enough currency and coin and whether hoarded currency would come out of hoarding on a large enough scale to supply minimum needs. By Tuesday or Wednesday it became evident that there was no widespread need to provide a temporary medium of exchange.

Proposals for meeting the emergency became intertwined with conflicting ideas for permanent reform of the banking system. Advocates of a unified banking system wanted to seize the opportunity to force all the forty-eight state banking systems into the Federal Reserve system. The state banking systems were fortified, however, behind tremendous influence in Congress and the fear of the South and West of domination by the big bankers. Other proposals for reforms ranged from conversion of Federal Reserve Banks into government-owned deposit banks to nationalization of the whole banking business. Such various reforms as the extension of branch banking, the segregation into separate institutions of the functions of commercial banks, trust companies, and investment banks, had their advocates and opponents.

The banking system lay unconscious on the table and the temptation to operate on it was strong. Mr. Roosevelt theoretically had a golden opportunity. He chose instead to postpone the operation and resuscitate the banking system as quickly as possible. If he had had completely worked out a permanent plan which commanded wide approval, he might have gone farther. But he did not have such a scheme and there was none which could be quickly developed without incurring widespread opposition and the risks of delay. Speed and the inspiration of confidence were the essence of his problem. Every day that the banks remained closed the economic system shriveled a bit more.

The plan that he adopted was, in a nutshell, to permit sound banks to reopen and to provide them with adequate currency to liquefy their assets. The main features of the emergency banking bill were these: The issue of new non-gold currency, to be called Federal Reserve Bank Notes, which the Federal Reserve Banks were to advance to its members up to one hundred percent of the value of government bonds and ninety percent of the value of other rediscounted assets. The Federal Reserve Banks were empowered to rediscount paper that previously had been non-eligible—"cats and dogs," as Senator Glass called them. Banks would reopen only under license from the Treasury. Completely sound banks would be licensed at once. Banks which were less than hopelessly insolvent would be placed under "conservators" and allowed to operate under restrictions or completely reopened as rapidly as they could be put in shape. Hopelessly insolvent banks were to be kept shut and liquidated.

The R.F.C. was authorized to subscribe to preferred stock in banks. All the proclamations and actions of the President and Secretary of the Treasury under the dubious Trading with the Enemy Act were confirmed, and the President was newly endowed with the wartime authority over gold and currency, with maximum penalties of $10,000 and ten years' imprisonment for violations of his regulations.

On Wednesday night, March 8, the President called the leaders of the Senate and House to the White House and told them what he had decided to do. Many of them were dissatisfied, but in this emergency there could be only one directing hand. At dawn the following morning, Secretary Woodin left the White House with the final draft of the emergency banking bill.

"Yes, it's finished," he said in answer to the quick questions of newspapermen. "Both bills are finished. You know my name is Bill and I'm finished too."

The Bureau of Printing and Engraving was already at work on a twenty-four-hour shift grinding out new currency. At noon the new Congress met and for three hours it organized. At three o'clock the clerk of the House read the President's message. Representative Bertrand H. Snell, the Republican floor leader, at once arose and said the President was the man responsible in the crisis and "we must at this time follow his lead." No one but a few leaders had even seen the bill. Cries of "Vote, vote!" drowned out the attempts of debate. At 4:03 P.M., thirty-eight minutes after it had been taken up, the bill passed the House by acclamation without reference to committee and went to the Senate. Senator Huey Long at once arose to make a fiery plea for the "State banks at the forks of the creeks of this country." Senator Carter Glass poured his scorn on "little corner grocerymen who run banks" and his venom on his foe of the winter's filibuster. After three hours of debate, the Senate passed the bill, 73 to 7. At 8:37 P.M. the President, seated before cameras in the Oval Room on the second floor of the White House, signed the first bill of his Administration. He promptly extended the moratorium to give the Treasury and Federal Reserve authorities time to work on their plans for reopening the banks.

An hour later the Congressional leaders of both parties trooped into the White House in answer to a presidential summons. Shortly after midnight they departed, a mixture of dazed, determined, and angry men. The President had laid before them the most drastic proposals for economy that ever had issued from the White House. He asked authority to cut more than $100,000,000 from government salaries and to revise the entire pension and veterans' compensation system at a saving of more than $400,000,000.

The President's incisive message to Congress the next morning stunned the veterans' lobby and drew ecstatic cheers from disciples of the budget-balancing school of recovery. It pointed out that for three years the federal government had been "on the road to bankruptcy." The total deficit for the depression years would reach approximately four billion dollars on June 30, 1933, the end of the fiscal year, and unless drastic economies were effected or new taxes imposed, another billion would be added to the year 1933–34.

The bill, appropriately entitled "A Bill to Maintain the Credit of the United States Government," contained the following main features: Reduction of all Civil War Pensions by ten percent. Repeal of all Spanish War pension laws. Repeal of all World War compensation and allowance laws. Creation of four groups of pensioners: 1. War-disabled veterans; 2. Veterans totally disabled in civil life; 3. Widows and orphans of veterans dying as result of military disability; 4. Widows and orphans of all veterans in service before 1917. Delegation of authority to President to classify all eligible pensioners and fix payments to each. Fixation of disability pensions at from $6 to $275 per month, and death pensions at from $12 to $75. Fixation of the end of World War on November 11, 1918.

Reduction of Congressional salaries from $10,000 to $8,500. Authorization for the President to reduce all federal salaries up to fifteen percent in ratio to the decline of cost of living since 1926.

For years Congress had been obedient to the demands of the veterans' lobby. The organized veterans and their families were a minority, but like the bone drys, a militant minority which held the balance of power in many Congressional districts. The well-conceived plan of President Wilson for the care of the veterans of the World War had been expanded and disrupted by successive laws over a twelve-year period. The obligation to care for the war-disabled and their dependents had been stretched to cover men whose disabilities had no connection with military service or were merely "presumed" to have had a connection through an unscientific and lax system. The veterans' organizations and Congressmen seeking votes had fostered the notion that the mere fact that a man had once worn a uniform—even though it had been under draft and on safe American soil—entitled him to special privileges for the remainder of his life.

The rising cost, when added to the pension systems for the earlier wars, amounted to nearly $1,000,000,000 yearly, or nearly one-quarter of the federal budget at its prosperity peak. Mr. Hoover's modest proposal to cut $127,000,000 from that quarter of the budget had been coolly ignored by the previous Congress. In the Congressional election of 1932 the veterans' lobby had held its own against the aggressive campaign of the National Economy League. Through the overstanding proposal to pay the bonus with greenbacks, generosity to the veterans had been linked with the inflationary sentiment of the farm states.

On broad economic grounds the opposition to economy could make a case. Reduction of the federal budget was deflationary when the prime needs of the country were inflationary. It was very little more deflationary, however, than the balancing of the budget by increased taxation instead of by economy.

On the other side of the argument were several persuasive points: The veterans system contained malignant growths that were indefensible even in the time of greatest prosperity. The Democratic party was pledged to reduce the current expenses of government by twenty-five percent, and that was impossible without the lowering of federal salaries and a huge cut into the veterans' payments. Whether sound or unsound, the idea that a balanced budget was essential to recovery had been popularized and was believed by important sections of society. It was devoutly upheld among the people who, by their relation to the financial system, could most greatly affect the security markets and credit structure. In five days, the Treasury had to refinance $694,000,000 in short-term obligations.

The Democratic majority in the House, from its leaders down, went to pieces before the impact of the economy bill. The new floor leader, Representative Joseph W. Byrns of Tennessee, refused to be its sponsor. Speaker Rainey endeavored to bind the party in caucus Saturday morning. A two-thirds vote was needed. But the rebels numbered more than one-third, and they included Assistant Floor Leader Thomas Cullen of Brooklyn, and the solid block of Tammany-Brooklyn legislators. Only the skillful parliamentary tactics of Representative McDuffie of Alabama, the defeated candidate for Speaker, prevented the caucus from adopting an amendment which would have destroyed the fundamental purposes of the bill by leaving all pension classifications intact and limiting the cuts in each to twenty-five percent. It was Mr. McDuffie who carried the fight onto the floor of the House, fought off eviscerating amendments and efforts to recommit the bill, and, after two hours of scorching debate, forced the roll call. The bill passed 266 to 138. Ninety-two Democrats deserted, but 69 Republicans crossed the aisle and saved the President from defeat at perhaps the most critical moment of his first weeks in office.

On Monday the economy bill was to be taken up by the Senate, where the debating habit presaged delay. On Sunday night, before he made his radio talk on the reopening of the banks, Mr. Roosevelt remarked to a few friends who had supped with him: "I think this would be a good time for beer." He sent Louis McHenry Howe to find a copy of the Democratic platform. When he had finished his speech, he wrote a 72-word message quoting almost verbatim the Democratic pledge to immediate modification of the Volstead Act. The message went to Congress Monday morning. That day economy won a test vote in the Senate, 60-20. On Tuesday the House voted 3.2 beer, 316 to 97. On Wednesday, the Senate passed the Economy Bill 62 to 13, and on Thursday it voted for beer (and 3.2 percent wine), 43 to 30. On Thursday, the President sent his farm relief bill to Congress.

In this electrifying atmosphere of swift governmental action, such as the country had not seen since war days, the banks were reopened. On Monday, March 13, the sound banks in the twelve Federal Reserve cities opened. On Tuesday, banks opened in the 250 other cities in which there were clearing houses. On succeeding days banks in the smaller communities opened.

One development during this period proved the wisdom of postponing banking reforms until the emergency had passed. Senator Glass's ambition to force state banks into the Federal Reserve System had guided his draftsmanship of the emergency banking act more than was generally realized. Huey Long's protest proved to be justified. Nearly everywhere state banks met insuperable difficulties in conforming instantly to the Federal Reserve requirements. An extreme deflationist and ardent reformer, Senator Glass would have preferred to see these banks remained closed. But the country, especially the states where the state banks greatly outnumbered the national banks, could not stand it. An amendment to the emergency act, facilitating the rediscounting of the state bank assets, passed the Senate Monday, March 13, and after some delays went through the House and was signed by the President.

The reopening of the banks, especially in the smaller cities, was a frenzied, heartbreaking job for the officials of the Treasury and Federal Reserve System. The condition of thousands of banks had to be checked in a few days. The borderline cases were numerous. Thousands of bankers and their friends bombarded the Treasury in Washington with long-distance calls and telegrams. There was no time to set up final standards of soundness which would be uniformly interpreted. Licenses to state banks which were not members of the Federal Reserve System had to be issued chiefly on the recommendations of forty-eight different state banking superintendents operating under forty-eight different state laws and with forty-eight different criteria of judgment and degrees of amenability to pressure. Errors inevitably were made. Repeatedly during this period, the Treasury ran into legal snags which had not been foreseen in the hasty drafting of the emergency banking act. Accompanied by Under-Secretary Ballantine or some other official posted on these technicalities, Mr. Woodin would go to the White House and lay the difficulty before the President. Mr. Roosevelt's reply usually ran something like this: "We can't start amending that law yet. Get an opinion from the Attorney General that what you have to do is legal." During the first two weeks of his unexpected tenure of the Attorney-Generalship, Mr. Cummings turned out opinions with the regularity of a machine and with the ingenuity of a subtle lawyer. Probably none of his predecessors ever had had to find defensible legal authority for the solutions of so many unprecedented problems in such a short time.

The progressive relaxation of the moratorium was watched from Washington with carefully concealed anxiety. But the country's fear had miraculously vanished. The lines of worried, determined men and women which had gone to the banks to draw out cash ten days before became good-natured throngs eager to deposit cash. In almost every city and town deposits exceeded withdrawals when the moratorium was lifted. The government had airplanes chartered to rush the new currency to the far corners of the country as rapidly as it came off the press. But they were not needed. Only a few thousand dollars' worth of the new Federal Reserve banknotes got into circulation. The rush to return gold became almost a stampede. In a week the Federal Reserve's gold holdings increased $327,000,000 (of which part came from its member banks), and currency in circulation decreased $269,000,000.

On Monday, March 13, the Treasury offered $800,-000,000 in new Treasury certificates, part for five months at 4 percent and part for nine months at 4¼ percent. The issues were oversubscribed in one day, and the government successfully met the critical refunding operation of March 15. The securities markets reopened Wednesday with a spirited rise all along the line from government bonds to the more speculative stocks.

In three quick blows, Mr. Roosevelt had broken as many iron bands which were strangling the country, actually or psychologically. He had broken the banking panic and salvaged most of the banking system. He had beaten the most feared lobby in Washington and established control of the federal credit. He had beaten the remains of the once all-powerful dry lobby, and broken the fourteen-year grip of Volsteadism. The country surged with enthusiasm and hope.

In these swift accomplishments Mr. Roosevelt had bipartisan backing both in Congress and in the Administration. He had had no time to install his own men in the government, excepting in the Cabinet and a few other posts. Under-Secretary Arthur Ballantine shared the main responsibility with Senator Glass, Attorney General Cummings, and Secretary Woodin for the drafting of the emergency banking act. The Republicans in the Treasury and Federal Reserve Board carried the brunt of the work of classifying and licensing the banks. Without Republican support, the economy bill would have met defeat or delay when delay would have been almost as destructive in its effects as outright defeat.

During this period Mr. Roosevelt was the hero of the conservatives, particularly in the East. The reopening of the banks had been effected in a manner which did little violence to orthodox banking and sound-money thought. (The gold embargo and ban on hoarding were thought to be temporary.) Economy in government and the release from Prohibition were the foundation of the conservative program for recovery. The defections in Congress were largely from the West and South.

But this period was short-lived; at the time it seemed an epoch, but it lasted only twelve days. On March 16, when he sent the revolutionary farm relief bill to Congress, Mr. Roosevelt turned away from the old order and began a steady march into unexplored fields.

IV

Good-by to Gold

THE farm relief bill began and ended the second period of the Roosevelt Administration in its first phase. March 16, the day that Mr. Roosevelt sent to Congress the revolutionary farm relief bill, had marked its beginning. April 19, the day that he formally renounced the gold standard and agreed to accept the Thomas inflation amendment to the farm relief bill, may be used to denote its end. In this interval of almost five weeks, Mr. Roosevelt rained on Congress bills to carry out the program of specific readjustments and reforms pledged in his campaign. This program as a whole satisfied very few people. It offended the tenets of the conservatives who had enthusiastically supported Mr. Roosevelt during the banking crisis. It did not offer relief that was quick and drastic enough for the seething farm belt. It failed to satisfy many other groups who had preconceptions or plans of their own, but it included several far-reaching innovations and was the real beginning of the New Deal.

The banking crisis and Mr. Roosevelt's action in coping with the emergency had been drastically deflationary, except insofar as the revival of the beer industry and the retapping of a lucrative source of municipal, state, and federal revenue, were to prove constructive. The need for prompt action to stimulate economic recovery was far more urgent than it had been a month before. Mr. Roosevelt could reassure conservative thought with a smashing economy program without relying on the theory that a balanced budget would produce prosperity.

Lifting the price of the basic agricultural commodities was the most imperative undertaking with which Mr. Roosevelt was faced. If the methods which he had proposed during the campaign were to be used, they had to be used in 1933. The summoning of the new Congress into an immediate special session presented a second opportunity to obtain legislative authorization for the experiment before the spring planting season was too far advanced. Secretary Wallace had begun conferring with farm leaders on March 6. By more or less common consent, they threw overboard the Farm Parity Bill that died in the old Congress, and made a fresh start. The same divergence of opinion which had led the farm leaders in November to propose that the Executive be empowered to choose between different plans again asserted itself. All realized the need for swift agreement. The farm bill that the President sent to Congress on March 16 was staggering in its scope. "Seldom, if ever, has so sweeping a piece of legislation been introduced in the American Congress," commented the *New York Herald Tribune*. Senator David A. Reed, of the Republican old guard, said later: "I can't permit the passage of such legislation. If the people of Pennsylvania knew what its passage would mean, they'd riot in the streets."

In his message to Congress, President Roosevelt said: "I tell you frankly that it is a new and untrod path, but I tell you with equal frankness that an unprecedented condition calls for the trial of new means to rescue agriculture. If a fair administrative trial of it is made and it does not produce the hoped-for results, I shall be the first to acknowledge it and advise you."

The basic idea of the experiment was the payment to the farmer of a bounty in return for reduction of his output. Instead of being bound to one device for carrying out this idea, the Secretary of Agriculture was given the most flexible powers. In general, however, four main plans of procedure were outlined. First, the Secretary could pay a benefit on that portion of a farmer's crop which was consumed domestically, following the general principles of the domestic allotment plan. Second, the Secretary was authorized to lease lands from individual farmers, such land to be left idle or planted in crops in which there was no surplus. Third, the Smith cotton option plan was included. Under this, a farmer reducing his cotton acreage could obtain a free option on a corresponding amount of the cotton held by the old Farm Board. If the price of cotton rose, with the reduction of the supply, the farmer would get his profit on share of the Farm Board's cotton. If the price of cotton fell, he would not be liable for the loss. Fourth, the Secretary could make marketing agreements with processors, associations, producers, and other agencies handling agricultural commodities or their products.

To obtain the funds to pay the farmers, the Secretary was authorized to levy a processing tax on any commodity subjected to control. The tax was to be sufficient to restore the farm commodity to its pre-war ratio to the general price level.

The magnitude and complexity of the mechanisms proposed for controlling the production of the most highly individualized sector of American economy were undoubtedly startling. So far as the individual farmer was concerned, co-operation was voluntary. He could take or leave the reward offered for reducing his production. But the powers given the Executive to impose taxes and to form and enforce producing and marketing agreements with processors involved elements of coercion which were terrifying to business men. The bill gave the Secretary the power to license and the power to withdraw licenses for violation of agreements, which were to have the force of law. It was commonly asserted that he had the "power of life or death" over individual units in approximately thirty percent of American business and industry.

Although seven of the leading farm organizations were united in support of the bill, it received a hostile reception in Congress. The Democratic Chairman of the House Agriculture Committee, Marvin Jones, refused to be its sponsor. Senator Smith, chairman of the Senate Agriculture Committee, liked it no better. Reduction of output violated the inbred beliefs and habits of the farmer, as well as the principles of efficiency in the production of such crops as wheat. The sharp cry from the farm belt was for immediate prevention of foreclosures, for generous government aid in meeting interest payments and taxes, and for a sharp rise in prices. The left-wing Farmers' Union, expanding rapidly with social unrest in the farming regions, wanted the government to guarantee the farmer his cost of production. Since the ultimate objective of the whole experiment was price fixing, it was argued, the direct approach was preferable.

It at once became apparent that Congress would not pass the farm relief bill in a hurry. Mr. Roosevelt had the alternatives of holding Congress in continuous session or of acquiescing in a recess of several weeks while he finished preparing the remainder of his program. Congressional leaders were weary from their winter of work; they had expected to go home after the inauguration, and

the emergency session of March 9 had been called without agreement as to how long it should continue after the
banking bill had been passed. With the prestige and running start that he got in the emergency period, it was obviously to Mr. Roosevelt's advantage to hold Congress in
session and drive ahead as rapidly as possible. On March
17, the party leaders in Congress agreed with him that
the best plan was to remain in continuous session.

Mr. Roosevelt was still operating a government in
which he had only a handful of his own appointees. But by
now he had one or more of his key men at work on almost
every important item of his program. As rapidly as each
project reached final form, he sent it to Congress. There
was no particular order to his procession of bills and messages. Legislation for some of the most acute problems,
such as railroad rehabilitation, could not be drafted
quickly. A few permanent pieces of legislation, such as
the securities bill, which had no particular relation to the
emergency, crept into the line simply because men who
were interested in them were able to get bills into shape.

The main Administration measures sent to Congress
during this period numbered six, in addition to the farm
relief bill. They provided for: the Civilian Conservation
Corps, $500,000,000 for direct unemployment relief, reg-
ulation of the marketing of securities, farm mortgage relief, home-owners mortgage relief, and the Tennessee
Valley Authority.

President Roosevelt sent the first two proposals to
Congress on March 21. It is difficult to recall the shock of
his terse proposal to put 250,000 or more men, recruited
from the unemployed, at work in the forests before summer. The idea was his own. It had developed in a vague
way out of his interest in conservation long before the

depression. When he had first mentioned it publicly, in his acceptance speech at Chicago, he had evoked derision from many quarters. Secretary of Agriculture Hyde, interpreting "reforestation" in a narrow sense, had explained that anyone familiar with the subject knew that only a few thousand men could be put to work planting trees. Even many of Mr. Roosevelt's friends had tolerantly explained the suggestion as one of his "brain storms." He had mentioned the employment of one million men in the forests. The subsequent reduction of the number was not dictated by lack of work to be done but by the problems of expense and of organization.

Organized labor at once cried out against the conscripting of labor and the proposed wage scale of $30 a month. William Green and his associates were still sulking over the appointment of Miss Perkins as Secretary of Labor. Representative William P. Connery, the Democratic Chairman of the House Labor Committee, refused to handle the Civilian Conservation Corps bill. As enrollment in the forest was to be voluntary, the protest on the ground of conscription made little headway. The objection to $30 a month, plus food, clothing, housing, medical attention, and sundry other benefits, including toilet kits, for men who were starving or living on the dole, quickly became a bit ridiculous. The equivalent of $2 a day met the existing wage scale in most parts of the country for this type of rough work. The labor leaders were not appeased by a compromise which left the fixing of compensation to the President or by assurance that skilled workmen would be employed at the union wage rates for the construction of cantonments and other more or less special work. It was partly the labor protest, too, which led to the decision to give young unmarried men the first preference in enrollment. After the bill had passed, Mr. Roosevelt skillfully pacified organized labor by the appointment of Robert Fechner, a prominent labor leader, as director of the work.

The bill was signed by the President on March 31. One week later the first 25,000 men were enrolled and beginning to move into conditioning camps. On April 17, the first forest camp was established near Luray, Virginia.

Despite the electrifying example of swift action during the banking action, the weight of inertia was heavy and the sense of helplessness in the face of a multitude of practical difficulties still held men paralyzed. The President's calm orders to have the unprecedented project under way within a week and to have the entire complement of men working in forest camps before July 1 overwhelmed a good many men in the government. Men and machinery in four different departments—War, Interior, Agriculture, and Labor—and corresponding portions of the governments of forty-eight states and the work of municipal relief organizations, had to be quickly coordinated. There were creaks and groans, but the new undertaking began to move. The Labor department took charge of the enrollment of workers. The Army transported them to conditioning camps and then into the forest camps. The army remained responsible for feeding, housing, and disciplining the corps. During working hours —limited to forty hours a week—the experts of the Departments of Agriculture and Interior were in charge of the men. After the arrival of the second bonus army in Washington, provision was made for the enrollment of a number of unemployed war veterans.

The mobilization of the members of the Civilian Conservation Corps and their movement into forest camps were completed more rapidly than the same number of troops were mobilized after our entry into the World War. On August 1, when the Corps was fully organized, it consisted of 240,000 young unmarried men, 30,000 war veterans, in 1451 camps situated in forty-seven states. In addition, there were 14,400 Indians in 150 Indian forestry camps. The basic cash payment to each member of the corps was $30 per month. Eight percent received $36, and five percent $45. Skilled woodsmen received more. Although each camp was under the supervision of army officers, there was no military discipline. For minor infractions of discipline, the penalty prescribed was a reprimand. Deductions from pay could be made for more severe infractions, and dismissal from the service was held in reserve for persistent loafing or disorder.

Among the projects to which these men were assigned were construction of 50,000 miles of truck and horse trails, and 12,000 miles of telephone lines joining forest lookouts, the improvement by thinning and fire control measures of 5,000,000 acres of land, the eradication of destructive insects and diseases on 10,000,000 acres of forest land. This work was being done in the national forests and parks, state and county lands, and to a limited extent, on private lands. The work on private lands was restricted to measures for the control of fires and diseases, particularly in large areas adjoining state and nationally owned forests, and arrangements were made whereby the federal government would be reimbursed eventually for most of its expenditure on private lands.

From the point of view of conservation, the Civilian Conservation Corps was a long stride forward. More than a quarter of a century ago, when we realized that the uncurbed exploitation which marked the development of the country was rapidly reducing our timber resources to the danger point, the National Forests had been set up. To a large extent conservation work insofar as it applied to the great natural resource of timber had been a rear-guard action against ruthless cutting and fire. Comparatively little had been done toward intensive development of the areas which were saved. The Civilian Conservation Corps condensed into a few months' time work which otherwise would have taken years to accomplish. No one could estimate how much it would mean in cold cash to the nation through the reduction of losses from floods and forest fires and the thinning of scrub woodland to permit high-grade timber to grow. The sums set aside for the purchase of additional lands, especially in the South, were designed to balance the forest system. Nor could one estimate the beneficial influence on our future national policy that the education of 300,000 young men in practical conservation work would have.

The immediate benefits of the enterprise were both definite and intangible. Nearly all the young men and most of the war veterans allotted from two-thirds to three-fourths of their cash allowances to dependents. That money helped to support perhaps one million people and enabled many families to be struck from the relief rolls. The money spent in maintaining the camps—$90,000 a day for food supplies alone—was a continual rivulet running into the stream of purchasing power.

The value of the undertaking in rehabilitating the young men physically and morally was beyond computation. For more than three years they had been poured out of schools and colleges into a world of rapidly dwindling opportunity for employment. Loafing at home, often in the despairing atmosphere of families supported by the dole, or living on the road and in shantytowns had been the only modes of life open to many of them.

As the second item in his immediate relief program, the President asked for an appropriation of $500,000,000 to be distributed through the states, and for the creation of the office of Federal Relief Administrator. The need for the additional appropriation was not pressing as enough was left of the $300,000,000 appropriation made the year before for distribution through the R.F.C. to last through May. The direct unemployment relief bill was finally signed by the President on May 12. Half the sum appropriated was to be matched by the states or their municipalities. The other half was available for unrestricted grants.

The third item in the relief program outlined by the President in his March 21 message was a broad program of public works, but the preliminary examination of a multitude of projects, for many of which applications for loans had already been made to the R.F.C., delayed determination on the amount to be appropriated and the methods by which the program was to be administered.

On March 29, Mr. Roosevelt sent to Congress his bill for federal supervision of the sale of investment securities. This was a long-range reform promised in the Democratic platform and it was of little or no service in the immediate problem of getting the country out of the depression, but the men who were working on this legislation thought they had a bill in final form and Mr. Roosevelt needed something to keep the House busy while the Senate still hesitated over the farm relief bill. Originally it had been planned to incorporate control of securities issues and regulation of the stock and commodities exchanges in a single bill. Samuel Untermyer, who had been counsel to the Pujo money trust investigation twenty years earlier and had prophesied accurately the disastrous results of unregulated finance, had been invited to draft this bill. Mr. Untermyer then went to California for his usual winter holiday. Meanwhile Huston Thompson, former Federal Trade Commissioner, and a few others had gone to work on the security-selling phase of the program. Mr. Untermyer was notified. He left the ship on which he was returning from California in Florida and flew to Washington with his own bill. Mr. Roosevelt got Mr. Untermyer and the Thompson group together in the White House. It quickly became apparent that they could not work together. Mr. Roosevelt broke the impasse by suggesting to the Thompson group that it go ahead with the securities bill while Mr. Untermyer drafted a separate exchange control bill. The Thompson bill was quickly completed. By the time Mr. Untermyer got his bill revised, Mr. Roosevelt had decided to defer everything except emergency legislation until the regular session of Congress. If the speculative excesses of the next few months had been foreseen, Mr. Untermyer's bill probably would have been placed in the emergency classification. The securities bill did not belong in that category. Everything considered, it was probably unfortunate that, if either half of the reform had to be acted on at the special session, it was not the half that dealt with speculation instead of the half that dealt with the original marketing of securities.

"This proposal," Mr. Roosevelt said, presenting the securities bill, "adds to the ancient rule of *caveat emptor* the further doctrine 'Let the seller also beware.'

"It puts the burden of telling the whole truth on the seller.

"It should give impetus to honest dealing in securities and thereby bring back public confidence."

The bill required that full information concerning all securities issues (except certain federal, state, and municipal issues) be filed with the Federal Trade Commission. The Commission was empowered to stop the sale of issues which did not comply with the act. Officers of companies were made personally responsible in both criminal and civil suits in cases of misrepresentation, whether willful or not. Similar restrictions were imposed on foreign securities sold in the United States. An amendment proposed by Senator Hiram W. Johnson provided for the creation of a Corporation of Foreign Security Holders to represent the interests of American holders of foreign securities which were in default.

The original draft of the securities bill proved to be faulty. The protests of bankers and security houses accelerated the amending process in Congress until the bill was nothing but hash. Mr. Moley then stepped in and brought Professor Felix Frankfurter down to make a complete revision. Professor Frankfurter's product was further modified by Congressional leaders, but the bill finally became law on May 27. The Securities Act was only a diluted version of the British Companies Act, but it imposed personal liabilities that frightened the purveyors of securities and became one of the favored explanations of Wall Street for the small quantity of new investments during the ensuing months. The enactment of the securities bill took much valuable time. Mr. Roosevelt and the Congressional leaders agreed to defer as much as possible of the rest of the permanent legislation pledged by the Democratic platform.

The reduction of the burden of farm debt and the

reorganization of the whole system of federal credits for agriculture had been pledged in the campaign. For almost twenty years the Federal Government had progressively assisted the financing of agriculture until, directly and indirectly, it was in the banking business on a large scale. But the federal credit agencies were scattered through several different departments. Mr. Roosevelt's first use of the authority to reorganize the government conferred on him by the old Congress was to combine these agencies into one—The Farm Credit Administration. The agencies thus joined were: the Federal Farm Board, created by President Hoover in 1929, minus the price-stabilizing functions through open market operations, which were abolished; the Federal Farm Loan Bureau, in the Treasury Department, which supervised the Federal Land Banks and the Joint Stock Land Banks and the Intermediate Credit Banks; the Agricultural Credit Corporation, a subsidiary of the Reconstruction Finance Corporation; and the Crop Production Loan Bureau and Co-Operative Loan Bureaus of the Department of Agriculture. In the words of Henry Morgenthau, Jr., Governor of the new Farm Credit Administration: "Our idea is to fix the credit structure so that a farmer can borrow money for planting, harvesting, and upon his land all in one spot." The completion of the merger was effected with the aid of a special bill.

The concurrent problem was to reduce the burden of existing farm debt. The outstanding total of farm indebtedness was estimated at more than twelve billion dollars, of which approximately eight and a half billions were in mortgages. The life insurance companies, mortgage companies, and other institutions and individuals holding the bulk of these mortgages were little less interested than the debtors, who were threatened with loss of their farms, in giving life to this dead weight of debt. The underlying idea of the Administration's plan was to assist in the orderly reduction of the principal and interest of mortgages. The more radical thought would have had the Federal Government refinance practically the entire farm mortgage debt at a low rate of interest. Rates as low as two percent were suggested. As that was cheaper than the rate at which the government itself could borrow money for long terms, the result would have been a continuing government subsidy. More conservative thought would have limited government assistance to friendly intervention in reducing principal and the provision of facilities for pooling and averaging mortgages, with a resultant lowering of interest rates. That did not offer sufficient relief.

The plan which Mr. Roosevelt sent to Congress was a compromise. The government undertook to guarantee interest, but not principal, on four percent Federal Land Bank bonds not to exceed $2,000,000,000 in total. The Land Banks could exchange these bonds for existing mortgages written down to fifty percent of the normal value of the farm plus twenty percent of the improvement value, or could sell them and use the funds to take over mortgages. The interest rate to be charged the farmer was limited to four and a half percent, and provision was made for postponement of payments on principal, where it was necessary, and for the lending of money to meet taxes. The bill contained many subsidiary features, including the liquidation of the Joint Stock Land Banks, a type of local enterprise under government authorization which had proved a failure.

Mr. Roosevelt sent a companion bill for the relief of home owners to Congress on April 13. The direct loan provision of the Federal Home Loan Bank Act of the preceding year had proved ineffective. The new Federal Home Owners Loan Corporation retained the Federal Home Loan Bank system and expanded its facilities for assisting organization of savings and loans associations. The new Corporation was provided with two hundred million in cash from the R.F.C. and with authority to issue two billions in four percent bonds on which the interest was to be guaranteed by the government. The procedure prescribed was similar to that created for farm mortgages. The main differences were that the home owner was to pay five percent instead of four and a half for his money and that relief was restricted to homes having a value of not more than $10,000.

Both the farm mortgage and the home mortgage plans were the result of balancing the urgency of need for relief against the need felt for protecting the credit of the federal government and for the limiting to a minimum the further encroachment of the government on the private investment field. A network of legal difficulties surrounded both undertakings: among them the fact that without special legislation in many states the new bonds were not legal investments for life insurance companies. Both undertakings raised hopes which could not be satisfied. Even under the most favorable circumstances neither afforded the quick and drastic aid on a large scale which was necessary if this type of approach to the problem of readjusting debt were to be of value. Both relied too much on voluntary co-operation by creditors. By the time the machinery began to operate—and it was extremely slow in the case of the home owners relief—the pressure on mortgage holders to co-operate was relieved by economic recovery.

On April 10, Mr. Roosevelt sent to Congress the message that heralded the end of the long deadlock over Muscle Shoals. The government had nearly $165,000,000 invested in the wartime nitrate plant and the huge Wilson Dam on the Tennessee River. For thirteen years the investment had lain practically idle while the power interests and Senator George W. Norris of Nebraska fought to a standstill over the issue of government operation. Presidents Coolidge and Hoover each had vetoed a Norris Muscle Shoals bill. Mr. Roosevelt's liberal power program as Governor of New York had been one of his chief attractions to the Progressives. In January he had visited Muscle Shoals with a group of Senators and Congressmen and power experts, including Senator Norris. About a week later he sat by the fireplace of his cottage at Warm Springs and talked to newspapermen for more than an hour about his plans for the harmonious development of the entire Tennessee Valley region. No one who was present on that occasion is likely to forget it, for Mr. Roosevelt talked with enthusiasm and earnestness and the detail that revealed an aspiration long and deeply nurtured. The press reports on that conference evoked many lightly patronizing editorial comments about dreamers. In January 1933, bold ideas were still material for cynicism instead of for action.

The Muscle Shoals program that Mr. Roosevelt recommended to Congress went far beyond the production and distribution of cheap electricity by the government. He asked the creation of a Tennessee Valley Authority of three members to plan and direct the development of the whole region of approximately 640,000 square miles. Its other major assignments were these: flood control, reclamation of river lands, the development of decentralized agricultural-industrial communities, the production of fertilizer from the nitrate plants.

"In short," Mr. Roosevelt said in his message, "this power development of war days leads logically to national planning for a complete river watershed involving many states and the future lives and welfare of millions."

This was probably the most far-reaching adventure in regional planning ever undertaken outside Soviet Russia. After a final subterranean brush with the power interests, the bill went through Congress with large majorities in both houses. Senator Norris called it the "best Muscle Shoals bill we have ever had," and Mr. Roosevelt saluted him as "the grandfather of this legislation." Mr. Roosevelt also let it be known that, if the Tennessee experiment began well, he was ready to recommend the similar developments of the Columbia and Missouri River valleys.

Mr. Roosevelt was moving with breath-taking speed and boldness. But he was not moving swiftly or boldly enough. On April 6, the day that beer flowed legally for the first time in thirteen years, the Senate passed, 53 to 30, the Black thirty-hour-week bill. The Democratic party was pledged to a shorter working week. But Mr. Roosevelt had not yet proposed any measure to further it. Congress had taken the matter into its own hands. The Senate Judiciary Committee had voted out the bill 11 to 3. After consultation with the White House, Senator Joseph T. Robinson, the Democratic leader, had tried to amend it to stipulate a thirty-six-hour week. He had been overridden by a vote of 48 to 41. The bill as adopted prohibited the movement in interstate or foreign commerce of goods produced in "any mine, quarry, mill, cannery, workshop, factory, or manufacturing establishment" in which persons were employed for more than five days a week or six hours a day. William Green, President of the American Federation of Labor, hailed the bill as "the first real practical step on the part of government to deal constructively with the problem of unemployment." The Senate Judiciary Committee estimated that it would give work to six million unemployed. No piece of labor legislation in seventeen years, since the Adamson Bill providing for an eight-hour workday for railroad men, had been so radical in relation to the thought and custom of the day. Two days earlier the companion thirty-hour bill by Mr. Connery had been reported favorably in the House. It contained an additional drastic provision: an embargo on the importation of any foreign goods manufactured in establishments employing persons more than thirty hours a week. This gave food for thought to the conservatives who wanted to rest on a balanced budget and were crying out against the radicalism of Mr. Roosevelt's program and his brains trust. The thirty-hour week was the sort of thing the country wanted. It was revolution boiling up from the bottom.

There were other signs that Congress was getting out of control. With the help of a gag rule the farm relief bill had been jammed through the House without impairment, but the Senate still balked. Mr. Roosevelt and the party leaders held several conferences but were unable to whip the Senate into action. In the farming regions the property owners' revolt against foreclosures was still spreading. It led shortly to the beating up of an Iowa judge. Milo Reno and the Farmers' Holiday Association were busy organizing a farm strike on a greater scale. The pressure for immediate relief asserted itself in the Senate in the demand for the cost-of-production amendment to the farm bill and inflation of the currency.

When Mr. Roosevelt imposed the gold embargo on March 6, the first question asked was "Are we off gold?" The inflationists hoped so. Their number had been growing rapidly. The process of deflation had gone below the level where only the debtor was oppressed. It had got well into the territory where creditors could not collect or realize on debts. Many insurance company executives and business men who were most dependent on the farmer's ability to buy and to sustain his debts had swung into line behind the movement for quick readjustment of the price level to the debt level by currency inflation. Their numbers were augmented suddenly by individuals afflicted with an odd ethical sophistry concerning the gold standard. Their argument was that the obligation of the government to preserve the existing gold standard was paramount to the welfare of the country but that once the citizens—or foreign speculators or central banks—had forced the suspension of the gold standard, that higher obligation was dissolved, and the government was free to manage the currency in the interest of the country's welfare. Behind that screen thinkers who decided they had been on the wrong side of the debate for many months were able to jump across without admission of previous error.

With gold securely under the control of the Treasury, the essential preliminary to currency management to bring about a rise of prices had been completed. American advocates of inflation, reinforced by tardy renegades from the gold cult, hopefully waited for the dollar to sink in foreign exchange, thus impelling a corresponding rise in domestic price of basic commodities. At his first press conference, on March 8, Mr. Roosevelt had made it plain that he was an advocate of a managed currency. He parried the question, "Are we off gold?" by reading, point by point, a financial writer's description of the characteristics of the American free gold standard. On some points, the President observed, we seemed to be off gold, on other points we were not off gold. On still others, anybody could draw a conclusion according to his taste.

However, Mr. Woodin, the Secretary of the Treasury, had already given the country an unqualified answer to the query. He had said emphatically: "We are definitely on the gold standard. Gold merely cannot be obtained for several days."

Instead of falling, the dollar rose from its pre-embargo slump, as European shorts scrambled to cover their commitments. And, as weeks passed, the dollar remained practically at parity with gold. The realization gradually spread that the United States was a creditor nation on a tremendous scale and that it had a continuing favorable trade balance. The normal foreign demand for dollars therefore exceeded the American demand for foreign currencies. The natural tendency was for the dollar to remain at parity with gold. It would not fall unless business men and speculators became convinced that there was going to be inflation of the currency. Mr. Woodin's positive "no" was enough to offset the opinion of a great many other individuals until about the middle of April.

Meanwhile two formidable facts stood out as the nation emerged from the banking crisis. One was that approximately five thousand banks containing approximately five billion dollars in deposits remained closed. The other was that two or three million workers had been added to the ranks of the unemployed. The banking crisis was thus shown to be the sharpest deflationary drop of the depression, with the possible exception of the stock market collapse of 1929. It came when the sagging economic structure could not afford it.

Prices of stocks and commodities rose sharply when the exchanges were reopened after the banking holiday, probably from a combination of short covering, the natural reaction from panic lows, a general resurgence of confidence, and belief that inflation was inevitable. But as the true devastation of the banking crisis became visible, prices, as a whole, began to fall back and continued to fall until enough speculators became convinced that inflation was in the wind to start them up again. Business was struggling out of the crisis with the greatest difficulty. For the week ending April 15, the steel output was only nineteen and a half percent of capacity, only one-half of one percent higher than for the week ending February 25. Car loadings and consumption of electricity were gradually rising from the crisis lows, but were still markedly below the corresponding periods of 1932.

On Tuesday, April 11, began a succession of events of extraordinary significance and effect. The dollar began to weaken. It weakened again the following day. On Thursday morning it sank abruptly, then suddenly rallied with the announcement that the Treasury had licensed a shipment of gold to Holland on the liner *Statendam* that day. That was the first gold shipment allowed for exchange purposes since the March 6 embargo, and it signified that the Administration had determined to defend the dollar. Six days later President Roosevelt renounced the gold standard and agreed to accept the Thomas amendment to the farm bill. Many elaborate theories were built up in succeeding weeks to explain this apparently sharp reversal of policy. Three-quarters of the explanation lay on the surface in a powerful sequence of events. It had become

apparent that the Administration could not get the farm
bill through the Senate without making concessions to the
more radical demands of the farm belt. The determination of the currency inflationists to force the issue to a
vote on an amendment to the farm bill gave speculators in
exchange their opportunity. When the dollar sagged on
April 11 and 12, New York bankers applied through the
Federal Reserve Bank to the Treasury for licenses to export gold. The first request was for approximately $10,-
000,000, which Mr. Roosevelt granted on Wednesday.
About $600,000 went to Holland on Thursday. That
same day the Senate defied the Administration by adopting, 47 to 41, the cost-of-production amendment to the
farm bill. It was Mr. Roosevelt's first defeat and it
showed the temper of the Senators from the farm states.
The publicity given to the gold shipment to Holland
caused the dollar to rally, but New York banks applied
for licenses to ship approximately $15,000,000 more in
gold. They were granted part of it. Stories were published
in European capitals that the House had refused to pledge
a caucus against inflation and that President Roosevelt
and Prime Minister Bennett of Canada had discussed a
one-third reduction of the gold content of the American
and Canadian dollars. It was the Easter week-end, and
foreign exchange dealings were light. But the New York
banks applied for licenses to ship more gold on Friday and
again on Saturday. From the first, each request was accompanied by the expression of ripe banking opinion that
only small shipments were needed. They would show that
the Administration was supporting the dollar and dis-
courage foreign speculation. However, each day the requests for shipments mounted in almost geometric ratio.
From various sources Mr. Roosevelt received the reports

that a group of speculators in Amsterdam had $125,000,-000 which they were using to depress the dollar. Some of the New York bankers were of the opinion that the Bank of England or the Bank of France or both were trying to draw out American gold. The belief that Great Britain was trying to force the dollar off gold arose mysteriously and persisted. One of Mr. Roosevelt's Cabinet officers appeared to be obsessed with it. The British had been using their pound stabilization fund to keep the pound about thirty percent below the dollar and other gold currencies. The operation of the fund resulted in the increasing accumulation of gold. The gold embargo had crippled the operation of the fund through New York, but the relaxation of the embargo would have permitted its resumption, with a continued loss of American gold. But the fund was used to depress the pound instead of the dollar. There was, however, about $750,000,000 in foreign short-term balances in this country. Mr. Roosevelt received reports, also, that large amounts of American capital, actuated by the fear that inflation was coming, were seeking refuge abroad. It seemed possible that the country would lose an unlimited amount of gold. Instead of preserving the dollar's international position, the relaxation of the embargo was merely depleting the nation's gold supply and inviting another panic. On Saturday night Mr. Roosevelt informed Secretary Woodin that he intended to conserve the gold supply and would not authorize any further exports. During the early part of the following week licenses were issued for the shipments for which oral promises had already been given. The publicity given these made Mr. Roosevelt's announcement of the ensuing Wednesday seem all the more abrupt. Through that brief lifting of the embargo, the country lost approximately $100,000,000 in gold.

On Monday, Senator Burton K. Wheeler's amendment to the farm relief bill, proposing the unlimited free coinage of silver at a ratio of 16 to 1, braved the Administration opposition voiced by Senator Joseph T. Robinson, and was defeated by the close vote of 43 to 33. Since January, free silver had won fifteen recruits in the Senate. Senator Thomas of Oklahoma at once offered his own inflation amendment, which included proposals commanding much wider support than free silver at 16 to 1. At eight o'clock the following morning, Senator James F. Byrnes of South Carolina, one of the Administration watch dogs, called Raymond Moley at his hotel and told him there was no chance of stopping the Thomas amendment in the Senate. Mr. Moley made an appointment for Senators Byrnes and Thomas to see the President. Senator Pittman was also called in. And the President took up the inflation question at his Cabinet meeting that afternoon. Mr. Roosevelt told Senator Thomas and other leaders that he was ready to accept authority to inflate the currency in certain ways. Senator Thomas and Senator Huey P. Long accordingly held up their amendments. After dinner that night Secretaries Hull and Woodin and the American experts for the international conversations which were then about to begin gathered at the White House for a rehearsal with the President. The President handed Mr. Moley a copy of the Thomas amendment and asked him to confer with Senate leaders and put it in satisfactory form. Budget Director Douglas and Herbert Feis, economic adviser to the State Department, were aghast and pleaded with Mr. Roosevelt to hold back. He good-naturedly defended his decision. He pointed out that he proposed to accept no mandate, but only discretionary powers, and that, with the budget under control, inflation could be controlled. The argument continued for some time. The President accepted the plea that there at least be a limit placed on the issue of greenbacks authorized by the Thomas amendment. According to reliable accounts, neither the Secretary of State nor the Secretary of the Treasury, the two ranking officers of the Cabinet, said a word on either side of the argument. The discussion was suspended to permit consideration of the international problems, but it was resumed later when several of the experts assembled in Mr. Moley's quarters. Mr. Douglas still fought doggedly for sound money. It was during the argument of that evening that he is reported to have uttered his dour warning: "This is the end of western civilization."

The following morning, Mr. Roosevelt confirmed his decision to the press. For concise explanation of his reasons he recommended Walter Lippmann's article in the *New York Herald Tribune* that morning. Mr. Lippmann had switched from the deflationary to the inflationary side with the gold embargo of March 6. His article of April 19 was the best short analysis of the situation, and it reached this conclusion: "Either the Administration, acting through the Treasury and the Federal Reserve System, will take charge of the inflation and manage it, or Congress will produce the inflation by statute. If neither the Administration nor Congress produce the inflation, we should still get it within a few months by means of budgetary deficits and the undermining of government credit. The choice is, therefore, between inflation by statute and inflation by monetary management, and there is a choice among several methods of producing the inflation and controlling it. But there is no choice any longer between inflation and no inflation. This choice has been abolished by economic developments and by the political sentiments which they now reflect."

The powers that Mr. Roosevelt agreed to accept were these: To reduce the gold content of the dollar up to fifty percent. To compel the Federal Reserve System to buy up to three billion dollars in federal securities. To issue up to three billion dollars in paper currency under the greenback law of 1862, this currency to be used only in retiring outstanding federal obligations and to be retired itself at the rate of four percent annually. To accept up to one hundred million dollars (inceased to two hundred millions) in war debt payments in silver during the course of one year at the rate of not more than 50 cents an ounce, this silver to be used as the basis for additional silver certificates. To provide for the unlimited coinage of silver and fix the ratio of gold to silver.

After a week's debate, the Thomas amendment was adopted by the Senate, 64 to 21. The House adopted it 307 to 86.

The foreign press, particularly in England and France, made furious protests, intimating or directly charging trickery. Prime Minister MacDonald and former Premier Édouard Herriot and their delegations were already on the high seas. It was generally acknowledged that Mr. Roosevelt had greatly improved his position to bargain at the international conference table. The State Department took pains to inform all American embassies and legations that the renunciation of the gold standard had been dictated solely by domestic considerations. The sound-money press in the United States regretted that Franklin D. Roosevelt was not a Grover Cleveland and took the

hopeful view that he was merely accepting these powers
to pigeon-hole them, thereby averting inflation by a neat
maneuver instead of by a sturdy veto. Mr. Roosevelt's
economics happen to be more advanced than Mr. Cleveland's. And the case for "sound" money had been relatively stronger in the eighties and nineties than it was in
1933. The United States had then been merely at the
threshold of its tremendous industrial expansion. "Sound"
money reassured capital, at home and abroad, and encouraged investment in new productive enterprises. The
expenditure on these productive enterprises threw out an
advance guard of purchasing power. In 1933 there was
no great field (at least none readily apparent) for productive expansion. The country already had a productive
plant capable of yielding a generous living for every citizen.

The inflationary powers accepted by Mr. Roosevelt in
the Thomas amendment arose from conflicting economic
theories and practical motives. The Federal Reserve System had conducted a huge experiment in the expansion
of credit by open-market purchases of government securities under President Hoover. The theory was that easy
credit would enable the banks to lend and thus promote
an upturn in business activity. Eventually the price of government securities would be lifted so high that they would
no longer yield adequate income, and the profit-making
motive would force bank funds into other channels. In
the last analysis, this type of inflation is the handmaiden
of the orthodox faith that private investment in new productive enterprises is the route to recovery. Actually all
this type of inflation accomplished was to set up a rotary
movement of cash and government securities between the
banks and the Federal Reserve System. The banks had

plenty of money to lend but could not find sound borrowers. By September 1933, although the operations had
not been large, the New York bankers, who earlier had
insisted that credit inflation was sound, were demanding
that the operations cease. They said they were drowning
in funds for which they could find no safe and profitable
outlets.

Reduction of the gold content of the dollar was a
means for suddenly establishing a new price level for the
basic commodities, such as wheat, cotton, and copper, of
which the United States had a surplus. Mr. Roosevelt
also received the power to change continually the gold
content of the dollar, an important device, in the eyes of
the commodity dollar school, in preserving a stable price
level. The remonetization of silver was encrusted with a
rare assortment of economic theories of venerable history which were kept alive by the demand of the silver-
mining states for a higher price for silver. The Democratic party and Mr. Roosevelt were committed to doing
"something for silver," and the Senators and Representatives from the silver states, including Senator Key Pittman, chairman of the Foreign Relations Committee,
were at hand to see that the pledge was not forgotten.

The word "greenback" gives nightmares to sound-
money people. The notes or "greenbacks" which the
Treasury was authorized to issue under the Thomas
amendment had to be amortized at the rate of four percent annually. Out of solicitude for the nervous systems
of the sound-money theorists, a bit of sleight-of-hand
was incorporated into this section of the law. The government could use the three billions in non-interest-bearing
notes or currency to retire outstanding obligations; it
could not use them to finance new undertakings, although

it could, of course, borrow anew for these new undertakings.

So far as the balance book of the Treasury is concerned, it makes little difference whether it borrows by selling long-term bonds, by selling short-term obligations, or by using currency which it must amortize annually. In each case the government assumes a debt which it is obligated to repay. In the case of long-term bonds it must pay more interest, in the case of short-term obligations usually less, and in the case of currency, none. But the worth of each of these types of obligations is dependent, not on the gold in the Treasury, but on the government's credit. If it can collect enough taxes to meet current expenditures and payments on outstanding debt, its credit is sound. In the way people act toward these three types of obligations there is, however, a great deal of difference. Currency which cannot be exchanged for gold will frighten the same man who will be perfectly satisfied with a government bond which cannot be exchanged for gold. When money is concerned, people act according to a strange combination of fetishes and beliefs, and thereby tend to give validity to theories of money which are logically irreconcilable.

Mr. Roosevelt's handling of the budget revealed an appreciation of the intangibles of money and credit faiths. During the depression years of the Hoover Administration we had had an uncontrolled inflation of approximately four billion dollars. The budget was not balanced; the Treasury made up the difference between income and outgo by issuing short-term securities. Mr. Roosevelt's audacious economies, especially his successful stroke in obtaining control of the expenditures on veterans, accomplished two purposes: it brought the regular budget into approximate balance and proved the power of the Administration to control its finances. After a reasonable lapse of time, Mr. Roosevelt let it be known that he intended to set up an extraordinary budget for relief funds, public works, and similar expenditures, and to finance it by borrowing. A few fanatics for economy cried out. It was true that this did not mean balancing the budget in the sense of "pay as you go."

But it was a good way of reassuring the great bulk of the investing public and, at the same time, of financing the new undertakings, which, of necessity no less than by reasons of sound economic theory, the government should undertake in times of depression. Mr. Roosevelt merely adopted the established practices of the business world (as they already had been adopted by most governmental units). He proposed to meet regular expenditures by taxation and to borrow to meet capital improvements and extraordinary expenditures. He proposed to impose additional taxes to meet the interest and amortization on this new debt. Between a four billion dollar creeping inflation by continual short-term borrowing under Mr. Hoover and a four billion dollar expansion or inflation under the conditions imposed by Mr. Roosevelt, there is a difference. It is the difference between the standing of the individual or business which borrows from day to day to meet a growing deficit and that of the individual or business which can go to the bank and borrow a large sum for a long period. It lies entirely in the lender's assessment of the ability of the borrower to repay the debt. In the case of a borrowing government, it is the lender's assessment of the ability of the government to collect sufficient taxes to meet current expenditures and amortize the debt. Mr. Roosevelt's first undertaking was to show that the government could balance its budget. With the re-establishment of the government credit, he became free to borrow. The extraordinary budget was a bookkeeping arrangement designed to substantiate the fact that the government had its fiscal affairs in order and was keeping track of them.

So long as the government has firm control of its fiscal affairs, uncontrolled inflation whether by borrowing or printing of the currency is an impossibility. The measure of inflation is the difference between the amount the government chooses to spend out of current taxes and the amount it chooses to borrow. That would be a truism but for the fact that a great many people do not think so and show their dissent by actions of various kinds which may have results that are either deflationary or inflationary, or combinations of both.

On April 19, the day that Mr. Roosevelt renounced the gold standard and proclaimed his readiness to accept the inflationary powers of the Thomas amendment, the dollar dropped precipitately in terms of foreign currencies—down to twelve percent below gold parity. Commodities and equities jumped correspondingly. A period of rising prices began which continued, with minor setbacks and interruptions, until the middle of July.

V

Upturn

THE third period of the first phase of the Roosevelt Revolution lasted approximately three months—from the President's acceptance of the Thomas amendment to the sharp drop in securities and commodities in the third week of July. Mr. Roosevelt used none of the powers to manipulate the currency which were conferred on him. That made no difference. The mere fact that he had those powers was sufficient. The country experienced the regular effects of currency inflation. The dollar fell, the prices of commodities, bonds, and stocks rose. There was a movement from money to goods and equities. The fear or expectation of higher prices caused persons with accumulated funds to invest in commodities and finished products. Retailers, jobbers, and manufacturers stocked up. As raw commodities rose, they created new purchasing power in the farming and mining regions. An active demand began for automobiles, clothing, and many other consumers' goods for which a tremendous latent demand had been piling up during the depression years. In short, the long downward trend was suddenly reversed. This change had tremendous psychological effects on the country as a whole, which were reflected in Washington. It reinforced the feeling of national self-reliance which Mr. Roosevelt had begun to restore on March 4. It developed a false sense of optimism and fathered a speculative spree, which became dangerous. Ironically enough, many

of the same conservative groups which most vehemently
contended that inflation meant ruin were the first to suc-
cumb to easy optimism when they began to feel the effects
of a depreciating dollar.

Against this moving background of inflation occurred
two major lines of action. Congress completed the temporary legislative framework for the domestic experiments of the New Deal and adjourned; and Mr. Roosevelt made an excursion into foreign affairs which centered
about efforts to preserve peace in Europe and to promote
international remedies for the depression. The interplay
of these three movements—inflation, the fundamental program of domestic readjustment, and the effort to restore
international commerce—produced many complications.
Mr. Roosevelt's acceptance of powers to inflate the currency improved his position in certain vital respects. It
broke the Congressional jam and opened the way for the
enactment of more of his program. The rise in prices
gradually subdued social unrest in the farming regions,
which was reaching a new peak at the end of April with
the continued spread of forcible prevention of foreclosure sales and the attempt of the Farmers' Holiday Association to organize a large-scale strike in several states.

But the rise in prices relieved the tension of the country
so rapidly that Mr. Roosevelt was seriously embarrassed
and the success of the most fundamental undertakings of
the Administration was threatened. Farmers increased
their spring plantings of corn and cotton and other crops,
thus aggravating the problem of tremendous surpluses
with which the farm relief experiment had to deal. Mr.
Roosevelt quickly lost the leverage which fear had given
him on Congress and on various groups in the country.
With prosperity returning before their eyes, neither the

conservatives nor the rabid inflationists (many of whom were extremely conservative on everything except money) saw much reason for submitting to dubious experiments. Spurred by the veterans' lobby, Congress revolted against economy in government with such force that Mr. Roosevelt felt compelled to make generous concessions.

Both currents of the domestic program—inflation and fundamental change—ran counter to the effort at recovery by international methods. The international economics of, let us say, Cordell Hull, was sharply revealed as more of an alternative than a supplement to the national program of the Administration. Mr. Hull's program aimed at the revival of international laissez-faire capitalism.[1] Its conflict with the main line of revolutionary development was brought out in a series of specific issues. Mr. Roosevelt settled each of these, as it arose, in favor of his domestic program. The overwhelming majority of the country realized or instinctively felt the collision between the domestic and international programs of the Administration. The great resurgence of national confidence as America began to climb out of the depression bolstered that profound distrust of anything savoring of internationalism which Wilsonism and the aftermath of the World War had developed. The Senate refused to give Mr. Roosevelt the power to embargo arms shipments in the form he wanted it. And after sizing up the temper of Congress he abandoned his plans for requesting powers to reduce tariffs up to fifty percent and to reduce war debts or accept token payments.

With the appeasement of the inflationists, Congress began to move. After a week of hot debate, in which the

---

[1] The next chapter will deal with Mr. Roosevelt's international program.

right-wing Republicans made sound money their first direct issue with the Roosevelt régime, the huge Agricultural Adjustment Bill passed the Senate, with the Thomas amendment and the farm mortgage relief bill as riders. The securities, Tennessee Valley Authority, and home-owners' loan bills followed in its wake.

The next problem that Mr. Roosevelt presented to Congress was rehabilitation of the railroads. For a year he had been devoting an extraordinary amount of time to study of the railroad situation. The railroads were doubly vital: as the backbone of the transportation system and as an important part of the credit system. Next to government securities, railroad bonds ranked with a few other classes of conservative first mortgages as the traditional and approved safe investments of savings banks and trust funds and conservative individuals. The public interest in the railroads as a transportation system had been recognized by the government in the creation of the Interstate Commerce Commission and in various special laws over a long period of years. So, too, the government had to recognize the public interest in the soundness of railroad credit.

Mr. Roosevelt himself belongs to a railroad family (his father was a vice-president of the Delaware & Hudson) and many of his warm personal friends, such as W. Averell Harriman and William H. Woodin (primarily through the equipment end), were actively associated with the railroad business. Throughout his campaign he was in frequent consultation with a committee of railroad executives, representatives of railway labor and investment groups, and such students of the problem as Professor Berle, Bernard M. Baruch, and General Hugh S. Johnson. After the campaign, and with the aid of the conclusions of the National Transportation Committee, of which Calvin Coolidge was chairman and Mr. Baruch was vice-chairman, Mr. Roosevelt's program expanded and took more definite form. He proposed to create a single national transportation agency with control over railroads, interstate highway transportation, inland waterways, pipe lines, coastwise shipping, and air routes. Among the major trends of readjustment which he proposed were: the orderly reduction of excessive capitalization, the integration of highway, air, and water transportation with the railroads on an equitable basis, with the elimination of superfluous railroad mileage and unnecessary competition, and the establishment of a new rate-making base. As soon as he entered the Presidency, Mr. Roosevelt turned the whole railroad problem over to Secretary of Commerce Roper with Joseph B. Eastman, "the great dissenter" of the Interstate Commerce Commission, as his expert deputy. Then began a series of hearings and conferences which lasted for two months. Almost every important aspect of the problem aroused sharp dissensions. On the administrative side, difficulties arose in trying to fit the I.C.C. into an administrative transportation agency. Historically the I.C.C. had been the protector of the producers of the South and West against oppressive railroad rates. A strong emotional attachment to the I.C.C. was reflected in Congress. Nor were railroad operators and large investors ready to surrender prerogatives. They wanted relief from restrictive legislation and regulation, not the strengthening and transfer of control to a branch of the executive department of government. Attempts to draw a line between the administrative and quasi-judicial functions of the I.C.C. lost themselves in confusion.

The immediate problem of putting the railroads on a paying basis was likewise surrounded by solid obstacles. Some railroad interests wanted higher rates and protection from the unfair competition of motor and water transportation enjoying the advantage of subsidized routes. Other railroad interests wanted to meet the competition part-way by reducing rates. The obvious fact stood out that the cost of rail transportation was far too high in relation to the cost of almost everything else. Yet it could not be sharply reduced without seriously damaging effects to either the credit structure or labor, or both.

Frederick H. Prince, of Boston, presented a plan which his experts estimated would save $700,000,000 annually in the cost of operating the railroads and thus yield a substantial margin over fixed costs for the Class I railroads even on the basis of 1932 traffic. He proposed to combine all the roads into seven or eight regional systems, concentrate traffic on the most economical routes, and rigorously eliminate other competitive expenses. This plan would have maintained competition between the main trunk-line terminals but abolished the subdivided kind of competition which the I.C.C. sought to maintain and which underlay the consolidation plan with which it had been trifling for a decade. But the Prince plan would have made labor pay the penalty for saving the railroad investors. The railway brotherhoods estimated it would throw 250,000 more men out of work. The railroad operators, as a whole, were no less vehemently opposed to such drastic reorganization, as many railroads would have lost their identity and many executives their jobs. Professor Berle and a committee of the railroad executives had developed a plan for a federal railroad co-ordinator. The basic issue was, how much power should the co-ordinator have? Should he be a dictator or a mere adviser?

The longer the discussions of the transportation problem continued, the more complex it seemed. The President therefore proposed to Congress only "three emergency steps." They were: repeal of the unworkable Recapture Clause of the Transportation Act of 1920 which had been designed to make part of the profits of the better roads available to support the weaker carriers; extension of I.C.C. regulation over railroad holding companies, through which Wall Street banks had fought for railroad empires, thwarted the I.C.C., and mulcted the public; and the appointment of a federal co-ordinator.

The co-ordinator was to work through three group committees, one each for the railroads of the South, West, and East. He was to try to bring about voluntary economies. In reserve he had the power to enforce economies under penalty of fines. The railroads could appeal from him to the I.C.C. The co-ordinator's decisions were exempted from the anti-trust laws. The railroad bill also made a fundamental change in the rate-making principle. The old principle was a "fair return" on the value of the property. For more than thirty years the chief element in determining the value of public utility properties, as established by the courts, was present value or reproduction value minus such items as obsolescence and depreciation. When first laid down by the Supreme Court the principle had been a victory for the public because prices had been falling. But then the long rise in prices began and the principle became a shield for over-capitalization and other financial malpractices, particularly in the electrical utilities. Until the depression began, it afforded, as practically applied, such a large margin for profit that most utilities, including the railroads, could not take full advantage of it. The railroad bill proposed to modify the unworkable rate-making principle. It instructed the I.C.C. to consider such factors as the effects of rates on movement of traffic, the need of adequate service at the lowest possible costs, and the need for adequate revenue to maintain such service.

The railroad bill passed both houses without a record vote, and Mr. Roosevelt appointed Mr. Eastman as Federal Co-Ordinator. The government's position as a huge railroad creditor through the R.F.C. was expected to furnish leverage for the co-ordinator. With that in mind, Mr. Roosevelt named Professor Berle special assistant to the directors of the R.F.C. The encouragement of financial reorganizations was one of the expressed purposes of the railroad act. The bankruptcy act passed during the winter had been devised to permit quick railroad reorganizations. The Administration hoped that a good many railroads would take advantage of that act and "go through the wringer." However, the quick economic upturn suddenly rescued the railroads and their banks and investors, and the Administration gradually lost its leverage. The co-ordination and financial reorganization of the railroads should have been begun two years earlier, when the railroads first applied to the government hat in hand. Instead of forcing the pace, the government, through the R.F.C., had passed out loans and demanded nothing in return. The railroad co-ordinator act was merely transitional. The whole national transportation problem was so complicated that it was perhaps wise to postpone permanent legislation while the railroad co-ordinator explored alternative plans in greater detail.

The weakness of the American banking system had been brought out clearly long before the crisis of 1933, which was at bottom a price crisis rather than a banking crisis in a limited sense. In the twelve years prior to 1933, approximately 10,500 banks in the country had failed. Until 1930 most of them had been small banks mowed down by the post-war agricultural deflation. The Federal Reserve System of 1913 had created the backbone of a unified banking system around the national banks. But most of the banks in the forty-eight different state systems remained outside the Federal Reserve. And the competition induced by the greater latitude of the state systems was a force on the side of laxer national bank requirements.

In long years of discussion, but no action, over banking reform, the big bankers were generally in favor of consolidation of the state and national systems. Compulsory membership in the Federal Reserve System was the most obvious way of bringing about consolidation. The concentration of all commercial banking in national banks and of trust companies under state authorities was another of the various solutions proposed. In addition the large banks advocated the extension of branch banking, which would tend to eliminate the small individual institution. The agricultural states—in many cases the very states which suffered the most from loose banking —distrusted the motives of the movement toward unification. The state bankers, themselves enjoying competitive advantages, opposed it. Farmers and small-town business men, fighting against the inroads of chain stores, feared the concentration of credit in distant hands. The West and South as a whole seemed to prefer bank failures to the loss of their sense of financial independence.

The Democratic platform pledged certain banking reforms. Chief among them were "quicker methods of realizing on assets for the relief of depositors of suspended banks," the complete divorcement of investment banking from commercial banking, and further restrictions on the use of Federal Reserve facilities and national bank credit for speculation.

The platform ignored the unification issue. On that the party was divided. Senator Glass, one of the authors of the Federal Reserve System, stood for unification by attraction or compulsion. Most of the Southern and Western Democrats stood by their state banking systems. They wanted security by government guarantee of deposits, or deposit insurance, not to mention inflation. The contest between unification and independence, abetted by Huey Long's filibuster, blocked a diluted Glass bill at the winter session of the old Congress. In the drafting of the emergency banking act, Senator Glass got in a few preliminary blows for unification. But the outcry from the West and South on behalf of the little banks—and the plain necessities of the emergency—led quickly to the liberalization of aid to the state banks. Undismayed, the peppery and stubborn Senator returned to the fray. On one side he had to fight the "little bank" group, led by Representative Henry B. Steagall, chairman of the House Banking and Currency Committee. On the other side, he had to fight the Administration. Mr. Roosevelt and Mr. Woodin were opposed to guarantee of deposits, which Senator Glass finally accepted in order to get the rest of his bill. They also disagreed with Glass on the fundamental question of the relationship between the Federal Reserve System and the Treasury. Glass thought the Federal Reserve System was the property of the banks and wanted it separated from political control. The Roosevelt Administration insisted on Treasury direction of the Federal Reserve System. The difference went to the very heart of the conflict between laissez-faire and the new order.

To one basic reform, however, all three groups in the party agreed: the separation of investment from commercial banking. During the boom of the nineteen-twenties the large commercial banks had invaded the historic domain of the private bankers on a great scale by the creation of investment affiliates. The profits from corporate financing, security selling, and speculation were enormous. Many of the biggest commercial banks became primarily stock-and-bond peddlers to their own depositors, their own employees, and the world at large, and the chief tom-tom beaters for the speculative frenzy. The Senatorial investigation of the National City Bank in February brought to a head the long contention over this kind of banking. Charles E. Mitchell's successor, James H. Perkins, made the separation of the National City Company from the National City Bank and the return of the bank to commercial banking the basic point of his policy. The Chase National Bank and its affiliate were next in line for Senatorial probing. Albert H. Wiggin, chairman of the board, had resigned in January, and been succeeded by Winthrop W. Aldrich, brother-in-law of John D. Rockefeller, Jr. The day following Mr. Perkins's action, Mr. Aldrich announced that for some time the Chase had been planning to divorce its securities affiliate. Commercial banks, he asserted, should not underwrite any securities except those of the federal, state, county, and municipal governments. He thought all commercial banks should be members of the Federal Reserve. Also, he thought, the Glass bill did not go far enough. No corporation or partnership should be allowed to take deposits unless subjected to the same regulations as commercial banks, and no corporation or partnership dealing in securities should be allowed to take any deposits. Lastly, all bank directorates should be small enough for their members to know what went on in the banks, and no officer or director or member of any corporation or partnership dealing in securities should be allowed to be an officer or director of a bank. This direct attack on the established practices and position of the private banks startled the country with the vision of open warfare between the Rockefellers and the Morgans. Some commentators suggested that Mr. Aldrich was merely trying to avert or remove the sting from the expected investigation of Chase by vigorous repudiation of the policies of his predecessor. Whether true or not, it was of little consequence. The shrewd politician does not question motives when he gets uninvited aid, and the duty of the statesmen is to make self-interest serve social purposes. Mr. Aldrich's pronouncement received a cordial reception at the White House. It did not stop the banking inquiry, which panicky Wall Street bankers and financiers were exerting tremendous pressure to have stopped on the high moral ground that it would undermine the confidence which Mr. Roosevelt was restoring. Several important Senators wavered, but Mr. Roosevelt insisted that the inquiry be resumed. But at his suggestion the Senate Banking and Currency Committee's inquisitorial nose was temporarily turned away from the commercial banks and toward the great private banking houses. With a new grant of power, Ferdinand Pecora, the committee's counsel, began to probe into the holy citadel of the financial world, J. P. Morgan & Co., and the lesser private houses, Kuhn, Loeb & Co., and Dillon, Read & Co.

Several reasons suggest themselves for Mr. Roosevelt's interest in having the private bankers examined immediately. With the support of Messrs. Perkins and Aldrich the fight for separation of securities affiliates from commercial banks was already won, and a strong impetus had been given to other reforms. Mr. Roosevelt was soon to begin conversations on war debts and other international economic problems. The House of Morgan was the chief fountain of propaganda for war debt cancellation and other items in the international bankers' solution of the depression. Through the personal prestige of some of its members, the wide ramifications of its influence in political, financial, and journalistic worlds, the Morgan firm had been for years a powerful and at times controlling influence in American policy, at home and abroad. If the United States had an invisible government, the House of Morgan held the chief portfolios. To put the House of Morgan on the defensive immediately was to the Administration's advantage. To establish definitely and expose its position in the economic and political world was a necessary preliminary to reforms that would go far beyond the improvement of the banking system.

The Morgan hearings were the most popular sideshow of the spring drama. For the first time in twenty years—since the Pujo money trust investigation—a Morgan was put on the witness stand and Wall Street's sanctum opened to the public view. For a time the Morgan hearing blanketed the main performance of the President and Congress. As in the Mitchell hearings, the sharpest public reaction was to the income tax disclosures. The public learned that the twenty partners in the firm had paid no income tax for 1931 and 1932 and only a trifling amount in the aggregate in 1930, thanks to the capital gains and losses provisions of the income tax law. The extraordinary methods by which three of the partners had legally avoided paying income taxes could only sharpen the ordinary tax payer's amazement at the ingenuity of big financiers and of their legal talent.

The imposing lists of politicians, financiers, industrialists, publishers, and other prominent friends of the firm who were invited in on the ground floor of Morgan stock issues. The list of 167 directorships held by Morgan partners. The array of great industrial concerns which kept deposits with the Morgan firm. The banks with which Morgan had connections through directorships and deposits. The building of the Morgan railroad and utility empires. The staggering profits of boom years. These, and many other revelations, confirmed the popular estimate of the House of Morgan as a mighty and sinister power. It was like looking at the inside of Tammany Hall. Power was maintained by prestige, patronage, and being kind to friends—what the reformers loosely and, of course, inaccurately, call graft. The jolly Mr. Morgan did not look sinister. His sincere exposition of the historic rôle of the private banker was reminiscent of a Tammany sachem's equally sincere exposition of the historic and important rôle of the benevolent Society of Tammany. There was a striking similarity between Mr. Morgan's simple and honest belief in the rightness

of his place in his system and John F. Curry's simple
and honest belief in the rightness of his. (Mr. Curry,
incidentally, is groomed like a banker and as sensitive as
Mr. Morgan to the imputation of wrong-doing.) Mr.
Morgan's suggestions for reform of the banking system
and of the world in general were about as fundamental
as Mr. Curry's for the reform of municipal government.
The analysis of the depression by Russell C. Leffingwell,
one of Mr. Morgan's partners, recalled the better Tammany explanations of inability to balance the New York
City budget. It was a recitation of the main episodes in
the sad tale of a boom followed by a deflation. I am unable to select a counterpart in Tammany Hall for Mr.
Morgan's attractive partner, George W. Whitney. His
plausibility and nimble thought suggested James J.
Walker, but it would be unfair (to Mr. Whitney) to
carry the comparison farther. The astute Thomas W.
Lamont reminded one of John H. Delaney. In turning
from the Morgan investigation to that of Kuhn, Loeb
& Co., one must cross Brooklyn Bridge from Manhattan.
Otto H. Kahn, with his affable admissions of uninten-
tional error and quickness to see the light, was the John
H. McCooey of the spring banking investigation. One's
reaction to the private banking revelations depended on
one's expectations. Those who had venerated the House
of Morgan were a bit shocked to find that it had left its
reputedly conservative hitching post for a gallop in the
speculative spree, and were grief-stricken by the dis-
closure that it had indulged in the crasser methods of
rewarding its friends. Those who had approached the
investigation from the other extreme, were disappointed.
The House of Morgan was less iniquitous than they had
been led to believe: certainly it appeared to be more re-

spectable and more conscious of a social obligation than many of its upstart rivals in the financial world. It had enormous power—entirely too much for twenty men aspiring to power and profits. But it did not have a monopoly over money and credit. The American economic machine of the twenties built up a surplus faster than the House of Morgan or any banking group could expand to handle it. The investigation showed that the competition in lending money had been keen and that some of the most vicious practices arose from excessive competition.

The investigation of private bankers, which was suspended until autumn after the Kuhn, Loeb hearings, evoked attacks by the Wall Street-baiters on two prominent members of the Roosevelt Administration. Mr. Woodin's name appeared on the lists of ground-floor subscribers to Morgan stocks—in 1929, when he was an industrialist little dreaming he would ever be Secretary of the Treasury. Norman H. Davis appeared on stock lists, as a personal borrower from the Morgan firm, and as the recipient of a handsome fee from Kuhn, Loeb, in connection with the flotation of a Chilean loan now in default. Mr. Roosevelt was unmoved by the demands for the resignations of these two gentlemen. He had been familiar with their Wall Street connections. Mr. Woodin's independence of Wall Street domination had been shown to the satisfaction of Mr. Roosevelt's friends by his support of Mr. Roosevelt for the presidential nomination. Mr. Davis's Wall Street connections were one of the chief reasons why he was in Europe working for disarmament instead of sitting in the Cabinet or handling economic and financial problems for the Administration in some other capacity.

Mr. Roosevelt was kept informed of the findings of preliminary investigation of the Morgan firm. He insisted that the public hearings go on regardless of embarrassment to any member of the Administration. Senator Glass's vitriolic attacks on Mr. Pecora's methods of investigation and the House of Morgan's resistance to the production of a few important pieces of information threatened to stop the inquiry. Each time that an obstacle was raised, Mr. Roosevelt exerted his influence to remove it. The investigation, as Senator Glass observed with indignant sarcasm, was "a circus." One wished that it had been conducted by a man with the knowledge of finance and the liberalism of an Untermyer or a Brandeis. Mr. Pecora's approach was that of prosecuting attorney unguided by a fundamental point of view. The job needed a social scientist inspired by the philosophy of the Roosevelt Revolution.

The Morgan hearings gave immediate impetus to banking reform. Senator Glass fought doggedly for his bill. Altogether it was killed fourteen times in the special session. By his acceptance of a deposit insurance plan Glass got the "little bank" support. But he did not get full Administration support. Chance events put the bill through: the veterans' bloc revolt and Mr. Roosevelt's failure to get Congressional adjournment on Saturday, June 10. In the following week the Glass-Steagall bill shot through. The House voted for it 262 to 19, and the Senate passed it by acclamation. "This bill has more lives than a cat," President Roosevelt remarked with a chuckle as he signed it. He also called it the "best piece of banking legislation since the Federal Reserve Act," though from his viewpoint it contained one or two objectionable features and was not as comprehensive as the permanent banking legislation which was needed.

Apart from deposit insurance the main provisions of the Glass-Steagall Act were:

1. The Federal Reserve Board was given broad powers to prevent the use of credit for speculation in securities, real estate, and commodities.

2. Payment of interest on demand deposits by member banks was prohibited, thereby removing a dangerous form of competition for deposits.

3. Within one year, member banks had to divorce their security affiliates, and private bankers had to cease either to sell securities or to accept deposits. If they chose to keep their deposit business, they had to submit to periodic examinations.

4. Beginning January 1, 1934, no member-bank officer or director could be an officer, partner, or director of a security-selling firm or of a private bank. By June 1934, no member bank could have more than twenty-five directors.

5. Mutual savings and Morris Plan banks were permitted to become members of the Federal Reserve system—another step toward unified banking.

6. National banks were put on a parity with state banks in the branch banking field. Nine states allowed statewide branch banking, sixteen permitted branch banking within certain limits, and eighteen states prohibited it.

The controversial deposit insurance plan set up a two billion dollar Federal Deposit Insurance Corporation directed by the Comptroller of the Currency and two presidential appointees. Beginning January 1, 1934, unless the President set an earlier date, a temporary insurance fund would insure all deposits up to $2500 each in the Federal Reserve member banks and all other banks meeting the requirements of the corporation. More than ninety-five percent of the individual deposits in the country were estimated to be less than $2500. Beginning July 1, 1934, the permanent insurance scheme was to become effective. That would insure 100 percent of all deposits up to $10,000, 75 percent on $10,000 to $50,000, and 50 percent above $50,000. After July 1, 1936, no state bank could obtain the benefits without membership in the Federal Reserve System. That delayed inducement to a unified banking system won over Senator Glass and others who fundamentally disapproved the insurance idea. The funds for the permanent insurance fund were to come from the government, the Federal Reserve Bank, and the participating banks.

The objections to deposit insurance were many. Eight Western states had tried it over twenty-five years and abandoned it with heavy losses. It was commonly said that it penalized good banking. Conservative bankers pointed out that many of the smaller banks probably could not qualify for insurance without calling loans and dumping assets with deflationary effects. Stronger state banks threatened to withdraw from the Federal Reserve System, unwilling to assume a share of the risks of their weaker competitors.

The Banking Act left untouched far-reaching problems centering about the place of a banking system in a régime of regulated or disciplined capitalism. The Securities Act tended to restrict irresponsible securities promotion. The Glass-Steagall Act severed investment banking from deposit banking, but placed no further control over investment banking. The flow of savings into new enterprise was potentially concentrated more than ever before in the hands of a few investment bankers compelled to exercise no responsibility except to tell the truth. There can be no security for either the investor or the depositor unless the economic machine functions. A handful of private bankers probably could make it function better than a large number of competing bankers did during the postwar decade. But only a few of the country's banking leaders had shown by their utterances any comprehension of the machine they were trying to run. A far greater measure of positive control over investment credit seemed indispensable to the objectives of the Roosevelt Revolution.

Another stroke severed one of the remaining strands between the dollar and the old gold standard. Mr. Roosevelt requested, and Congress, after sharp debate, overwhelmingly voted, a resolution annulling the gold clause in both public and private contracts. The federal government had outstanding approximately thirty billions of dollars in currency and debts which it had promised to redeem in dollars containing 23.22 grains of gold. Between sixty and seventy billions in private mortgages and securities contained gold clauses. This general use of the gold clause was peculiar to the United States. The President's powers to inflate the currency, particularly his power to change the gold content of the dollar, were worthless so long as the gold clauses were binding in this tremendous volume of federal and private obligations.

Mr. Roosevelt pointed out that there was only enough gold in the country to pay one twenty-fifth of these obligations. The sound money adherents tartly pointed out that the obligations did not all become due simultaneously. They shrieked against the abrogation of sacred contracts, wept over the stultification of the national

honor. Mr. Roosevelt was more thoroughly roasted by
the Tories for proposing to annul the gold clause than
for accepting inflationary powers. The gold clause annul-
ment was a definite indication that he did not intend to
return to the old gold standard. It was possible that,
following a recent British precedent, the Supreme Court
would in effect annul the gold clauses. But a declaration
of policy from Congress, which had supreme power, was
deemed helpful preparation for a test case. Senator
Borah stated the point succinctly: "There is no limitation
upon the power of Congress. The government cannot
contract away its sovereignty. Neither can it legislate
away its sovereignty. All contracts are subject to the
power of Congress to regulate money."

Several minor developments showed the trend of the
times. Congress expressed its feeling about high salaries
in private business. An amendment to the insurance relief bill prohibited the R.F.C. from lending to any bank,
railroad, or insurance company which paid any person
more than $17,500 a year. Its adoption was prevented
only by immediate, though over-due, action of the R.F.C.
to force reductions of moderate proportions in executives' salaries in businesses to which it lent money. A
Senate amendment to the Independent Offices Appropriation Bill specified $17,500 as the maximum yearly
salary to be paid to officers of air and ocean mail-carriers
receiving government-subsidized contracts. The Senate
passed unanimously Senator Costigan's resolution order-
ing four public bodies—the Federal Reserve Board, the
R.F.C., the Federal Power Commission, and the Federal Trade Commission—to furnish the salary schedules
of executive officers in all businesses under their supervision.

Another index of the times was the passage of the Wagner bill setting up Federal unemployment exchanges. For two years that bill had made front-page news. After Senator Wagner finally got it through the Senate, President Hoover vetoed it. In the leftward sweep of 1933, it passed both houses by acclamation with scarcely a word of discussion and barely received mention in the daily press.

A third straw was the insistence of the House on making the producer instead of the consumer pay the tax on electricity.

The National Industrial Recovery Act was the crowning piece of legislation of the special session. The dominating place in the Roosevelt program which this law quickly acquired was in strange contrast to its seemingly fortuitous origins. The depression had produced a host of plans for the regulation and stimulation of industry. The long-range plans sought the reshaping of the organization of American industry and business along lines deemed better suited to our advanced stage of productive development. The short-range plans were concerned primarily with artificial stimulants to recovery. In the more elaborate plans, the long- and short-range elements were combined in various ways. In the hands of some of the liberal economists they became complete blueprints for a planned economy.

The fundamental purpose of the long-range plans was to correct certain evils of the competitive system or to supersede it altogether. At least four legal barriers prevented effective dealing with some of the obvious evils of the competitive system: the body of anti-trust legislation, the tremendous disparities in legislation governing the conditions of work and in the power of labor in the individual states, lack of power to discipline recalcitrant minorities, and the constitutional limitation upon the Federal Government's authority to interstate commerce only. The anti-trust legislation, built up over two generations, was the clumsy defense of the small entrepreneur and the agricultural consumer of industrial products against the great financiers and industrialists. Competition, rugged individualism, equality of opportunity, democracy—all were wound up into a vague unity which was at the very heart of traditional American thought. The anti-trust laws were aimed at curbing the exploiting monopolies. Partly because of uncertain enforcement, but mostly because of their intrinsic unsoundness, they failed to check the growth of great industrial and merchandising units or the concentration of economic power in a few hands. In uneven ways they did succeed in preserving certain elements of competition. Through fair-practices legislation administered by the Federal Trade Commission and in other ways, the government sought to regularize competition. But business itself was legally hindered from making stabilizing agreements. In certain lines of business which were not naturally monopolistic, because they required little capital or for other reasons, the anti-trust laws actually put the small man at a disadvantage, since he could not agree with his small competitors on fair practices and prices. Consequently his choices frequently proved to be either to close up shop, to be swallowed up by a stronger competitor, or to join in an illegal agreement of some kind. The "racket" was in reality an illegal method of stabilizing certain highly competitive types of business.

During the depression years even the most enthusiastic defenders of competition became aware that it was being preserved at the expense of labor. Several development ments in the post-war decade had temporarily improved the position of the rank and file of wage and salary earners. Among them were: the restriction of immigration; the unprecedented prosperity cycle which easily permitted a rise in real wages; the growth among business men of a more or less hazy idea that high wages were desirable because workers were consumers as well as producers; stricter labor legislation in some states; the creation and enlargement of pension and insurance systems of various kinds by some of the more prosperous industrial units.

Offsetting these gains, however, were many trends which undermined the position of the employed classes. Among them were: the destruction of the I.W.W., which left the great masses of unskilled and other workmen outside the trade unions without a militant comprehensive organization; the dwindling membership of the American Federation of Labor and its failure, under effete leadership, to organize the mass production industries; the movement of certain types of industry, especially in the textile group, from states where labor was strong and state labor legislation and taxes were burdensome into states, especially in the South, where labor was unorganized, wage standards and taxes were low, and factory legislation was practically non-existent; the deterring effect of this movement on further improvement of labor conditions, either by collective bargaining or by statute, in the more progressive states; prodigious technological advances, which steadily reduced the element of skill in certain types of industry, and, even in the face of rapidly rising production, provided an unemployed labor surplus estimated at four million persons

in the peak year of 1929; a movement off the land to
the cities; the soporific effect of the phantasmagoria of
prosperity on the rank and file of employed classes (because they were better off than they had ever been before
they thought they were getting their share of the national income, which they weren't; lured on by the pros-
pects of becoming millionaires through speculation they
completely lost sight of their own interests and tried to
act like capitalists—which some of them were on a small
scale).

The depression caught wage and salary earners in a
defenseless position. Enlightened employers—and in a
broad relative sense there were a great many of them
—were equally defenseless in a great many lines of en-
deavor. Cut-throat competition for dwindling business
relentlessly broke down wage standards. Employers who
tried to hold up wages and conditions of work and in
some cases maintain pension and insurance systems were
increasingly at the mercy of what General Johnson aptly
termed "the chiseling fringe." The realm of the sweat
shop and the blight of child labor—which the United
States had tolerated in the heyday of prosperity—
spread. In the worst spots, women and children worked
seventy-two hours a week for a dollar or two, and conditions rivaled those of the barbaric early stages of the
industrial revolution in England.

With this process of dissolution as its exhibit, big
business could base its plea for relief from anti-trust
legislation on the broadest social grounds. In 1931,
Gerard Swope, President of the General Electric Company, outlined an approach to the problem of industrial
stabilization. It was important, not because it was the
first plan or very comprehensive, but because it was con-

structed from existing materials and took cognizance both of the strong emotional attachment of the agricultural regions and small business men to the anti-trust laws and of the business man's aversion to governmental control of his affairs. Mr. Swope's suggestion grew out of the current agitation over unemployment insurance. The trade association was his main implement. He proposed that the Federal Trade Commission be empowered to clarify and relax the anti-trust laws by approving specific agreements drawn by trade associations to govern competitive practices, the interconnection of the old age and unemployment insurance schemes of individual units, and the like. Mr. Swope's original suggestion provoked a great deal of public argument, which led him to amplify his views. Assuming that the Federal Trade Commission or any other federal agency entrusted with the power was composed of men who could adequately represent the public interest, the plan had much to recommend it. It left the anti-trust laws on the books but furnished a means to specific exemptions after the nature and purpose of the exemptions had been reviewed. After that the burden of enforcement fell on the trade associations, with the government retaining supervising authority. The idea at least opened a road toward industrial stabilization under government supervision. It was elaborated in a great many ways by other industrial and financial leaders. But it made comparatively little headway in the agricultural regions, which were absorbed in their own problems, had seen the Federal Trade Commission's activity wane, and distrusted anything that big business proposed, especially with relation to the anti-trust laws. At the other extreme of the more widely publicized early industrial planning proposals was Senator Robert M. LaFollette's scheme for an economic council, which, like other schemes of this type, worked down from the government rather than up from industry.

In the other field of purely emergency plans were ideas for the mobilization of industry, for the simultaneous resumption of production at a high level with a government guarantee against losses over a stipulated period, for the subsidizing of expenditures on plant improvement and enlargement. Some of them were simple, some highly complicated. In this category would have to be placed also the various types of plans for large expenditures on public works.

Dozens of these plans, long- and short-range, were public property. All of them—by Gerard Swope, Fred I. Kent, Bernard M. Baruch, M. C. Rorty, Henry S. Dennison, LaFollette, Henry I. Harriman, and many others—were well known to Mr. Roosevelt and his brains trust. In several of his speeches, particularly the Commonwealth Club speech, Mr. Roosevelt argued for the substitution of planning by business in co-operation with the government for unbridled competition. But he did not go into detail and he avoided direct discussion of modifying or relaxing the anti-trust laws—a ticklish subject in the agricultural regions which were the main base of his drive for the presidential nomination and election. It was plain to everybody who talked with him on the subject that he did not look with favor on the more rigid and complicated plans for imposing a planned productive system through an economic council. On the other hand, he was favorably interested in the plans which placed the chief burden of organization and enforcement on industry itself.

In the discussions with the brains trust, attention was

given also to the emergency mobilization devices. The occasion for a decision did not arise during the campaign, but it was generally understood in the inner circle that in conjunction with the public works program there would be some plan for obtaining a firm industrial base along the lines of wage and hour agreements.

The priority given the agricultural problem, balancing the budget, railroads, and other difficulties of tremendous scope, and the high pressure of events after March 4, deferred the crystallization of a plan, either long- or short-range. But rising demands from several different quarters forced the issue. In addition to the railroad industry, which was being dealt with separately, the oil industry was clamoring for the assistance of the Federal Government in rescuing it from chaos. The efforts of the oil producing states to curb production and distribution had failed. Oil was being bootlegged across the state lines. The opening up of the East Texas field threatened to sink the whole industry. Sales of oil for as little as 8 cents a barrel were reported at one time in East Texas. The oil industry, large and small, wanted government assistance—though it was bitterly divided on the question of the type of assistance it wanted. The anarchic bituminous coal industry was also clamoring for help.

The passage by the Senate of the Black thirty-hour bill on April 6, forced the broad issue from another direction. That was organized labor's drastic but crude effort to spread work. Miss Frances Perkins promptly pointed out that a minimum wage provision was a necessary companion to a shorter week. With a general assignment from the President to make something workable out of the Black bill, a Cabinet committee under her leadership worked out a substitute for the nearly identical Connery

bill which was before the House. The main features of
the substitute were: the five-day week would apply to
all industry and the thirty-hour week would apply with
certain exceptions to be permitted by the Secretary of
Labor to meet seasonal requirements and other special
needs. A forty-hour week was to be the maximum. The
Secretaries of Commerce and Labor would appoint a
fair wage board in each industry—one representative
each of employers, employees, and consumers, to submit
within thirty days recommendations as to minimum wages
for the entire industry or with adjustments to localities.
The Secretary of Labor could accept or improve these
recommendations and put them into effect through a
"directory order," which would have the force of law.
Violations would be punishable by fines and prison sentences. The Secretary of Labor could relax the anti-trust
laws to authorize the making of trade agreements of
various types. The fair wage board scheme was developed, I believe, by Sidney Hillman, President of the
Amalgamated Clothing Workers of America.

The Perkins substitute evoked cries of "Sovietism,"
"left-wing radicalism," "dictatorship," from the conservatives. Miss Perkins expressed astonishment and
"some amusement" at the protests against her "modest
plan to make the Black bill workable." Employers of all
types swarmed into Washington for the public hearings
and vented their objections without hesitation. The testimony given at the hearings made it evident that, even
with further modification, the plan was too rigid to be
workable in some fields and could not command the co-
operation of most employers.

The shock caused by the Black and Perkins bills gave
sharp impetus, however, to other plans to meet similar

objectives which were already under way. The smoke had hardly cleared away after the banking crisis before the more active authors and promoters of schemes for industrial mobilization and stabilization began their activities in Washington. James H. Rand, Jr., a group at the Brookings Institute and a committee of the National Manufacturers' Association were working on a mobilization plan. Henry I. Harriman and the United States Chamber of Commerce group were busy with another plan.

Mr. Moley, who was in touch with some of these groups, talked to Senator Robert F. Wagner, the leading Democratic sponsor of progressive industrial legislation, about incorporating a mobilization plan with the public works program on which Senators Wagner, LaFollette, and Edward P. Costigan were working. Wagner was primarily concerned at the moment with driving through a large public works program, and the outlook was none too reassuring, in view of the Administration's insistence on balancing the budget and Mr. Roosevelt's cautious attitude toward public works.

During the following week, the first in May, 1400 industrial and business leaders gathered in Washington for the annual meeting of the United States Chamber of Commerce. From this meeting came a demand for government co-operation in the regulation of competition which was literally astounding. Undoubtedly it was bred of desperation, but it was genuine. Of the forty-nine principal speakers more than half advocated a larger measure of government control of industry. Only nine definitely opposed it. The others ignored the issue. Paul W. Litchfield, President of the Goodyear Tire & Rubber Company, said: "We have failed to take the neces-

sary steps voluntarily, so the element of force, government compulsion, becomes necessary. . . . Our continued
decline in employment is leading us into state socialism
or complete anarchy." Gerard Swope solemnly warned
industry that, if it did not seize its opportunity to regulate itself with government co-operation, the regulation
would be done "from without." With the backing of
Harriman and Swope, the Chamber placed itself on
record in favor of industrial regulation and planning
through trade associations under government supervision.
A committee had already called on President Roosevelt
and asked his aid. The crux of the problem from industry's viewpoint was an effective curb on the "recalcitrant
minority." In his speech to the Chamber, Mr. Roosevelt
promised them "the co-operation of your government in
bringing these minorities to understand that their unfair
practices are contrary to a sound public policy." He also
asked them to increase wages as rapidly as they could.
But he committed himself to no definite plan. Three
days later, in his second radio address to the nation, he
went a little farther. He promised "well-considered and
conservative measures" which would attempt "to give
to the industrial workers of the country a more fair wage
return, prevent cut-throat competition and unduly long
hours for labor, and at the same time to encourage each
industry to prevent over-production." Using the cotton
goods industry as an example, he expressed the belief
that ninety percent of the cotton manufacturers would
agree to eliminate starvation wages and stop long hours,
child labor, and over-production, if the other ten percent
could be compelled to conform to the agreement.

Mr. Roosevelt was mildly reflecting the plan which
had taken tentative form in the hands of the Wagner

group. He had already withdrawn Administration support from the Black-Perkins bill, to which so many practical and emotional objections had been brought out in
the House Labor Committee hearing. Among those active in the Wagner group were Senator David I. Walsh,
Miss Perkins, John Dickinson, Assistant Secretary of
Commerce, an economist, lawyer, and college professor,
Donald Richberg, counsel to the railway brotherhoods,
William Green, and Assistant Secretary of Agriculture
Tugwell. After study of a wide range of plans, the assembling of a mountain of ideas, a glance at the corporative
laws of Fascist Italy, and other studies, they had produced a complex plan for industrial self-government under government supervision through trade association
codes of fair competition. Mr. Roosevelt had not committed himself to this bill and there were strong counsels
in his inner circle on behalf of caution.

Independent of the Wagner group, a fresh driving
force had been brought into the situation. Soon after the
start, in late April, of the rapid inflationary price rise,
General Hugh S. Johnson came to Washington. In a
talk with his old colleague in the brains trust, Mr. Moley,
he pointed out the imperative necessity of doing something in a hurry to boost mass purchasing power in the
wage and salary earning classes. Mr. Moley asked General Johnson, with whose ideas on the subject he was
already familiar, to go to work immediately. He presented him with his file of industrial plans, and one of
his secretaries, Robert K. Straus. General Johnson locked
himself in a hotel room and put in twenty-four hours of
straight work. He went through all the main plans and
emerged with the rough two-page draft of a bill. He
proposed to combine a swift distribution of funds for

public works to stimulate heavy industry with a sudden
lifting of wages and reduction of working hours. He
had no codes or elaborate arrangements. He sought action by the simplest and quickest methods. He wanted
a blanket rule. Exceptions could be granted, but the main
purpose was to get an instantaneous result. A great marshaling of business leaders, labor, and the general public
in a campaign modeled on wartime lines was the Johnson plan of procedure.

The National Industrial Recovery Act in its final form
was a merger of the Johnson and Wagner-Dickinson
plans. The final drafting was done primarily by Senator
Wagner, General Johnson, and Donald Richberg. The
fight over fundamental points continued to the end.
Senator Wagner and most of the Administration group
felt that industry, through trade associations, should
have the first chance to prepare codes. Johnson insisted
that the process should be reversed. Cautious counsel
wanted the minimum of government dictation all the
way through, the disciplining of recalcitrants left largely
to industry and punishment for violations to be obtained
solely through prosecutions. Johnson pleaded the necessity for a rigorous licensing power. The whole thing
would break down unless the government had extraordinary and swift authority to discipline minorities. Johnson hammered home the fact that the bill had to have
sharp teeth in it. Senator Wagner and the Administration group were insistent on the protection of collective
bargaining, to which, I believe, General Johnson was
more or less indifferent or opposed, not by principle, but
because he wanted the fewest possible impediments or
complications in the way of quick action.

Title I of this legislative leviathan set up the plan for

government "partnership" with industry. It declared a
national emergency. Any genuinely representative trade
or industrial association might draft a code of fair competition which would become effective on approval by
the President. He might amend it, amplify it, make
exemptions, impose requirements for the protection of
consumers, employees, and others. When approved by
him the code assumed the character of law, with punishment by fines for violations. The federal courts and district attorneys were authorized to take steps to enjoin
violations. As his most potent weapon the President could
impose licenses on balky industries. He could also enter
into voluntary agreements.

Every code was required to contain a guarantee of
the right of employees to "organize and bargain col-
lectively through representatives of their own choosing."
No employee and no one seeking employment could be
required to join any organization or to refrain from
joining any labor organization. Every employer had to
comply with maximum hours, minimum wages, and other
working conditions approved or prescribed by the President. Employers and employees had the first chance to
reach such agreements. But if they failed, or the President did not approve their agreement, he could impose
one of his own. These agreements were to have the same
effect as a code of fair competition.

Any action under the provisions of the bill was exempt
from the anti-trust laws. The President could cancel or
modify any arrangement at any time. He could delegate
his authority to any persons whom he chose. He could
embargo imports which interfered with the purposes of
the act. He could establish an industrial planning and
research agency. All of the provisions of the act were

to remain in force two years, except the licensing power, which was limited to one year. But the President could declare the emergency terminated, thus annulling the act at any time.

Title II of the bill authorized the President to create a federal emergency Administration of Public Works, to spend $3,300,000,000 on public works in their broadest sense: naval construction, highways, parkways, conservation of natural resources, federal buildings, low-cost housing, and slum clearance, and almost every other kind of project. He could make loans or grants to state and local governments for public works, finance railroad maintenance and equipment, fix minimum wages and maximum hours for labor on these projects.

The President was authorized to obtain the money for the public works program by borrowing. He requested $227,000,000 in new taxes to pay interest and amortization on the debt. After the usual fight over taxation, the Senate Finance Committee framed the revenue section: an increase in the gasoline tax, assorted corporation taxes, and readjustment of the capital gains provision of the income tax law. A special oil regulation clause was also written into the bill, empowering the President to appoint an oil conservation board, to prevent interstate commerce in oil shipped in violation of state laws and to prohibit new drilling.

There, with all the trappings of co-operation, were the greatest powers ever conferred on the President of the United States. The country gasped. The bill was jammed through the House. In the Senate it encountered trouble. Every important phase of the bill, and Title I in toto, came under heavy fire. Senator Borah and other foes of monopoly attacked the price-fixing provision, and it was defined to preclude monopolistic practices. Business men, large and small, who had clamored for government co-operation in industrial government were aghast when they saw it concretely outlined. The collective bargaining clause was naturally a storm center. Theoretically it was designed to protect genuine collective bargaining, to outlaw "yellow dog" contracts, and at the same time to protect the great open shop industries from unionization by outside leaders. In reality that was next to impossible.

In two weeks the revolt, in business and in the Senate, became formidable. Prices were rising, business began to get out of the red and into the black. The psychology of employers underwent a sudden and wondrous change. Laissez-faire boldly raised its voice. Business and banking pundits proclaimed the arrival of recovery from "natural causes."

"Dictatorship" was a much-used word in the spring of 1933. The discretionary powers delegated to the President were, of course, enormous. Within defined limits Mr. Roosevelt became a temporary "dictator" over portions of the country's economic system. But the political processes remained unchanged. Anyone who feared that the nation was slipping away from its established form of government had plenty of material for reassurance in the last two weeks of the special session of Congress. Congress revolted in a familiar manner against the drastic cuts in payments to veterans.

The struggle between the Executive and Congress, with the veterans' payments and the National Industrial Recovery Bill as the main bones of contention, kept Washington in turmoil for two weeks. It frustrated Mr. Roosevelt's plan to obtain a Congressional adjournment on Saturday, June 10, before the week that war debt payments were due and the World Economic Conference was to open, and it tested his skill in legislative management. The old guard Republicans who had saved the March economy bill from defeat by Democratic bolters jumped en masse to the side of the veterans and locked arms with the Progressive Republicans for the first time within memory. It was the second party issue drawn by the Republican old guard in the session. The first had been the gold standard. "Sound" money and the unbalancing of the budget—a rare combination. Prices were going up, the long-sought corner had been found and turned, prosperity was in sight, and politics reasserted itself.

Thanks to the zeal of his budget-balancing assistants, Mr. Roosevelt was vulnerable on the veterans' issue. The new regulations had gone beyond all expectations. Instead of the $385,000,000 at first estimated, the cuts approximated $480,000,000. Without question, battle casualties with specific injuries had been cut too deeply. That was a blunder—perhaps the worst tactical blunder of the Administration's first months. It prejudiced the defense of the new veterans' system all along the line. The veterans' organizations had begun mobilizing for the counter-attack as soon as they revived from the stunning blow of their March defeat. They had fought it with terrific pressure on every Congressman and with direct pleas to the President. Through the Independent Offices appropriation bill, which President Hoover had pocket-vetoed, Congress had another chance to make amends to the veterans.

Convinced that the Administration was in partial error, Mr. Roosevelt announced that the service-connected cuts had been "deeper than was originally intended." He promised to review these cases and give further study to all the regulations. He also suspended the plan to close regional offices of the Veterans Administration, except where they were clearly proved unnecessary, and promised that no governmental hospitals would be closed until the whole hospital situation had been reviewed.

But Mr. Roosevelt could not allay the storm. The Senate adopted an amendment limiting to twenty-five percent the reductions in pensions of service-connected World War veterans and of all veterans of earlier wars. Vice-President Garner voted for it, breaking a tie, to prevent worse emasculation of new regulations. Mr. Roosevelt was confronted with the loss of $170,000,000 of his economies and a vital impairment of the whole new system. The veterans' bloc in the House eagerly prepared to do even more for the veterans. Mr. Roosevelt called the House leaders into consultation. He could have vetoed the bill when he got it, made a plea to the country, and kept Congress in session, and Budget Director Douglas and others urged him to do it. But there was some merit to the case for the veterans and some consideration was due Congressmen who were about to return home to face angry constituents.

Out of the give and take came Mr. Roosevelt's compromise. He agreed to limit pension cuts for war-disabled to twenty-five percent. He agreed to leave on the rolls 154,000 veterans whose disabilities were "presumed" to have originated in the war, pending individual review of their cases. He promised to give the presumptive cases the benefit of the doubt. Senators Cutting and Steiwer, Republicans, battling for an amendment which would definitely restore all "presumptives" to the rolls, subject only to the general twenty-five percent reduction, refused to compromise. The President refused to recede farther. With the threat of a veto, he whipped the House into line behind his compromise.

The Senate again asserted its independence, and adopted the Steiwer-Cutting amendment. The House again threatened to break away. Mr. Roosevelt refused to budge; the Administration lines held; the House rejected the Senate amendment on June 15. Shortly after midnight the Senate capitulated. Nine Democrats returned to Mr. Roosevelt's support; the Administration compromise was adopted 45 to 36, and Congress adjourned. Meanwhile, during the ten days of turmoil, Congress had passed the National Industrial Recovery Act, the Glass-Steagall Act, the largest appropriation bill in the history of the country: $3,610,079,670.24 for public works and other emergency expenditures, apart from the $631,802,546 Independent Office bill.

Thus ended the 99-day extraordinary session of the 73rd Congress and the first 105 days of the Roosevelt Administration. Whatever lay ahead, the new government had wrought a feat in legislation which shattered all precedents:

The Emergency Banking Act, supplemented by the state bank act, which met the crisis.

The Economy Act, which brought the budget under control and created a new pension system.

The Agricultural Adjustment Act, which authorized the vast experiment in controlling agricultural surpluses, invested the President with powers to inflate the currency, and provided means for reducing the farmers' debt.

The National Industrial Recovery Act, which instituted the even more extraordinary industrial experiment, authorized a large public works program, and imposed new taxes.

The Tennessee Valley Authority Act, which authorized the long-range experiment in regional planning.

The Civilian Conservation Corps Act, which combined unemployment relief with conservation work.

The Home Owners Loan Act, which provided for the refinancing of home mortgages.

The Railroad Co-Ordinator Act, which began work on the complex problem of revamping the nation's transportation system.

The Glass-Steagall Bank Act.

The 3.2 Beer Act, abetted by the Medicinal Liquor Act, which relaxed the restrictions on the sale of whisky.

The $500,000,000 Emergency Relief Act.

The Securities Act.

The Wagner Employment Exchange Act.

The Gold Clause Resolution.

Legislation revising the power of the R.F.C.

Mr. Roosevelt gayly signed the final bills, gave his various experiments a push forward, and departed for his vacation sail up the New England coast as skipper of a 45-foot schooner. The nation was bewildered, thrilled, happy with hope. The orthodox economist, the international banker, the open-shop employer, the hard-headed farmer, the home-owner about to lose his property, could have his doubts. But the nation had been yanked out of the pit and put on its feet. The government functioned. The new President had delivered with a vengeance the "action" which he promised on March 4. The nation was launched on an adventure.

VI

The New Deal Meets the Old World

THREE sore spots in the world were of grave concern to the United States at the close of the 1932 campaign: the old European World War area, the Sino-Japanese conflict, and Cuba. Without the backing of President-elect Roosevelt, the Hoover Administration was powerless to take effective action abroad. But an undeclared war in the Orient and the deepening omens of a general conflagration in Europe forbade drifting.

In Europe, economic and political difficulties were hopelessly interlocked. The World War had severely dislocated European economy, as well as altered the entire balance of world economy. The Versailles Treaty had imposed boundaries which economically were indefensible, yet could not be altered or ignored without imperiling the dominant position of France. The fear of war led each nation to seek so far as it could economic self-sufficiency. The allies had theoretically imposed the cost of the war on Germany, and actually had contrived a system designed to extract from Germany enough to pay their debts to the United States, with a little left over for the French. They could not make it work without permitting Germany to export goods which competed with their own for dwindling export markets. We were faced with the same dilemma of accepting goods or services or of forgoing the receipt of payments. Instead of more goods, we wanted fewer. We were insisting on exporting a larger and larger surplus. We met the dilemma with loans. As the American surplus had kept the World War going, so it now became a large factor in the resuscitation and functioning of the post-war European system. It makes no difference whether we say that we lent money to pay the reparations and, in turn, the war debts to ourselves, or that we lent the money to buy our own surplus. We exported goods and tourists. We received some goods and services and a little gold in exchange, and made up the difference by converting our foreign balances into loans and direct investments, many of which were for the construction of factories, American or foreign-owned, which directly competed with our own. It was a crazy system, which could be kept going only by larger and larger American loans or the acceptance of an unfavorable trade balance and its consequences to our internal economy. When we ceased lending, the system began to collapse. We fortified ourselves behind the Smoot-Hawley tariff, and the movement toward self-containment was accentuated throughout the world. Each nation strove to protect its own economy behind higher tariff walls, quota systems, exchange restrictions and other devices. The gold standard went to pieces. Great Britain, home of free trade, sought to bind its political empire into a protected economic empire with the Ottawa agreements. The pains of economic disintegration intensified the political dissatisfactions of Continental Europe and the rest of the world.

The international bankers and their attendant bevy of economists and European-minded intellectuals were preoccupied with the break-up of the international economic system. The Hoover Administration followed the internationalists, while denying, of course, that Republican protectionism was inconsistent with this mode of thought.

Mr. Hoover's effort to save Germany by a moratorium on intergovernmental obligations had been hobbled by the French. The private bankers had accepted the inevitable with the moratorium for German short-term obligations. Frightened by the movement of Germany toward either a communist left or a militaristic right, and by general collapse all around, the European nations belatedly got together at Lausanne in the summer of 1932. Their solution of this dire situation was to agree to a settlement of reparations at the rate of ten cents on the dollar, subject to a corresponding reduction in war debts by the United States, and to call a World Economic Conference.

On good advice, they postponed the mass appeal to the United States. But the November ballots no sooner had been counted, than the attack began. The next debt payments were due December 15. The debt cancellationists in the United States went into action. Mr. Hoover invited Mr. Roosevelt to confer. On November 14, Mr. Roosevelt thrust the full responsibility for the December 15th problem back on Mr. Hoover. The cancellationists at once turned their fire on Mr. Roosevelt. They had envisioned the outgoing and incoming Presidents taking joint responsibility for forcing Congress to accept the "realities" of the war debts. Although Mr. Hoover and Mr. Roosevelt were pledged not to cancel the debts, there was at that time a rather firmly held opinion in certain circles of the intelligentsia and of international finance that these pledges were only political persiflage to appease the ignorant, emotional inhabitants of the American hinterland. It was assumed in these circles that all really intelligent people knew that the war debts were one of the main causes of the depression and that their cancellation was a sure step toward restoring prosperity to the United States and the world. With infinite pain the cancellation propagandists had endeavored to make the American public understand the recondite complexities of the transfer problem and international banking economics as a whole.

The cancellationists surrounded the war debts with an economic ideology which most of them would have been horrified to have applied to private debt. The war debts were only part of the problem of international debt and international debt, in turn, only a fraction of the problem of debt. Fundamentally there was as much, and, no more, justification for canceling the war debts than for canceling the debts of the American farmer. In fact, everything considered, assumption by the American taxpayers of the American farm debt probably would have helped much farther toward recovery than their assumption of the European debt.

However, years of propaganda had educated the citizens of the Allied nations to believe that the war debts were the source of their troubles, that they weren't real debts, that the United States had got rich out of the war, etc., and that only an insufferable miser like Uncle Shylock would refuse to cancel the debts. The American citizen saw that the World War did not bring the happy results that Mr. Wilson and the Allied propagandists had prophesied and began to feel that he had played the part of a sucker; he saw the allegedly impoverished nations of Europe spending more on armaments than they had before the war and generally behaving like ingrates toward their transatlantic benefactor. The hard political facts were that the debtor nations were determined to stop paying their war debts and that the American public would not forgive these debts unless it received very substantial compensations. Having despaired of convincing the American public that the cancellation of the debts was in its own interest, the cancellationists had invented a varied assortment of proposed "trades," some genuine, others not. Among them were: the cancellation of war debts in return for a beginning toward European disarmament, writing down of the debts in proportion to the debtor nations' purchases of our exports (a sugar-coated form of cancellation which possibly might have some use in stimulating trade but again raised the question: Would we accept payment in goods for those new exports?), cancellation of the British debt in return for resumption of the gold standard by Britain. The Hearst press proposed that we swap the debts for British and French possessions in the Caribbean—which was the nearest to a substantial trade that anybody suggested. On the other hand the most avid cancellationists said that the war debt system was so dead that there was no bargaining power left in it and that we had better take what we were offered in the way of a lump sum and forget the rest.

Fundamentally the conflict was between the American taxpayers and the European taxpayers, plus the American purveyors and private owners of European obligations, about eleven billion dollars which had been thrown into the scrapheap of the war.

After disclaiming responsibility for the immediate issue of December 15 payments, Mr. Roosevelt accepted Mr. Hoover's invitation, and the first of their meetings occurred at the White House on November 22. Mr. Roosevelt was accompanied by Mr. Moley and Mr. Hoover was attended by Secretary of the Treasury Mills. At that meeting the whole European situation was surveyed. Two statements the following day revealed the main lines of cleavage between the viewpoints of the old and forthcoming Administrations on the handling of the war-debt issue. They agreed on four long-established points of American policy: first, that the debts were actual loans; second, that each debtor must be considered individually; third, that the debt settlements took into consideration capacity to pay; fourth, that the war debts bore no relationship to reparations.

With those four points their agreement ended. Mr. Hoover felt it imperative to have the World Economic Conference meet as soon as possible. He wanted Congress to set up a debt-review agency with complete or partial identity of membership with the delegations to the World Economic Conference and General Disarmament Conference. Mr. Roosevelt, on the other hand, asserted that, as a general policy, a debtor must always have access to his creditor and that the most convenient and effective method of access was through the regular channels of diplomatic intercourse.

On December 15, the British paid their debt installment with the assertion that it was the last under the existing agreement and requested an immediate review. The Herriot government fell on the issue and the French "deferred" payment. Mr. Hoover at once resumed his efforts to persuade or force Mr. Roosevelt to pursue the policy of Mr. Hoover. Mr. Roosevelt stood his ground. Mr. Hoover could proceed to receive the representations of debtor nations through diplomatic channels with the understanding that the incoming Administration would in no way be bound. The interchange ended with Mr. Hoover's testy announcement that Mr. Roosevelt had refused to co-operate and Mr. Roosevelt's indignant reply that he had proposed a method of co-operation consistent with the policy of the new Administration and that, if Mr. Hoover wanted to co-operate, he could adopt it.

Mr. Hoover would have used the war debts for trading purposes. At that time the prevailing cry of the international bankers and classic economists was for the return of the pound sterling to gold. That was supposed to give a firm base for a rise in commodity prices and world recovery. The agenda for the World Economic Conference was drawn with that in view. It was an international bankers' agenda, centered about the return to an international gold standard. Fortunately the British had insisted on writing in important qualifications: each nation was to determine when and at what level it should return to gold.

Mr. Roosevelt probably had many reasons for refusing to support Mr. Hoover's economic policies abroad. The whole subject was ticklish politically and Mr. Roosevelt could not afford to fritter away his public prestige and influence with Congress. The backbone of his recovery program was domestic and, if possible, he wanted to avoid the complication of international negotiations until after his domestic program was well under way. Neither he nor his advisers could see a suitable "trade" for the war debts. A measurement of debts against monetary stabilization or anything else was difficult to apply. They shied away from the theory that the basis of recovery lay in the return to gold of the pound and sterling-attached currencies, thus indicating that Mr. Roosevelt had already reached the conclusion that we probably would emulate the British example ourselves. So far as trade concessions went, there was plenty of bargaining in our own tariff position. At the same time Mr. Roosevelt's formula furnished better opportunity for trading if the occasion arose. By keeping the war debts in the hands of the President, he removed them from the public forum, where they fanned popular emotions on both sides of the Atlantic.

Behind the scenes Mr. Roosevelt directed some important changes in the agenda of the conference. Early in January, after their return from the first meeting of the agenda committee, the two American representatives, Dr. Edmund E. Day and Professor John H. Williams, were brought to Hyde Park by Dr. Tugwell to see Mr. Roosevelt. They returned to the second meeting of the agenda committee with the requests to make the agenda inclusive and particularly to include tariffs, which Mr. Hoover had wished to omit, and the regularizing of the production of such basic commodities as wheat, copper, silver, and cotton. The broadening of the agenda was recognition that the collapse of the international gold standard was only a symptom of more profound disturbances. Mr. Roosevelt's most active lieutenants during this period were Messrs. Moley and Tugwell, neither of whom placed much stock in the World Economic Conference or international remedies except as a supplement to the domestic program.

The momentarily broken connections between Mr. Roosevelt and Mr. Hoover were quickly repaired by Mr. Norman H. Davis, who returned from the Disarmament Conference and the committee on arrangements for the World Economic Conference with a doleful picture of the state of Europe. Then, in early January, Secretary of State Stimson and Mr. Roosevelt had a long talk at Hyde Park. They got along well. From this meeting came concrete developments: Mr. Roosevelt's endorsement of some of the policies of the Hoover Administration and a second meeting with President Hoover.

First, Mr. Roosevelt backed up the Hoover-Stimson Manchurian policy, which then rested on the formula of non-recognition of political changes wrought in violation of existing treaties. Mr. Roosevelt's support was vitally important at that juncture. The mobilization of world opinion, which Mr. Stimson had done so much to bring about, was just about to reach its culmination in the report of the League of Nations Committee of Nineteen. The leading European powers had slowly swung around to the point of view of the United States and the small nations. Doubt as to the attitude of the new Administration in the United States was undermining this belated formation of a moral front. Mr. Roosevelt was presented with the practical choice of seeing through a movement which already was approaching its fulfillment or of repudiating the Stimson policy, which would have amounted to an endorsement of the Japanese partition of China. He, of course, backed up Mr. Stimson. The Committee of Nineteen made its report; it was adopted by the League, with only Japan dissenting; and Japan promptly withdrew from the League. That was Mr. Roosevelt's last open action with reference to Japan. The Japanese advance through Jehol to the Wall of China continued. In the spring months more exciting events pushed the Sino-Japanese war off the front pages of American newspapers. That was a wholesome development. World opinion had been registered. Unless we proposed to fight, a less active policy became the only sound course.

However, Mr. Roosevelt endorsed Mr. Hoover's request for the power to join with other governments in embargoing the shipment of arms. When the delegation of this authority to the President had first been proposed, the previous year, it had been with the intimation that it was for use in curbing the little wars in South America. But it was theoretically of greater value in hampering the warlike activities of Japan. Later it looked as if it were intended for Germany. All that was made clear was that arms embargo was an integral part of the Roosevelt policy.

The second conference between Messrs. Hoover and Roosevelt, in January, grew out of the British request for a review of their war debts. The British were apprehensive about the whole European situation and, on their own behalf, were undoubtedly anxious to take advantage of the favorable opinion created here by their full payment of their December debt installment. Preliminary exploration with the dying Hoover Administration, of course, meant nothing. There were strong reasons why the British request should be granted. We shared in a small degree the British interest in the peace of Europe, and we wanted their co-operation in the Far East. The fidelity of the British to their bond merited a friendly hearing of their pleas, particularly in view of the default of the French. Furthermore, the British were entitled to special consideration because we had been less generous in the debt settlement with them than with our other creditors. Although it complicated and endangered his domestic program, Mr. Roosevelt agreed to receive British representatives immediately after his inauguration. Specifically, he agreed to receive a "representative" (singular) to discuss debts and "representatives" (plural) to discuss other world economic problems. Thus he kept war debts separate from the World Economic Conference and securely in his own hands. The implication of the singular "representative," of course, was that he would be a man corresponding in rank to the President. Speculation at once hit on the obvious man: Prime Minister J. Ramsay MacDonald.

The details of the arrangements were entrusted to Secretary Stimson and Sir Ronald Lindsay, the British Ambassador, and Mr. Roosevelt went on to Warm Springs, Georgia. A few days later, Sir Ronald made his flight to Warm Springs. He was going home to report to his government. The relaying of the views of the incoming President through Mr. Stimson had raised difficulties. Mr. Roosevelt himself suggested to Mr. Stimson over the long-distance telephone that it would simplify matters to have Sir Ronald come to Warm Springs. It violated precedent, but it was sensible. Mr. Roosevelt and the British Ambassador had been personal friends since the days of the Wilson Administration. What Mr. Roosevelt told Sir Ronald was not disclosed. But with Sir Ronald's return to England, a change in British policy became apparent. The British became less hurried about discussing war debts and prepared to co-operate in reviewing the whole problem of world recovery. Meanwhile Mr. Roosevelt had begun cajoling the French, tactfully ignoring for the moment their "deferred" December payment.

In preparation for the economic conversations with the British, Professor Moley was detailed to assemble experts and data. This brought about another extension of the group which was loosely called the brains trust. The most active additions were: Herbert Feis, economic adviser to the State Department; James P. Warburg, young New York banker, and William C. Bullitt. Mr. Bullitt's dramatic past in the Wilson Administrations and recent cavortings over Europe, accompanied by stories that he was Mr. Roosevelt's personal representative, had surrounded him with a certain amount of glamour.

At this time, also, Senator Cordell Hull was introduced to the situation as Mr. Roosevelt's choice for Secretary of State. At Mr. Roosevelt's inauguration, Mr. Moley was planted in the State Department as an Assistant Secretary. Thus the fundamental conflict between the New Deal and old-fashioned Democracy, between bold experimentation and Adam Smith economics, was personified and sharpened. Mr. Hull saw the international route to recovery in its theoretical whole and believed in it devoutly. He would have none of the lop-sided Republic mercantilism; he saw that to sell goods, we had to buy them, and he was willing to take the consequences. He distrusted the liberal men and experimental measures with whom Mr. Roosevelt surrounded himself. Yet, as the ranking Cabinet officer, he had as one of his titular subordinates the very symbol of the new order. Because of his varied activities, the titular subordinate saw many times as much of the President as Mr. Hull did and knew better what was going on in the President's mind. Moreover, he was in full charge of the preparation of data for the World Economic Conference, which Mr. Hull regarded as the nation's and the world's supreme opportunity, and was the President's chief expert on war debts, a problem so delicate that the President did not confide it to his Secretary of State.

The Roosevelt Revolution at home and concerted international action toward recovery along certain lines, were not mutually exclusive. In fact, the synchronizing of the domestic efforts of different nations and the control of the production of basic commodities could be distinctly helpful. Within limits the reopening of trade channels, in which Mr. Hull was interested, was highly desirable from our point of view. We had to buy abroad rubber, tin, coffee, and many miscellaneous commodities. There were many other goods from abroad which we could take without adverse effects on our own production. It was extremely desirable to reopen foreign markets for wheat, cotton, lard, and other farm products. Our surplus in these primary agricultural products was one of the roots of our problem. The gigantic task before the AAA would be reduced correspondingly by the recovery of foreign markets. The realists in the Administration saw, however, that the reopening of trade channels would be a slow business.

With remarkable tact and forbearance on both sides, Secretary Hull and his powerful subordinate might have been able to get along with each other if their fundamental views had not been irreconcilable. But Mr. Hull was a theorist and a visionary. If he had been a college professor, the gentlemen of the brains trust would have shunned him as they shunned many of their professorial colleagues who had only one formula. Mr. Moley was a realist who saw that economic self-containment was the order of the day and that the domestic experiments of the new régime would require, at least temporarily, more, rather than less, insulation of American economy from the remainder of the world. A rising undercurrent of personal feeling widened the breach in viewpoint. Instead of correlating his own ideas to the domestic program, Mr. Hull assailed economic nationalism with increasing vehemence. In fortifying his own position, Mr. Moley expanded his theory of the origin of the depression in a way which probably gave less emphasis to the international causes than he would have given a year earlier.

The banking crisis in this country and the Hitler revolution in Germany postponed the visit of Prime Minister

MacDonald. Mr. Roosevelt's handling of the banking crisis instantly gave him world prestige. The Hitler revolution made Europe tremble with the fear of war and sent Mr. MacDonald flying over the continent to preserve the peace. Meanwhile Mr. Roosevelt had expanded his plans for international conversations. Something had to be done about the French. They were the key to the continental impasse. The futility of confining preparatory conversations to the British had been proved by Mr. Hoover's experience with the London Naval Conference. Beginning with our post-war refusal to guarantee the French domination of Europe, our sympathies and active help had swung slowly over toward the side of the dissatisfied nations. Mr. Roosevelt's family and wartime associations made him naturally sympathetic to the French point of view. Most of his close associates thought Mr. Hoover had badly mishandled the French. Mr. Roosevelt evidently thought that with kindly understanding of the French he could get somewhere with the European situation and perhaps coax them to pay their war debt and co-operate in a world-wide effort at economic recovery.

So the French were added to the list of special visitors. Ambassador Claudel asked President Roosevelt if he had any suggestions as to whom the French should send as their chief representative. Mr. Roosevelt replied that, of course, he could make no suggestions and would welcome any emissary the French Government might choose, but that, as the Ambassador knew, a man who was known to favor payment of the French war debt, such as M. Herriot, would be assured a warm public reception. So M. Herriot, who was not a member of the French Government at that time, was detailed to come.

Now, were you going to ignore the Italians? They were

our good friends, as the diplomats say, and Mussolini, with his Four-Power Pact, had ceased to be a firebrand and was acting as a fire-extinguisher for Europe. Nor could you ignore the Germans, or the Argentinians, or a lot of other people. Mr. Roosevelt decided to invite all the nations with which we had diplomatic intercourse to the preliminary bi-lateral conversations. Eleven were invited to send special representatives: Great Britain, France, Italy, Germany, Japan, China, Argentina, Brazil, Chile, Mexico, and Canada. With all the other nations, excepting Soviet Russia, the Administration held preliminary conversations through their regular diplomatic representatives in Washington.

The perfectly natural desire to get acquainted, to get his finger on the world's pulse by those same personal contacts with which he felt the nation's pulse, was undoubtedly one of Mr. Roosevelt's motives. Secretary Hull's enthusiasm for international economic action was also an impelling force. If the conference was to accomplish anything, much preparatory work had to be done.

The parade of diplomats accomplished some useful purposes. Among its immediate effects was the screening of the war-debt issue. Its economic insignificance was established even though its political importance remained undiminished. Also the groundwork was laid for Mr. Roosevelt's supreme effort to break the European political deadlock, which had to be broken soon if it was ever to be broken peacefully.

On the other hand, the succession of conversations in Washington diverted the attention of the Administration and of the public from the main line of recovery at home. Mr. Roosevelt could keep in mind that international action was a supplement and not a substitute. But the corre-

lation of international action with the American domestic
program was difficult to translate into concrete terms,
especially since no one could foresee the full practical implications of the American domestic experiments. Some of
Mr. Roosevelt's advisers wanted only the international
program, some could not see that the domestic experiments would have any effect on an international program,
and others disagreed as to what the effects would be. It
was not surprising that the public was unable to diagnose
the situation. But the Roosevelt Administration unmis-
takably emerged in the eyes of the public at home and
abroad as the chief sponsor of the World Economic Conference and the international approach to recovery. Before we knew it, we were back in the familiarly vulnerable
position of "leadership" in European affairs. Mr. Roosevelt's policy of being a "good neighbor" began to look
suspiciously like the old rôle of the rich uncle.

At the very moment that the conversations were to begin, while Mr. MacDonald and M. Herriot were still on
the high seas, Mr. Roosevelt said farewell to gold for a
second time and accepted inflationary powers. The French
were stunned and said they might as well turn back;
possibly a lot of wasted effort would have been saved if
they had. Mr. MacDonald was perturbed. Instead of wel-
coming us to the fold of managed currencies, the British
criticized us for abandoning gold "voluntarily." The dollar had been forced off gold as surely as the pound. In
America, because of a gold standard that permitted every
citizen to obtain gold coin, the run was primarily internal.
The external run was halted by the embargo of March 6.
When Mr. Roosevelt relaxed the embargo temporarily,
the outward movement was immediately resumed on a

large scale. During this spell of British criticism the British gold holdings were the highest on record. Theoretically the pound and the dollar could both have been returned to gold, if the respective governments had been willing to take the consequences. If the British argument lacked logic, it covered up previous error and current division of opinion on monetary policy. It also met the standard requirement that policy be clothed in language appeasing to the Anglo-Saxon's subtle moral sensibilities and compatible with that stern code of ethics in financial matters which the British had to preserve among their debtors.

Of course, our farewell to gold made the British worry about their export trade and the trembling peace of Europe. The French were in agonies of fear about their own ability to hold to gold. Their budget was unbalanced, but they did not want to raise prices. Untroubled by internal surpluses of basic commodities, they had succeeded in maintaining their price level by adjustable barriers against imports. They had devalued the franc eighty percent after the war, and their millions of small investors were heartily opposed to any further loss of their savings. If the franc toppled from gold, the prestige of France in Europe would be shaken at the very moment that the Hitler revolution was giving the French their worst fright in years. The British feared a French swerve to the right and a "preventive" invasion of the Reich. The British accordingly modified their stabilization operations, which were causing a drain on French gold and arranged to leave their franc balances in France as loans. The Germans, having ridden inflation once to its ultimate conclusion, were now riding deflation toward its bitter end. Like the

Italians, and the other so-called gold countries, with the exception of Holland and Switzerland, they were adhering to gold only by severe restrictions on exchange.

After the first flutter of excitement over the departure of the dollar from gold, the international conversations in Washington went along fairly pleasantly. Mr. Roosevelt was well aware of the interrelation of politics and economics in Europe and had developed a well-rounded peace and disarmament plan, which received an agreeable reception from Prime Minister MacDonald and M. Herriot. The atmosphere of the White House was exceedingly friendly and encouraging. Optimistic communiqués flowed forth. The experts got together and talked. The Administration knew that Mr. MacDonald was only the figurehead for a Tory Government and that M. Herriot was more liberal than the French Government at that time. But it tended to forget it.

Now, despite all the confusion then and until the end of the World Economic Conference, Mr. Roosevelt did have one international economic objective. It was to raise the world price level. That was an estimable goal which theoretically could be achieved by a variety of economic and monetary methods. The American attitude during the economic conversations was partly exploratory, but our experts did have a program, even though it was bred of conflicting economic theories and conflicting views concerning the American program. The American monetary formula, later presented at London in the Pittman resolution, proposed a reduction in the gold cover of currencies and the optional use of silver as part coverage. That was a plan for the eventual restoration of a revised international gold standard. According to some monetary theorists, the more economical use of gold and the employment of silver would have a price-lifting effect. When and with what gold content each currency was to adhere to this standard was left open. Other main points in the American program were: synchronizing of public works programs, control of production of basic commodities, elimination of extreme trade barriers and a beginning on the reduction of tariffs, the raising and stabilization of the price of silver between 50 and 75 cents an ounce. On the tariff there was a cleavage. Secretary Hull and the State Department career men were keen for multilateral reductions. Senator Pittman and the brains trust (with the exception of Mr. Taussig, who stood by Mr. Hull) were in favor of reciprocal trade agreements after the British model. Purely from the point of view of tactics, there was much to be said for a demand for general tariff reductions. Our earlier leadership in tariff protectionism had created the popular fiction that we were the worst offenders, whereas in fact we had long since been outplayed at the game. There was also a blithe hope among our low-tariff people that we could win the British away from their newly assumed protectionism, and, particularly, bring about a modification of the Ottawa pacts.

The relative influence and aggressiveness of the various American experts greatly affected the course of the conversations. Senator Pittman's chief interest was in doing something for silver. His power as chairman of the Foreign Relations Committee, and his skill and persistence in exposition, kept silver to the front. Most of the other nations considered silver relatively unimportant but were willing to help raise the price if it meant anything to us and would bring them something substantial in return. Senator Pittman made more headway than anybody else, with the result that the importance of silver to us

was undoubtedly magnified in the minds of our visitors.
Mr. Hull did not get far with the tariff, but his determination remained unshaken. When the organizing committee for the conference met in London in early May, Norman H. Davis proposed a tariff truce on behalf of the
United States. He finally got it adopted, but the exceptions and interpretations made by the eight participants
were numerous and vitiating. The British, who had just
cornered Argentina's exchange in a discriminatory trade
agreement, coolly went ahead with the formation of their
protected trade system. Shortly afterward Mr. Roosevelt
himself faced the question of the real meaning of the
truce. For a day or two he withheld approval of preparations for the application of a cotton processing tax because it meant a compensatory rise in the tariff on cotton
products. Then he changed his mind and gave the word
to go ahead.

The gravest deficiency of the American group of experts was on the monetary side. Senator Pittman knew
something about money but was not a specialist in banking and finance. Mr. Warburg, the chief financial expert,
was very able, but he was an international banker and a
conservative on money matters. In fact, he was more conservative than the British Treasury experts. One of Mr.
Roosevelt's imperative objectives was to get internal
prices and debt back into workable relationship with each
other and to keep them there. He had accepted currency
manipulating powers. But there was no one among the
experts qualified by knowledge or disposition to discuss
the place of currency management in the maintenance of
a stable internal price level or the relationship of that
problem to the maintenance of an international monetary
standard.

As soon as the dollar began to fall, Mr. Warburg and Treasury officials began working on plans for stabilizing it. The idea that the dollar would quickly find a "natural" level was widely held in Washington. About a ten or fifteen percent drop from the gold level was the conservative estimate. Few prognosticators could be found in Washington who thought that the dollar would sink beyond the level represented by a $4.25 pound, assuming the pound was held at its fairly well-established point below the old gold parity. There was tremendous pressure from the conservative side for temporary stabilization with the pound at $3.75 or $3.85.

The speculative character of the fall of the dollar and the rise of American commodities, based on the fear or expectation of currency inflation, was only gradually realized. The discussion of de facto stabilization plans by Mr. Warburg and the Treasury group undoubtedly gave visiting experts the idea that the dollar would soon be pegged. Secretary Hull, however, left the subject severely alone. With his comprehensive theoretical view of the whole problem of restoring international trade, he could see no point in trying to stabilize currencies unless trade barriers were to be razed or lowered at the same time.

During the international conversations, Mr. Roosevelt apparently left entirely open the time and level of dollar stabilization. At least he did in every formal statement. Some of his eager aides were perhaps misled by his habit of giving off-hand encouragement to everybody around him who is trying to do things. Several weeks after Mr. Warburg had begun to work on plans for de facto stabilization and discuss them at the White House, he apparently was surprised to find that he had not yet sold the idea to the President.

"But this is de facto, not de jure stabilization," Mr. Warburg is reported to have said.

"Ah," Mr. Roosevelt responded with a gay laugh, "at last I know what you mean by de facto stabilization."

The Roosevelt-MacDonald communiqué of April 26 stated the Administration policy: "The necessity for an increase in the general level of commodity prices was recognized as primary and fundamental. To this end simultaneous action needs to be taken both in the economic and in the monetary field. . . . The *ultimate re-establishment* of equilibrium in the international exchanges should also be contemplated.

"We must, *when circumstances permit,* re-establish an international monetary standard which will operate successfully without depressing prices and avoid the repetition of the mistakes which have produced such disastrous results in the past. . . . The achievement of sound and lasting world recovery depends on co-ordinating domestic remedies and supplementing them by concurrent and simultaneous action in the international field."

The Roosevelt-Herriot statement, April 28, which had to meet the French views as well as the American, referred to "progressive and simultaneous disarmament and the restoration of stable monetary conditions in an atmosphere of general security." Again it spoke of "a rapid revival of world activity and the raising of world prices by diminishing all sorts of impediments to international commerce, such as tariff, quota, and exchange restrictions, and by the re-establishment of a more normal monetary and financial situation."

The Roosevelt-Bennett statement, April 29: "We are agreed that our primary need is to insure an increase in the general level of commodity prices. . . . It is recognized that *as soon as practicable* an international monetary standard must be restored, with arrangements that will insure a more satisfactory operation of international monetary relationships."

The Roosevelt-Jung statement, May 6: "We are in agreement that a fixed measure of exchange values must be re-established in the world and we believe that this measure must be gold. The entire problem of raising world prices and restoring the opportunity to work to the men and women who today wish to work and can find no employment is a unit."

All of these left open the time of return to an international standard. There was, however, a strong belief in the Administration that the French would soon be forced off gold. That was expected to expedite the restoration of an international standard with relationship to which each nation could establish the new base which it chose for its internal price level.

All close observers saw that the Washington conversations were leading nowhere. That was only a challenge to Secretary Hull, who renewed his attacks on economic nationalism with increasing ardor. Mr. Moley saw that the ballyhoo attendant on the visits of foreign statesmen had misled the country and that the reaction from the assured failure of the London Conference to do what Mr. Hull thought it ought to do would be embarrassing to the Administration. He boldly stepped to the radio and gave the warning that not too much should be expected, that the causes and remedies for the depression lay primarily within each nation, and that the chief results to be gained at London were a friendly exchange of opinion and co-operative action toward raising the world price level.

Instead of improving, the European situation got

worse. The disarmament conference broke down when Germany objected to the counting of Hitler storm troops and Steel Helmets as soldiers in calculating German military strength. More ominous threats of re-armament came from Germany; Vice Chancellor von Papen rattled the saber. On May 12, Hitler summoned the Reichstag, which he had recently dismissed, to meet on May 17 to hear a pronouncement on disarmament and German foreign policy. In Washington, Mr. Roosevelt immediately called in Louis Howe, Secretary Hull, Under-Secretary Phillips, and W. C. Bullitt.

Mr. Roosevelt proposed to make immediate use of his disarmament and peace plan. At intervals for four days, the President and his small group secretly worked on a message. Probably nothing that bore Mr. Roosevelt's name was ever more carefully prepared. At the first meeting of the group, Mr. Roosevelt wrote down a paragraph, read it aloud, inviting criticisms. Bit by bit, the message was built up and revised. It was worked over again the following afternoon. The next night, Sunday, the group reassembled. The final draft was molded. Each word and phrase was tested for ease and accuracy of translation into the major tongues so that there could be no possibility of misunderstanding. The following morning, Mr. Moley returned from a week-end out of town and revised the message further before the President gave it his final approval. Early Tuesday morning, the message sped over cables to the heads of fifty-four governments, including Soviet Russia. The stroke was spectacular and precedent-breaking in a truly Rooseveltian manner.

Hitler seized the opportunity. His speech the following day was a conciliatory but masterly exposition of the German case. The French were greatly disappointed in the message. Important members of the Administration were surprised. They had thought the French would be delighted, Hitler embarrassed. But that was minor. Tension in Europe was momentarily allayed. The Disarmament Conference was resumed. Four days later, Norman H. Davis supplemented the President's message with a speech.

Mr. Roosevelt stated persuasively the practical approach to disarmament: the reduction and ultimate elimination of offensive weapons, such as bombing planes, heavy mobile artillery, tanks and poison gas, a process which would relatively strengthen fixed fortifications and lessen the fear of attack. He placed the United States behind the broad outline of the MacDonald disarmament plan, then before the Conference. He urged that the time and procedure for taking the next steps toward disarmament be agreed upon and that in the meantime no nation increase its existing armaments beyond the limitations of treaty obligations.

Lastly, he proposed that all the nations of the world enter into a pact of non-aggression by which they agreed, subject to existing treaty rights, to send no armed force of any kind across their frontiers.

Mr. Davis, at Geneva, presented the other important item in Mr. Roosevelt's policy. In the event of a threat to peace, we were willing to consult with other states with a view to averting a conflict.

"Further than that," stated Mr. Davis, "in the event that the states, in conference, determine that a state has been guilty of a breach of the peace in violation of its international obligations and take measures against the violator, then, if we concur in the judgment rendered as to the responsible and guilty party, we will refrain from any action tending to defeat such collective effort which these states may thus make to restore peace."

The American internationalists triumphantly proclaimed that our isolation was gone. American isolationists unlimbered their guns and trained them on Mr. Davis, and, indirectly of course, on Mr. Roosevelt. The French sharply dissented. To them, we were just as far from guaranteeing the peace of Europe as we had been since the downfall of Wilson. The whole result was an unfortunate inversion. The desirable effect was to make the French think we were abandoning our isolation, and to make the American public—internationalists and isolationists—think that we were not.

A White House statement strove to reassure the American public that all this business about consultation was dependent upon the quick achievement of a substantial degree of disarmament. Politically that was advisable. But so far as the substance of the Roosevelt policy was concerned, the French were correct in seeing that it was not a means of guaranteeing the *status quo* in Europe.

Mr. Roosevelt enlarged or clarified American policy in four principal ways. First he proposed a common-sense definition of an aggressor: anyone whose armed forces cross the frontier of another nation in violation of treaties. That helped to plug the loopholes in the Kellogg Pact, through which so many nations were waging war without declaring it. Also, as Mr. Roosevelt promptly confirmed, it definitely renounced our old policy of sending marines into Latin-American countries. Under a pact of the definiteness proposed by Mr. Roosevelt, we would not have sent the expedition to Vera Cruz in 1913, or marines into Nicaragua, Haiti, or the Dominican Republic. We had marines in Haiti, under a treaty expiring

in 1936, we had special obligations in Cuba under the
Platt Amendment, and we had small armed treaty forces
in China. Those were our only exemptions from the
Roosevelt non-aggression proposal.

Second, Mr. Roosevelt stressed especially for the benefit of the French one of the features of the MacDonald
plan: continuous inspection of arms by a permanent, mobile supervisory body. Through such a supervisory body,
representatives of foreign governments would have the
right to inspect us, to see that we were not violating a
disarmament agreement—but only if we also had the
same right to inspect the armaments of all other nations.
The idea may be distasteful, but it is none the less sensible. The first objective of the continuous inspection proposal was, of course, to reassure the French concerning
the rearming of Germany. If Germany were secretly
manufacturing weapons of offense, the fact would be
brought out. If it were not, there would be a stop to the
French rumors, fears, and charges of secret German war
preparations.

Third, Mr. Roosevelt proposed to consult in case of
threatened violations of the peace. And fourth, if we
agreed with other states on the identity of the aggressor,
we would not interfere with their efforts to restore the
peace. In short, under such circumstances, we would not
insist on our rights as a neutral to trade with the aggressor. American opposition to anything that savors of
"entanglements" is so sharp that President Hoover would
not support a consultative agreement at the London
Naval Conference in 1930. Yet in the case of the Manchurian problem, Messrs. Hoover and Stimson made the
United States the most active proponent of a united world
front against Japan. We invoked all the pertinent pacts

and got into deep water in a vain effort to preserve the *status quo* in the Far East.

Whether or not the United States is drawn into a war is dependent on a multitude of factors, including the skill and cool head of the President. If properly used, Mr. Roosevelt's formula would help to keep the United States out of war, rather than get it into war. Consultation need not impair independence of judgment. And in many cases of threatened war it would undoubtedly be sounder policy for the United States to withdraw from the firing zones rather than insist on its rights as a neutral to trade with all belligerents. The Roosevelt formula would be of particular value in preventing the British fleet and American trade from getting tangled up with each other. Since the failure of the United States to join the League of Nations, the British have been troubled by the question of what the United States would do in the event of a League blockade of an aggressor. The same issue would arise under any other guarantee pact. The sensible procedure is for the United States and Great Britain to let each other know in advance what each proposes to do. If the United States would not insist on its right to trade with a nation deemed to be an aggressor by the guarantors of the *status quo,* other nations would be free to go ahead with their sanctions. On the other hand, the refusal of the United States to waive its neutral rights would, in many instances, tend to act as a deterrent. However, Mr. Roosevelt's formula caused the isolationists considerable worry. In the background stood the arms embargo resolution, which the old Congress had refused to pass, even with Mr. Roosevelt's backing. The new House put it through. The Senate Foreign Relations Committee balked. Mr. Roosevelt wanted power to join other nations in embargoing the export of arms to a single nation. The Foreign Relations Committee amended the resolution so that, if arms were embargoed, all belligerents would be affected alike. After several vain efforts to straighten the matter out, the Administration dropped it.

In the same way, the country's distrust of the internationalist vein of the Administration, as reflected through Congress, led Mr. Roosevelt to drop his plans to ask for authority to reduce tariffs and to handle war debts. Meanwhile, the Disarmament Conference failed to reach an agreement prior to the World Economic Conference. Mr. Roosevelt's spectacular play had smoothed over a tense moment in Europe, and that was all.

As delegates to the London Conference, Mr. Roosevelt chose Secretary Hull, James M. Cox, Mr. Roosevelt's running mate in 1920, Senator Pittman, Ralph W. Morrison, a wealthy Texan who had been a campaign contributor, Representative Samuel D. McReynolds, Chairman of the House Foreign Affairs Committee, and, after considerable scouting for a suitable Republican, Senator James M. Couzens of Michigan. All of these gentlemen knew their own country. Three were more or less internationalistic in their economics: Hull, McReynolds, and Cox. Three were nationalists: Pittman, Morrison and Couzens. None had ever before attended an international conference.

Mr. Roosevelt also arranged with Secretary Hull for a series of liaison men to carry verbal reports. Warren Delano Robbins, Mr. Roosevelt's cousin and the new Minister to Canada, was selected as the first man. He was to go to London ahead of the delegation, make various arrangements, and remain until about June 18. Mr. Moley was to be the second messenger. He was to leave about June 11, when it was thought Congress would be adjourned, and report on the domestic situation. After a week in London he was to return and be followed by a third man. The system was to continue throughout the conference. The delay in adjournment of Congress correspondingly delayed Mr. Robbins's return and Mr. Moley's departure.

Mr. Roosevelt's parting instructions were to emphasize a rise in prices. As the delegation got ready to sail, stabilization of the dollar came to the fore again. The delegation was instructed to leave it alone, but Mr. Roosevelt approved consideration of the problem through central banks. Dr. Oliver M. W. Sprague, former Harvard professor, had been taken from his post as economic adviser to the Bank of England and attached to the Treasury in Washington as a special adviser.

There was very strong opinion in the Administration that the moment to hitch the dollar to the pound had arrived. The pound was around $4.00. It was argued that the continued slump of the dollar had been maintained primarily by the delayed conversion of foreign balances into dollars. When business men and bankers began bringing home their funds, the dollar would rise. Therefore the dollar was probably as low as it could be forced without actual currency inflation of some sort or sufficient reduction of the dollar's gold content. This opinion underestimated the flight of American capital and the force of speculative activities in exchange, but it was widely held. Mr. Roosevelt gave serious thought to de facto stabilization but he did not commit himself to it. He definitely barred consideration of any stabilization methods which would require the shipment of gold or a Treasury guarantee against losses to the Federal Reserve Bank.

Whether those restrictions left any room for a steadying of exchange was a problem for technical experts. Any agreement which would oblige the United States, formally or morally, to refrain from inflation was prohibited.

From now on, the interplay of events becomes a bit complicated, and a time table is useful.

May 31. Secretary Hull, Delegates Pittman, McReynolds, and Morrison, and most of the American experts and clerical staff sail from New York on the steamer *President Roosevelt.*

June 2. By a curious coincidence the sound-money people sail on one boat: the *Olympic.* Messrs. Cox and Warburg form one party. George L. Harrison, Governor of the New York Federal Reserve Bank, and J. E. Crane, Vice-Governor of the Bank, form a separate party. Dr. Sprague is aboard as a special representative of the Treasury, unattached to the delegation.

June 7. Secretary Hull toasts "the Irish Republic" at Cobh, which startles the British and whets their curiosity concerning the events soon to follow. President Roosevelt and Congress near breaking point on the veterans issue, and opposition to the National Recovery Bill looms formidably.

June 8. Secretary Hull and party reach London.

June 9. The *Olympic* party reaches London. Temporary stabilization talks begin with Montagu Norman, Governor of Bank of England, and Clarence Moret, Governor of Bank of France. Messrs. Harrison and Crane appear to be active in them. Dr. Sprague appears to be participating. Mr. Warburg is hovering somewhere in the background. The outlook for the inflationists is ominous. Mr. Cox sets out to get the chairmanship of the monetary committee of the conference. The Americans have been promised the chairmanship of one of the two important commissions. The French furiously oppose Mr. Cox. They might as well save their breath. He is a hard-money conservative, better suited to represent the views of France or the Bank of England than those of the American experiment. Mr. Roosevelt, at the peak of his battle with Congress, definitely announces he has postponed until the regular January session any intention of asking authority to reduce or raise tariffs by fifty percent. That ruins Mr. Hull's tariff program, and he naturally becomes despondent.

June 10. President fails to get Congress adjourned. National Recovery Bill and veterans compromise still held up.

June 11. Sunday.

June 12. Conference opens. Prime Minister MacDonald brings up war debts. The Americans are resentful—perhaps unjustifiably, as no statesman for a debtor nation can command confidence at home without taking a jab at the war debts. MacDonald admits war debts are not on the conference agenda. The British and French begin their drive for temporary stabilization. Messrs. Harrison and Sprague say they have no authority but will consult Washington. The dollar sags to a new low: a gold value of 80.6 cents. The pound, steady against gold, rises to $4.18, the highest since September 1931. The British want $3.75 or less, the Americans are insisting on $4.25, with the expectation of striking a bargain around $4.00 to $4.10.

June 13. The dollar rallies sharply, American stocks and commodities fall. Reports that temporary stabilization is imminent begin to spread. Mr. Roosevelt is still battling Congress over the veterans issue while he handles

the last-minute war debt negotiations. Following Mac-
Donald's example, other delegation leaders cry out
against war debts in rising crescendo as opening round of
speeches at London continues. Mr. Hull fails to appear
at the hour set for his speech. The wholesome idea
spreads that it is because of American annoyance over the
injection of war debts into the conference speeches.
American diplomacy is thereby credited with a finesse
which it does not deserve. What really happened was
this: en route to Europe, Mr. Hull wrote his most im-
passioned denunciation of economic nationalism. Persons
who saw it describe it as a "Cross of Gold" speech, containing the quintessence of Mr. Hull's feeling and literary
ability. Mr. Hull desired to include in the speech a blessing from President Roosevelt that would show that Mr.
Hull's views were those of the Administration. Several
members of Mr. Hull's party thought that the speech
gave the impression that the United States was in a help-
less state and that it should be revised to make note of
the domestic progress toward recovery and give more
attention to other phases of an international program
than tariff production. Mr. Hull assented, and the press
representatives of the legation, Charles Michelson and
Elliott Thurston, amended the speech before cabling it
to Washington. Mr. Roosevelt made suggestions for further changes and sent word to London that no presidential blessing was necessary, as no one would question that
the Secretary of State represented the Administration. By
the time Mr. Hull's speech had been amended in London
and Washington, it was too late to prepare press releases
before the scheduled hour. That is why its delivery was
postponed for a day. Mr. Hull had also considered following the precedent set by Secretary Hughes at the

Washington Naval Conference by placing all the main American proposals before the conference at the outset. He was persuaded that that would be poor tactics. As things turned out, there might have been less confusion and bewilderment during the next few weeks if Mr. Hull had followed his original plan.

June 14. The dollar strengthens, and stocks and commodities dip. Britain makes token payment on debt. Mr. Hull makes his speech, asking that economic nationalism be declared "discredited." He notes briefly the need for a rise in the world price level. Between one burning indictment of "bootstrap methods" of recovery by individual nations and another vehement attack on the futility of separate national efforts, he pays this compliment to the American experiment: "Each nation by itself can to a moderate extent restore conditions by suitable fiscal, financial, and economic steps. Thus the administration of President Roosevelt has within three months adopted an effective domestic program to promote business improvement in the fullest possible measure."

June 15. Dollar rises; pound quoted at $4.02; stocks and commodities slump. Europe blazes with headlines that currency pegging for duration of conference has been agreed on. French default on war debt payment. Mr. Cox wins chairmanship of monetary committee and is quoted as confirming French reports that $4.05 "would shoot very close to the mark" on the dollar-pound ratio. (Mr. Cox denied later having said it.) In Washington, Secretary Woodin, at presidential prompting, repudiates all these reports, saying any stabilization plan will have to be submitted to President and Treasury and that none has been received.

June 16. Congress adjourns shortly after one in morning. Dollar weakens slightly and markets rise, thanks to Mr. Woodin's statement. Details of proposed currency truce published abroad: ratios of pound, dollar, and franc will be maintained where they are the day the truce is adopted; the truce will hold for a limited period, six weeks being proposed; co-operation between Federal Reserve Board of New York and British exchange equalization fund. The New York Federal Reserve Bank wants a guarantee against losses; that means Treasury backing. Most of the American delegates are dubious of advisability of the truce, but it is not their affair—it is in the hands of the central banks. Mr. Roosevelt lets it be known that he thinks France is trying to stampede the United States and unqualifiedly reiterates nothing can be permitted to interfere with management of dollar in interest of domestic price level. The Harrison-Warburg-Sprague plan arrives. Mr. Roosevelt cables his rejection, but leaves door open for some kind of exchange steadying. He signs National Recovery Act, cleans up desk, leaves Washington for his vacation cruise.

June 17. American prices rise. Mr. Roosevelt's rejection of currency pegging plan produces consternation in London. Harrison sails for home. The speculative character of the American rise in prices has been brought out sharply. The way is still open for an exchange "steadying" operation by the central banks, but, without guarantees against losses, the New York Federal Reserve Bank will not undertake it. In London the delegates are shocked to read that they have proposed a three-point tariff program, including a ten-percent horizontal cut.

June 18. Senator Pittman issues a statement denying that the delegation has proposed a ten-percent horizontal cut in tariffs. The foreign press, steadily growing more anti-American, makes the most of this bewildering performance. This is what had happened: the American tariff experts had drafted the three-point tariff program, which coincided with Hull's views. They had taken it to him and got his approval. He apparently thought he was approving it for discussion by the American delegation. Some hours later the press officers heard that it had been placed before the members of the economic committee. They at once sought Hull. He had gone to Windsor. When they reached him, he felt confident that his intention would not be misconstrued. They told him that, regardless of his intention, the economic committee had the resolution and that it would be construed as a proposal of the American delegation and should be recalled at once. By then, in fact, the resolution had been made public as an American proposal.

Senator Pittman repudiated it with an implied criticism of the League secretariat which left everybody in the American delegation appeased.

June 19. Hull wires explanation of tariff mix-up to Washington. Pittman introduces his monetary resolution. It proposes: use of gold for currency backing and settlement of international balances; reduction of metal cover of currencies to uniform minimum of 25 percent, of which one-fifth may be silver, at option of each country; restriction of silver sales by leading producing countries and those with large holdings; remonetization of subsidiary coinage, with a higher silver content.

Concerning stabilization, the resolution said: "It is in the interests of all concerned that stability in the international monetary field be attained as quickly as possible."

Mr. Moley, preparing to leave for London as President's messenger, announces that Bernard M. Baruch will use his office and serve as a liaison officer between the President and the American delegation, and that Herbert Bayard Swope will accompany him to London, both at the request of the President. As far back as December forecasts had been printed that Mr. Baruch would be the chairman of the American delegation to the World Economic Conference. He had given generously during the campaign and had been of service in many ways. It was thought that he really wanted the delegation chairmanship, and he was, in fact, slated for the job. However, it became impossible to make Mr. Baruch chairman. Secretary Hull wanted to go, and as the ranking Cabinet officer, he naturally had to be chairman. Furthermore, Mr. Baruch was on the wrong side of Hull on the tariff issue. The President's closest advisers felt they ought to do "something" for Mr. Baruch. Mr. Roosevelt found a happy solution: he told Mr. Baruch he wanted him to remain in the United States to advise him on the World Economic Conference as it progressed. Accordingly, Mr. Moley let it be known that Mr. Baruch would occupy his office.

Mr. Baruch's close friend, Herbert Bayard Swope, was also a man to whom Mr. Roosevelt and his friends felt indebted. After supporting Alfred E. Smith for the Democratic nomination, Mr. Swope had been helpful in persuading Mr. Smith to take the stump in behalf of Mr. Roosevelt's election. Mr. Moley suggested that Mr. Swope's services be recognized by putting him on the expedition to the Conference, and the President assented.

June 20. Moley flies to *Amberjack II* off Cape Cod for final conference with the President. The episode is dramatic. A carefully guarded statement from *Amberjack II* says Moley is taking American delegation first-hand information on developments at home and "the President's views of the effect of these developments on the original instructions given the delegation before it sailed." The gist of what the President told Moley was to reassure the American delegation that the American Recovery program, now reinforced by the NRA, was progressing well, to remember that the primary international objective was raising the world price level, and to get in touch with J. M. Keynes and Walter Lippmann and swing the Conference to the left on the money question. He was particularly keen to have a general discussion of the various plans for commodity currencies and the problems of fitting them into an international monetary standard. Mr. Moley left a memorandum by himself, Baruch, and Swope, which was adverse to pegging the dollar.

June 21. Stories that Mr. Baruch is "Acting President" spread over land. The American delegation remembers that a rise in the world price level is the main objective. The delegates at once get busy. Moley and Swope sail.

June 22. American delegation produces two resolutions. One renounces efforts at temporary currency stabilization. The other proposes a world drive to raise prices. Nobody pays much attention. Moley is coming, with instructions from Mr. Roosevelt. The Conference marks time. The French decide to wait and see if Moley is bringing authority to peg the dollar. Stories that Hull is going to be displaced or resign fill London and other capitals.

June 23. The conference waits for Moley—"his master's voice." Abashed by an excessive dose of publicity, Mr. Baruch seeks a storm cellar.

June 24. Secretary Hull denounces trouble-makers and denies that there is any contradiction between the Administration's policy and his own. He formally records his belief in the American domestic policies.

June 25. The Conference marked time while waiting for Moley to save it.

June 26. The Dutch guilder weakens. The French are in a panic. American commodities and stocks skyrocket. Senator Couzens, sole Republican delegate, speaks on world price raising; he opposes tariff reductions, favors large public works programs.

June 27. The guilder is wobbling. The pound reaches $4.28. Wheat passes $1 and 168 stocks reach new highs for year. Delegate McReynolds, disagreeing with Delegate Couzens, asserts lower tariffs are key to recovery. Mr. Roosevelt is fogbound on Maine coast. Moley and party reach Cobh. Moley toasts "the Irish Free State and the Irish." An airplane awaits to carry the Moley party to London. Desiring to avoid overnight trip from Plymouth to London, Moley has inquired about air lines from Cobh. Others, swift to please him, have ordered a special plane. At Cobh, Mr. Moley begins to get the European reaction to his visit, and cancels the airplane flight. Moley reaches London late at night. The gold bloc prepares to mob him.

Secretary Hull's patience is exhausted. The main program of the Administration offends his fundamental beliefs. The President seldom has consulted him, and has failed to request power to reduce tariffs. Repeatedly Hull has felt publicly humiliated. He has made no secret in London of his feeling that the President is not backing him and of his profound regret that he ever left the Senate. Now his apparent insignificance is accepted by the statesmen of the world, as they ignore him and prepare to flock around Moley. Mr. Hull's dissatisfactions are concentrated in a hatred of Moley, which one newspaper man described as "psychopathic." Although Mr. Hull publicly denies it, his friends feel he is at the point of resigning.

June 28–29–30. Apprised of Mr. Hull's tense feeling, Moley ostentatiously subordinates himself. At press conference with Hull he insists he is only a "messenger" and refers to Hull as "my chief." He informs Hull and press of President's pleasure with Mr. Hull's performance at London. Europe doesn't believe Moley is a mere messenger. All the French want to know is whether he has authority to stabilize the dollar.

Treasury officials in Washington begin study of Keynes sliding-scale stabilization plan. Dollar breaks to 77.3 cents; sterling rises to $4.37½. The French franc wobbles.

"Stabilize or we quit"—gold bloc ultimatum.

The French franc is still wobbling. Moley calls on MacDonald and is implored to help save conference. He consults with Warburg, Sprague, and others, who have never ceased to work with foreign finance ministers and central bankers in search for a formula which will receive approval of both Roosevelt and the gold bloc. While Moley was on the water, Warburg submitted a revised plan, which Mr. Roosevelt rejected. Moley knows the President's formula: no stabilization of the dollar, no gold shipments, but a willingness to let central banks co-operate in "steadying" exchange fluctuations and eliminating speculative activities, centering in London, Paris, Amsterdam, and Brussels. The finance and banking group have been working toward that end, and the British have developed a declaration intended to meet the situation. Moley is convinced the Conference will break up unless the gold countries are appeased and that the gold declaration already worked out provides a suitable basis for a solution. He sends word to Hull by Bullitt that he is taking over the problem. Hull naturally gives his formal consent, though he has refused to touch stabilization in any form without specific orders from the President. The Moley thesis: he is not a member of the delegation; every message to and from delegation as such must be made available to all delegates, which is equivalent to publishing them and adding to speculative movements; Moley can serve as vehicle of transmission to President. Moley meanwhile gets in touch with Keynes and they discuss plans for a world-wide inflationary drive.

Mr. Roosevelt sails gayly into Campobello, ending vacation cruise. At hints of stabilization from abroad the dollar strengthens to 79 cents, sterling drops from $4.43 to $4.25, American markets sag.

A denatured gold declaration is put in final form at a meeting of the financial emissaries. Present are: Bonnet, French Finance Minister; Leith-Ross, British Treasury expert; Sprague, Swope, Moley, others. Unofficially, Pittman and Couzens are present. The declaration falls into two parts. Part I is a rephrasing of the Pittman resolution, agreeing that gold will be re-established as a measure of international exchange value, but reserving to each nation the full right to decide when it would return to a gold standard and undertake stabilization. The countries still on a gold standard agreed to remain on it. Part II pledges the non-gold countries to adopt such measures as they deem effective to limit "exchange speculation" and to ask their central banks to co-operate to that end.

There is no statement in this declaration to which the most rabid inflationist can take exception. Keynes, an inflationist, would go even further toward reassuring the gold countries. The non-gold countries agree to try to limit only the fluctuations due to exchange "speculations." British and Continental experts and Sprague say this is feasible, as most of the big speculators are known. In a forty-eight-minute transatlantic telephone conversation, Sprague explains the declaration and the mechanism of checking speculation to the American Treasury group hastily gathered in Secretary Woodin's apartment in New York for the occasion. (Among those present are Woodin, Acheson, Harrison, Baruch, and Douglas.)

Moley approves the declaration, subject to the President's decision, and cables it to Campobello with message saying that in his opinion the declaration is necessary to save the Conference, that the experts are agreed that it does not mean stabilization, but that the declaration must be gauged by its probable effect on the American price level, and that only the President can decide that.

Hull meanwhile has expressed to members of the American party his displeasure at not being kept informed of the currency negotiations by Moley. The American delegation is disrupted by the tariff issue. Couzens, apparently backed by Pittman and perhaps strengthened by Moley, is demanding that Hull's low-tariff resolution be withdrawn since it is incompatible with the American domestic program. The presence of Pittman and Couzens at the American Embassy during the final drafting of the gold declaration arouses the suspicion of the low-tariff advocates that stabilization is being traded for support of Pittman's silver plan.

Hull, about this time, drafts a message to the President which is tantamount to his resignation. A few persons hear of it. Pittman takes Moley to see Hull, pro-

vokes free talk, which momentarily clears the air.
Whether Mr. Hull communicated his thoughts to the
President at this time remains undisclosed.

Friday morning, June 30. Mr. Roosevelt receives at
Campobello the text of the gold resolution. But it is in
garbled form. It has been sent in a State Department
code from London to Washington, deciphered, trans-
lated into a Navy code and again deciphered before reaching Mr. Roosevelt. He tells the correspondents that his
views on pegging the dollar are exactly what he has been
telling the would-be stabilizers in the Treasury and cabling
to London at intervals for three weeks. Later in the
afternoon he gets a revised final draft of the gold resolution. He dispatches a formal message rejecting it "in its
present form." Two-thirds of the message is taken from
the anti-stabilization memorandum of Swope, Baruch,
and Moley. His opinion of the practical effect of the
resolution differs from the opinion of Moley and the
Treasury advisers. He thinks it will be interpreted as
stabilization and that it will impose a moral obligation on
the government to ship gold or guarantee the Federal
Reserve Bank against losses. He authorizes the issue of
a statement in his name conveying the views expressed in
this message of rejection. Back of all this, one suspects, is
Mr. Roosevelt's by now thinly worn patience with the
American monetary conservatives in the Treasury and at
London and with the French. Both groups have been trying to force his hand. He knows that most of the Treasury experts who said the gold declaration did not mean
stabilization are at heart zealous for stabilization. The
French, who have not paid their war debt installments,
who have been cool to the American disarmament proposals, and, all in all, are very trying, undoubtedly seem

to Mr. Roosevelt to have the American representatives badly on the defensive.

July 1. With the idea that it will smooth over feelings which have been sharpened by a series of small incidents, Moley proposes that, when the President's approval is received, Secretary Hull go to Downing Street and inform MacDonald. Mr. Hull probably thinks he is being converted into a messenger. Mr. Moley's gesture is inspired by generosity and a desire to be proper. He has no doubt that the President approves the declaration. He is suggesting that Hull receive the accolade of Europe for saving the Conference. The delegation unanimously approves his proposal.

Then Mr. Roosevelt's rejection arrives. The veto stuns the Conference. Moley is publicly deflated. The declaration had been heralded abroad as the "Moley plan," and it was assumed by everybody that the chief of the brains trust was an infallible index of the President's mind. Most of the American delegates—Cox was a notable exception—are delighted by the President's decision.

Mr. Roosevelt boards the cruiser *Indianapolis* for his return journey to Washington. He receives a message saying that somebody is not inconsiderably relieved by his decision. He thinks it is from Hull. It is really from Moley.

July 2. MacDonald hastens back to London in despair. Moley and others gather in Hull's room and draft the statement authorized by the President explaining the American viewpoint. Hull has announced there will be such a statement Monday. The statement is cabled to the President for approval.

July 3. Instead of approving the message drafted in London, the President cables his own message, written aboard the *Indianapolis*. He would consider it a "catastrophe amounting to a world tragedy" if the Conference should allow itself to be diverted from its great purposes "by the proposal of a purely artificial and temporary experiment affecting the monetary exchange of a few nations only." He denounces this "specious policy," the "basic economic errors" of the past, and "all fetishes of so-called international bankers." He lunges at the French with a reference to unbalanced budgets. He asserts that the sound internal economic system of a nation is a greater factor in its well-being than "the price of its currency in changing terms of currencies of other nations," and says that the United States seeks "the kind of dollar which, a generation hence, will have the same purchasing and debt-paying power as the dollar value we hope to attain in the near future." He reiterates that gold and silver can well continue to serve as a metallic reserve behind currencies.

Mr. Roosevelt is giving his representatives a lesson in tactics. They have supinely and ineptly let themselves be out-maneuvered and out-shouted by the French, and have lamentably failed to bring the Administration's point of view forcibly to the attention of the Conference. Colonel Howe, who is always alive to the domestic, political reaction, is on board the *Indianapolis*. Possibly Mr. Roosevelt has in mind the favorable domestic reaction to a belligerent message, although he can hardly hope to improve on his current popularity at home.

The Conference reels. Europe explodes with resentment and wrath. Mr. MacDonald speaks of Mr. Roosevelt as "that person." The American public cheers the repulse of the foreigner. In a laudatory article, Mr. Keynes says Roosevelt is "magnificently right." "Magnificently left," remarks Moley. Moley has been rebuffed—but with his own views on money. The American delegates are lost. They don't know whether the commodity dollar is incompatible with the Pittman resolution or not. Mac-Donald, crushed, sends for Moley. The American delegates decide a recess or adjournment should be taken—most of them have wanted it for some time. Hull, according to one correspondent, is "a stricken man."

July 4. The gold bloc determines to force adjournment of the Conference, placing the blame on the United States. Some of the gold leaders want to indict President Roosevelt by name. MacDonald is convinced it is useless to go on. Hull is sorrowfully ready to quit; most of the other American delegates are eager to quit. But some of the party, including the press representatives, see the unfavorable consequences of an adjournment blamed on Mr. Roosevelt. They bestir Mr. Hull to action and he persuades the steering committee to postpone a decision until Thursday morning, July 6.

Hull cables the President his message is breaking up the Conference, etc. Moley sends his own cable—a very important one—to prepare Mr. Roosevelt for a transatlantic telephone conversation as soon as Mr. Roosevelt reaches the White House that night. Mr. Moley's cable is a confidential message for the President alone. He proposes a recess of from two to ten weeks to permit preparations for pushing the President's program for price raising by monetary action. He suggests that some reconstruction of the American delegation be considered, saying that Senator Pittman is the only member of the delegation with sufficient understanding and sympathy for the President's views to push them before the Conference. He reports that the staff of experts needs strengthening on the progressive side. He also tells the President to pay no attention to what anyone else may say about his July 3 message: that it was fine, the very type of bold attack needed to make the world sit up and pay heed to the American program.

If it is remembered that Mr. Moley has in mind the President's left-wing monetary doctrine, as reiterated in the July 3 message, his diagnosis is unquestionably correct. In his dispatch to the *New York Herald Tribune,* published the following morning, Walter Lippmann said publicly and more forcefully what Mr. Moley said in his confidential cable to the President: "Likewise, Mr. Roosevelt cannot have understood how completely unequipped are his representatives here to deal with the kind of project he has in mind. For one thing, they do not know what is in his mind. For another, there is not among them a single man who understands monetary questions sufficiently to debate them. For another, they have been so frequently repudiated that they are demoralized. For another, they are divided among themselves. How can a delegation, which lacks authority, which lacks technical competence, which lacks unity, which lacks contact with the President, hope to undertake the kind of difficult negotiation for far-reaching reforms which the President desires? It cannot be done. Mr. Roosevelt's purposes may be excellent. He has completely failed to organize a diplomatic instrument to express them. If Mr. Roosevelt means what he says, he must send a new delegation to London which knows what he means and has power to act for him."

Mr. Roosevelt opposes a recess or adjournment, saying that, if the Conference ever breaks up, it will never get back together. Moley gets Keynes and Lippmann together at the American Embassy and they work until 3:30 the following morning drafting a supplementary statement of the American position designed to draw together all the nations outside the gold bloc.

July 5. The American delegation votes for a long recess. Mr. Roosevelt, back at the White House, takes command by transatlantic telephone: no recess, advance the price-lifting program. The Keynes-Lippmann-Moley statement is enthusiastically approved by the American delegation. MacDonald is delighted with it. In politer language it says what the President said. Its publication eases Conference tempers. The gold bloc wants to adjourn but begins to see signs that it can't put the blame for ruining the Conference on Mr. Roosevelt.

July 6. Mr. Hull goes before the Conference steering committee, makes a fervent plea for continuation of the Conference, and exposes with relentless logic worthy of a Frenchman the absurdity that a bounding dollar is the source of the world's troubles. The British Dominions, Japan, the Scandinavian countries, swing into line behind Hull. Britain follows. The gold bloc is isolated. The French veer away from the idea of forcing an adjournment, as they see the blame for a break-up being maneuvered onto them. However, they insist there shall be no further discussion of money, tariffs, and quotas, until stabilization has been achieved. Moley, Swope, and Sprague leave for home as per schedule.

July 7. The monetary committee of the Conference overrules the gold bloc and votes to continue work. Mr. Roosevelt sends a memorandum to the delegation suggesting for discussion such methods of price-raising as currency management, production control, shorter working hours and higher wages, etc. Formation of a price-raising bloc is implicit in his program. The Dominions are with him. Britain is forced to talk higher prices.

July 8. Hull puts the American suggestions before the Conference. The Conference goes ahead innocuously. The American public ceases to follow it.

Eventually everybody went home. Senator Pittman brought back part of what he sought in the form of agreement to cease debasing silver coins and a more specific arrangement by which the silver-holding countries would check their sales and the governments of the silver-producing countries would buy more of the metal for Treasury use.

Meanwhile the Hull-Moley problem had come to a head. Mr. Moley did not know it, but a copy of his confidential cablegram to the President was sent from the American Embassy in London to Secretary Hull. Mr. Hull naturally was aggrieved to find that his titular subordinate had cabled the President that no member of the delegation except Pittman was equipped to advance the President's views. The reconstruction of the delegation that Mr. Moley urged apparently meant eliminating everybody except Pittman. The message, in part or in whole, was shown to other members of the delegation. Couzens, whom Moley had particularly praised to his face, was no less aggrieved than Mr. Hull. The other delegates were aggrieved. Pittman explained to Hull that he knew nothing about the message and that, of course, Moley had not thought of Hull as a delegate, but as Secretary of State, chairman of the delegation, and his "chief." The experts heard that Moley had cabled the President saying that they were no good. And they were aggrieved. The blow would have been softened a little all around if it had been understood that the views of the

President to which Mr. Moley referred were those on money.

Here enters a strangely evanescent message. Beneath his restrained, courteous exterior, Mr. Hull harbored a long list of objections to Mr. Moley and to everybody associated with Mr. Moley or whom he suspected of being associated with Mr. Moley. Several persons thought they saw such a list of criticisms of Mr. Moley and his real or supposed friends in the form of a long cablegram to the President. The message did not contain Mr. Hull's resignation, but the deduction was easily made. Officially this message was and is non-existent.

Reports spread through London and across the Atlantic that Mr. Hull was coming home either to resign or get Moley out. With them came rumors that, if Mr. Hull resigned, Ambassador Bingham would resign also. They were fellow-Southerners and friends, and their views on economics were similar. Reports were bruited that the noisy night sessions of Mr. Moley and his party had blasted the quiet and dignity of the American Embassy, where Mr. Bingham had put workrooms at their disposal. From these small beginnings, rumors grew hourly. The resignation of Mr. Hull—alone, or with Mr. Bingham—would have caused a perhaps irreparable cleavage in the Democratic party. Mr. Hull was one of the most highly respected members of Southern Democracy, which was a bit dizzy from the American Experiment. Mr. Roosevelt wrote a cablegram to Mr. Hull praising him for his splendid work in saving the Conference, inviting him to Hyde Park, and telling him he would talk to no one else about occurrences at London until he had talked with Mr. Hull. Part of the message was made public.

Mr. Roosevelt soon shifted Mr. Moley to temporary

duty in making a survey of federal methods of abolishing kidnaping and racketeering. Mr. Moley seemed destined for a wide variety of important duties at a safe distance from the State Department. When Mr. Hull got back, the President welcomed him at Hyde Park with open arms. Mr. Hull's grievous disappointment at the failure of the London Conference to do much was already relieved somewhat by his own personal triumph. His transparent sincerity and lofty tone had elevated him above the petty nationalism of the day. While Maxim Litvinov, the Soviet Commissar of Foreign Affairs, was the only statesman to get anything tangible for his country during the Conference, Mr. Hull captured personal respect.

Mr. Roosevelt's warming smile and radiant enthusiasm were a tonic. The Pan-American Conference at Montevideo was coming. Repulsed at London, we would carry the fight for lower tariffs and international trade into Latin-America. Already, in fact, Mr. Roosevelt had instructed the State Department to institute bilateral discussions of trade agreements.

The World Economic Conference and the European problem as a whole were thrust on Mr. Roosevelt before he was ready for them. Broadening the application of Mr. Lippmann's observation, Mr. Roosevelt failed to forge a diplomatic instrument. The American performance at London had its ludicrous aspects. But as a whole the London Conference had such profitable benefits to the United States that it must be put down as a success. It showed that at the present time it is impossible for the principal nations to get together to any great extent on their economics. It brought the internationalist tendencies in the Administration up against the hard realities of world politics with enough force to bring most of the daydreamers to their senses. That was a good thing to have happened as soon as possible. The Conference also showed that the United States had a President whose first regard was the national interest—which is a good thing for the world and the nation to know. The Conference did nothing concrete and as a result we are much better off.

Among the miscellaneous bits of useful information which some of the internationalists picked up at the Conference were these: that Great Britain was canalizing its trade with very successful discriminatory trade agreements; that Great Britain had no intention of returning to an international gold standard until after the United States had returned to it; that every nation was moving further toward self-containment rather than away from it; that the statesmen of most nations usually represent their national interests; that the war debts were not the obstacle to economic recovery; that Europe was in a bad mess which it was wiser to sympathize with at a distance than to try to clean up with American idealism.

The London experience was reassurance that, for at least a time, the foreign policy of the United States would be dominated by the principles of the "good neighbor" rather than by the solicitude of a doting uncle.

The change in tone was marked when Norman H. Davis returned to Europe in September for the next, and perhaps last, effort to bring the Disarmament Conference to a conclusion. Mr. Roosevelt stood by his formula of the spring. Mr. Davis was instructed to co-operate in every way, but not to try to lead. The United States shared the really vital interest of the world in the reduction of armaments. Our interests were relatively less important than those of most other nations. If the armed nations of Europe were ready and able to limit their armaments, so much the better. For some inexplicable reason the idea had been developed on this side of the water that by limiting their armaments the nations of Europe would be making a generous concession of some sort to the United States, for which they should be adequately rewarded.

The June 15 crisis was bridged by an ingenious device: Great Britain acknowledged its debt "pending final settlement," and made a token payment. Mr. Roosevelt expressed the personal opinion that this did not constitute a default. Six debtor nations paid $11,359,540, or approximately eight percent of the total payments of $143,359,-540 which were due. Seven, including France, paid nothing. Those which paid something used silver, which was selling in the open market at 36 cents an ounce and which was accepted by the United States at 50 cents an ounce under the Thomas Amendment to the Agricultural Adjustment Act. All the indications were that the token payment device would have to be used to bridge the December 15 payments, since only Congress can modify the debt arrangements.

Practically, we appeared to be confronted with two choices. First, to accept small final settlements at the rate of 10 cents on the dollar—the funds for these settlements probably to be obtained largely by loans floated in the United States. Second, to let the debts stand and the debtors default or pay what they would. The interest rates might be lowered to an even level to remove the great disparities in the terms of settlement or might be canceled altogether, and a system of token payments might be regularized. The repeal of the Eighteenth

Amendment suggested the possibility of American markets for wines and liquors, which would enable some of the
debtors to make payments. From the point of view of
American policy there was much to be said for letting at
least the principal of the debts stand. As a monument to
folly they were much too valuable to be torn down, especially since the tearing down would help to clear the way
for a reversion to the short-sighted practice of giving
away American surplus in the form of foreign loans. In
the event of a European war, the impulse would be markedly strong to enjoy a momentary fling of prosperity by
lending the sinews of war. So long as the war threats hang
over Europe, the war-debt structure is at least one reminder that the lending of war materials is a very unprofitable business to which the disastrous sequel is likely
to be our own involvement in war.

The cultivation of closer relations with Latin-America
was one of the basic points in Mr. Roosevelt's foreign
policy from the beginning. The Hoover Administration
had started the liquidation of the domineering practices
which alienated Latin-American sentiment from the
United States. Mr. Roosevelt was determined to complete
the liquidation and establish a new era in our relations
with Latin-America.

At the outset, however, he was faced with one extremely difficult obstacle—Cuba. Cuba looked as if it
were ripe to become for Mr. Roosevelt what Mexico had
been for Woodrow Wilson. American investments dominated Cuban economy. Mr. Roosevelt's renunciation of the
policy of protecting American property in Latin-America
by armed intervention did not stop European nations from
forcing intervention by demanding protection for the lives
and properties of their own nationals. The United States

had a special obligation to preserve orderly government in Cuba under the Platt Amendment to the Cuban Constitution. Elihu Root, when Secretary of State, formally interpreted this obligation to mean that the United States should intervene "only to protect the Cuban Republic from foreign attack, or when a veritable state of anarchy exists within the republic." The United States had intervened four times, either with armed forces or special diplomatic missions.

By the winter of 1932–33, Cuba was in a desperate condition as a result of the loss of much of its American market for sugar and the relentless drop in the world price of sugar. It was ruled by the iron hand of President Machado, who had made himself the darling of the New York bankers by borrowing so liberally and with such generous regard for bankers' commissions and by relentless squeezing of the remnants of Cuban economic life to meet payments on the top-heavy debt. Civil liberties were suspended, the opposition leaders driven out or slaughtered. Machado held his power through a well-paid army and a reign of terror. The counter-terrorism of the A.B.C. and other revolutionary groups mounted. If the opposition could not overthrow the Machado régime as long as the army remained loyal, it could create a state of growing turmoil probably leading to the state of anarchy which would force American intervention. This is what the Cuban opposition appeared intent on doing, if assured that the incoming Administration would not intervene to save Machado. The main objective of the Hoover Administration in its dying days was to prevent a Cuban eruption before March 4. Through unofficial but direct contacts with the leaders of the Cuban revolutionary junta in the United States, friends of Mr. Roosevelt worked toward the same end. Given time, they felt that the Cuban problem could be handled without heavy bloodshed.

Mr. Roosevelt began formulating his Cuban policy in the summer of 1932. Apart from the numerous sources of information which any man in his position would have, two members of the brains trust, Professor Berle and Mr. Taussig, were familiar with Cuban conditions. In January 1933, they went to Cuba, made a detailed survey, and reported to Mr. Roosevelt at Warm Springs. The basis of Mr. Roosevelt's Cuban policy was recognition of the fact that the fundamental sources of trouble in Cuba were economic. He proposed to fulfill our special obligations for the welfare of Cuba by co-operation in the restoration of Cuban economy. The inclusion of Cuba in a closed sugar production and consumption area with the United States and its insular possessions was the backbone of his plan. That involved the allotment to Cuba of a sugar quota sufficient to give the island a minimum foundation of economic stability—perhaps 2,000,000 tons annually— and the negotiation of a new trade treaty with perhaps a greater preferential for Cuban sugar. Other necessary steps were the refunding of the Cuban government debt at lower interest rates and the restoration of employees of the large sugar plantations to a self-sustaining basis on small pieces of land.

It was also plain that Machado's efforts to live up to the New York bankers' conceptions of a model Cuban President had led him into a pocket from which there was no easy escape. He could not relax his dictatorship without being deposed. The deep hatreds which his terrorism had created were beyond appeasement. Cuba could not be pacified until the Machado régime was ended.

Immediately after March 4, Mr. Taussig was quietly

working on the formidable task of convincing the sugar
growers that they should agree to limit their production
and bring Cuba into an American closed sugar economy.
By zealous watchfulness, Mr. Roosevelt managed to keep
in the farm bill a general clause permitting control of
sugar production. Dr. John Lee Coulter of the Tariff
Commission was detached to guide the preliminary work
on a sugar agreement.

Finding a diplomat of sufficient caliber for the Cuban
post was difficult. Mr. Roosevelt finally turned to Sumner
Welles, a young career diplomat whom he already had
brought out of retirement and made Assistant Secretary
of State in charge of Latin-American affairs. Mr. Welles
was extremely popular with the Latin-American diplomatic corps. He willingly surrendered his comparatively
safe post in the State Department to undertake the
hazardous Cuban mission.

With extraordinary skill and some luck, Ambassador
Welles broke the Cuban impasse. Machado went out and
the provisional de Cespedes government, supposed to represent all factions, stepped in with comparatively little
disorder. The transfer of authority was effected by a complicated series of resignations, leaves of absence, and provisional appointments which satisfied minutely the requirements of the Cuban Constitution. Thus the United States
was spared the embarrassment of recognizing a revolutionary government in contravention of its Central American policy. For three weeks the United States enjoyed
the pleasant experience of a diplomatic triumph. It was a
short-lived triumph. The de Cespedes government gave
way without a struggle before a more profound upheaval.

The second revolution, which put the Grau San Martin
government in power, supported by the "sergeants'

army," presented the United States with a thorny problem. The possibilities of avoiding intervention dwindled. There was no question of approval or disapproval of the revolutionary government. The question was whether the new government could preserve order, consolidate its power, and save Cuba from complete anarchy. Mr. Roosevelt invited the diplomatic representatives of the leading Latin-American powers to the White House, put before them all the information he had on the Cuban situation, assured them that the American government was seeking every means to avoid intervention, and asked their co-operation. He also directed the dispatch of 33 naval vessels to points off the Cuban coast. The naval concentration was disconcerting to those who hoped that intervention could be avoided, and it provoked a flurry of anti-American feeling in Cuba. The move was precautionary and it had temporary effects in strengthening the Grau San Martin government. Mr. Roosevelt announced that the United States would recognize any orderly government which was satisfactory to the Cuban people. But the Cuban treasury was drying up and social dissolution was progressing. A month later American vessels were still patroling the coast, while public demonstrations led to fighting in the streets of Havana.

The Roosevelt policy for Cuba was enlightened and soundly based on the desire to help Cuba. It was easy to pick flaws in its execution, but until the rapid course of events reached a conclusion or breathing spell it was impossible to judge which were the real flaws, which the skillful strokes, and which the rightly conceived actions that failed to achieve their purpose merely because the situation was in a state of flux. Ambassador Welles and his chief consultants in Washington appeared to err in their estimate of the strength and importance of the various leaders and groups in Cuba. But once the lid was off, probably no conservative or middle-of-the-road government could hold in check the forces of social revolution.

The recognition of the Soviet Union was impending throughout the first phase of the Roosevelt Revolution. Mr. Roosevelt included Mikhail Kalinin, titular head of the Communist state, in the heads of governments to whom he sent his May message on peace and disarmament. Comrade Kalinin responded cordially. Mr. Roosevelt instructed Laurence A. Steinhardt, the new minister to Sweden, and John V. A. MacMurray, the new envoy to Estonia, Lithuania, and Latvia, to report to him on conditions in the Soviet Union. He authorized the R.F.C. to lend the Amtorg Corporation, the Soviet trading company in the United States, some $4,000,000 to buy cotton. Negotiations for a $50,000,000 credit from the R.F.C. for the purchase of copper, meats, and more cotton began soon thereafter.

Mr. Roosevelt's preoccupation with other more urgent affairs was one of the main reasons for the continued postponement of Soviet recognition. The absence of diplomatic relationships between the United States and the U.S.S.R. had long been an absurdity. On the other hand, it was doubtful whether recognition would open the way to the large and profitable trade claimed for it by some of its advocates. The Communists wanted goods and American technical experience, but they could not absorb much of them without credit. American loans would have been much more safely placed in the rising Communist colossus than in some of the economically second- and third-rate nations into which our bankers poured our funds in the nineteen-twenties.

Credit to remove burdensome accumulated surpluses of raw commodities could be justified by the emergency. The resumption of foreign lending for the disposal of the American surplus as a long-range policy would revive old issues. Politically, however, there were strong reasons for closer ties between the United States and the Soviet Union. The two nations had a similar interest in the preservation of peace. They were the only first-class powers in the world between whom there were no major conflicts in interests abroad.

As the first phase of the Roosevelt Administration came to a close, American foreign policy had two important bases, without prejudice to our friendly relations with the world at large. One was Great Britain. The willingness of Great Britain and the United States to adjust their differences as they arose by amicable, even if hardhearted, negotiation was one of the most reassuring elements in a troublesome world situation. The second base was Latin-America. Soviet Russia looked very much like a third base.

VII

The NRA

THE organization and first trials of the new experimental apparatus formed the fourth period of the Roosevelt Revolution in its first phase. That period ran through July and August and into September. The NRA dominated the scene. The mobilization and reorganization of all the industrial and commercial life of the country under the National Recovery Administration were an undertaking of revolutionary nature. The NRA had picturesque and driving leadership. More than the other experiments, it collided with vested interests and with the ingrained thought and habits of the country. It had to compromise fundamental class and group differences. It had to create and use the wartime psychology of coperative action, and in doing so it practically cornered the publicity. The launching of the companion experiment in controlling agriculture under the Agricultural Adjustment Administration was the second arresting spectacle of the period. As is usual and natural, the agricultural experiments were forced into second place in the metropolitan press. The agricultural undertaking was more diffuse and less easy to visualize. The element of conflict between classes and groups was smaller within the AAA than within the NRA, although the interaction of these two major experiments stirred a very lively sense of conflicting interests between farmers and wage earners. Behind these two most novel and fascinating spectacles, the lesser experiments moved at a more sedate pace.

Perhaps the best date to take for the beginning of this period—the NRA period—is July 19, when the speculative rise in stocks and commodities, begun in April with the departure from gold, ended with a crash.

Spurred by Mr. Roosevelt's refusal to peg the dollar at London, stock and commodity prices had soared with a speculative energy reminiscent of 1929. On July 18, stock price averages were more than double the low for the year. Wheat sold at $1.25 a bushel, approximately three times its low for the year. Other grains and cotton had jumped with amazing agility to new highs. The fall of the dollar was the main theoretical gauge of the speculative rise. Actually the decline in the dollar in ratio to gold accounted for less than half the gain in commodities and stocks. A short crop accelerated the rise in the price of wheat until it reached the point that imports from the Argentine would become profitable. Anticipation of further inflation, a remarkable spurt in the production of consumers' goods, and the approaching repeal of the Eighteenth Amendment were other factors behind the boom. Automobile production was racing ahead. Steel production rose rapidly against the normal seasonal trends, until it passed fifty percent of capacity. The cotton textile industry was going at full blast.

In addition to this speculative rise in stocks and commodities and a genuine business upturn there was a very substantial amount of speculative manufacturing, which was particularly evident in the cotton and shoe industries. This speculative manufacturing was partly induced by the AAA and the NRA. Manufacturers hastened to pile up stocks at low wages before going under the NRA codes. In the cotton industry there was an additional incentive to full-speed production: the imminent processing tax on cotton.

The Administration began to worry about the speculative rise some time before the actual crash. Some of the President's advisers felt that the exchanges should be closed. As the whole sweep of the early recovery was speculative to such a large extent, the Administration was hesitant about applying a brake to the speculative machinery. But the results of the President's refusal to peg the dollar quickly exceeded expectations. It was evident that there would soon have to be a set-back; the problem was to induce a moderate set-back without causing a crash which would destroy the recovery. While the Administration leaders were still discussing the problem with the President, the markets vaulted high and then crashed.

The great drop came on July 19. In four days, stock averages fell nearly twenty percent, the prices of grain, cotton and other commodities collapsed, and the country recalled the black days of October 1929. Indeed, speculative habits in the United States had not changed much since 1929. The drop uncovered at least one notable plunger, Edward A. Crawford, a formerly obscure Southern doctor. When the crash came, Crawford was long from 300,000 to 1,600,000 shares of stock. His assortment of commodity holdings on slender margins included 18,200,000 bushels of rye, 16,000,000 bushels of wheat, 13,000,000 bushels of corn, 180,000 tons of rubber, 700,000 tons of sugar, more than 3,000,000 eggs, and sundry other articles; the holdings of one man, when shaken loose, were enough to demoralize markets which were heavily loaded with thinly margined commitments and honeycombed with stop-loss orders. At the prodding of Washington, the Chicago Board of Trade temporarily fixed minimum prices for grain futures and imposed limits on daily fluctuations. These were only temporary measures designed to afford time for the straightening out of the tangled affairs of "Doc" Crawford. As the price of cash wheat continued to fall, the wheat pegs soon had to be withdrawn. Crawford was only one spectacular example of the "New Deal plungers," whose ranks included many old hands at the game of manipulating markets.

The vast experiments in lifting the purchasing powers of farmers and workers were launched on a down-grade. The organization of the NRA had begun the day that the President sent the bill to Congress. Mr. Roosevelt asked General Johnson to draft a blue-print for the administration of the act and get a skeleton organization together. The first home of the NRA was a vacant room on the second floor of the State Department near Mr. Moley's office. General Johnson used the room while he worked on the bill. His staff consisted of two secretaries. On May 18, he began the gigantic task of whipping together an administrative staff. One of his first moves was to send for Alexander Sachs, the statistical economist of the Lehman Corporation, who had been a minor member of the brains trust during the campaign. Unlike so many of the Wall Street economists, Mr. Sachs believed that the primary causes and remedies for the depression lay within the nation. He became chief of Johnson's research division. Before the National Industrial Recovery bill passed Congress, General Johnson had moved his rapidly growing skeleton staff into vacant quarters in the Commerce Building and, in a series of rapid movements, had spurred some of the big industries into beginning work

on codes. When the President signed the act, General
Johnson was ready to plunge ahead. Mr. Roosevelt ap-
pointed him temporary Administrator of both the NRA
and the public works program and placed over his head a
Cabinet committee. The Secretary of Commerce appointed an Industrial Advisory Board of forty-one members, all leading executives—of whom Walter Teagle,
chairman of the board of the Standard Oil Company of
New Jersey, Gerard Swope, president of the General
Electric Company, and Louis E. Kirstein, of Edward
Filene & Co., Boston merchants, became the most active.
Representing labor was an advisory board under the
chairmanship of Dr. Leo Wolman, liberal economist and
industrial arbiter, with two organized labor men at his
elbow, William Green, president of the American Federation of Labor, and John L. Lewis, president of the United
Mine Workers of America. A consumers' advisory board
was set up under Mrs. Mary Rumsey. General Johnson
appointed Donald Richberg as chief counsel, and named
deputy administrators as rapidly as he could find suitable
men. The quick assembling of a trustworthy staff was in
itself a tough job. There were few men with the practical
knowledge of the various industries of the country whose
interests were not bound up with those industries. Finding independent experts fitted to advise the Recovery
Administration on the detailed problems of many industries was next to impossible. In the first drive, General
Johnson was forced to rely most heavily on his personal
friends.

During Mr. Roosevelt's sailing holiday in June, his
Cabinet committee split wide open over the public works
program. The conservatives led by Budget Director
Douglas wanted the program held back. They argued that

recovery was on the way and that the money could well be saved, or, at least, used sparingly until the need for it became apparent. The left-wingers, led by Dr. Tugwell, realized the insubstantial character of the speculative rise. They urged that the entire $3,300,000,000 be flung out with a sweeping gesture. When Mr. Roosevelt returned in early July he struck a compromise. He announced that all the money would be spent but that care would be exercised to see that none was wasted on unnecessary projects. Secretary Ickes was perturbed about the dangers of graft and ensuing scandal that would wreck the entire Administration. He made his point so well that Mr. Roosevelt appointed him Public Works Administrator. At the same time, he relieved General Johnson's NRA administration of the embarrassing and retarding supervision of a Cabinet committee.

In his preliminary surveys with General Johnson of the launching of the NRA, Mr. Roosevelt had agreed that the first job was to shorten hours of work and boost wages. The code for each industry was to be as simple as it could be made for accomplishing that purpose. The long-range regularizing of competition through elaborate codes was to be postponed insofar as it was possible. As a rule price-fixing was to be avoided. Speed was the essence of the emergency problem, for prices were soaring away from the buying power of wage and salary earners. Mr. Roosevelt made one particularly important suggestion: that all lawyers be barred from conferences and hearings. If the NRA were to let itself be bound by the tedious practices of established governmental bodies, such as the I.C.C., industry would never be organized. Industrialists naturally would employ their counsel in drafting proposed codes. Lawyers hung around the fringes and took part in code hearings, but legal formalities had no standing in General Johnson's court. Nor were any other intermediaries, except the recognized committees of business men and the recognized representatives of labor, permitted to complicate and hinder the work. General Johnson brought the heads of industry and labor together with no buffers between them.

General Johnson tore into action as if a war were to be won or lost in thirty days. He was practically unknown to the country. The fresh shock of his blunt manner and amazing energy had the effect of a hypodermic.

The Cotton Textile Institute, representing two-thirds of the cotton textile industry, had been making swift preparations to lead the way into the new industrial era. No industry in the country illustrated so glaringly the vices of excessive competition and mobility. Child labor, starvation wages, the stretch-out system (by which the same number of, or fewer, workers handled more machines at higher speed), and peonage had made the textile industry, especially in the South, a fruitful field for the Communists. The country had been shocked repeatedly by bloody industrial warfare in the Southern states. The Southern mill-owners shortsightedly had repulsed the efforts of the conservative American Federation of Labor to follow the Communist battering-ram and take over the organization of labor in the industry. As the depression cut deeper, the industry fell into a hopeless morass. Under the leadership of George A. Sloan, the majority of manufacturers were frantically eager to do something to stabilize the industry. Mr. Sloan had a code ready to submit almost the moment that General Johnson was empowered to receive it. It proposed a maximum forty-hour week and minimum wages of $10 a week in the South and $11 in the North.

The hearings of the cotton code in late June were an event of which the revolutionary significance was felt by all who participated in them. General Johnson presided. Organized labor, led by William Green, presented its case; the committee of the cotton industry presented its case. Expert testimony was taken. General Johnson succeeded in jacking up the minimum wage scales to $12 in the South and $13 in the North. Then came the dramatic moment when the cotton manufacturers offered an amendment abolishing employment in the mills of persons under sixteen years of age. The hearing room broke into cheers. After years of struggle between reform and industrial bourbonism, child labor was being abolished as a mere incident in the reorganization of the industrial system. It was not much of a concession on the part of industry, to be sure. The new minimum wage levels were making child labor unprofitable. But it was a striking illustration of the potentialities of the NRA. It caught the emotions of the country and gave the whole movement an initial impetus.

Labor fought for minimum wages of $14 and $16 and a thirty-hour week, but this code, like others to follow, was a compromise. Minimum wages of $12 and $13 for a forty-hour week seemed very low, but they were a sharp advance for an industry in which wages in some cases were as low as $4 a week and hours practically unlimited. Considerable effort was lavished on making the cotton code a model for others to follow. After all negotiations had been completed, the President himself made several amendments which extended the minimum wage and maximum hours to miscellaneous employees and white-collar workers and otherwise tightened the code. The code set up a governing authority representing employers, employees, and the public. The stretch-out problem was left unsettled in detail pending the report of a special committee. The President gave the industry until January 1 to work out a plan for abolishing the mill-town system. It was estimated that at current production the code would put 500,000 more people to work, 100,-000 more than ever had been employed in the industry. Seventy-seven percent of the industry subscribed to the code at the beginning. The problem of lining up the recalcitrants remained to be solved.

The cotton textile code went into effect July 17. The NRA had wrought a feat. Nevertheless, in one month, it had produced only one code. Several other industries in the textile group were brought under the cotton textile code with comparative ease. Many minor industries submitted codes. The great objective was to bring the big basic industries with large numbers of employees under codes as rapidly as possible. The big industries were hanging back; their problems were infinitely complex. Such industries as coal and oil were torn by bitter rivalries. The collective bargaining condition of the law made open-shop employers shiver. A.F. of L. organizers had gone to work at a furious pace; they were telling workers not only that they could join unions under the protection of the government, but, in some instances, that they had to join unions. Independent labor organizers and agitators sprang to the opportunity all over the country. The great open-shop industries such as steel, which had fought and beaten organized labor in several battles in the past, were determined that the United States Government should not force unionization down their throats. They

hastily began to set up company unions which would
have the appearance of really representing the employees.
Their best legal minds sought ingenious means of writing protective clauses for these company unions into the
codes. The desire to pile up stock at low wages also led
some industries to hang back. A great array of miscellaneous employers who were willing to co-operate in the
venture could not find out how to go about it. The quick
organization of thousands of types of business under
codes was beyond human accomplishment.

General Johnson had realized from the start the un-
suitability of the code system for rapid action. He had
sent to Kansas City for Charles F. Horner, one of the
organizers of the wartime Liberty Loan drives. By mid-
July, Mr. Horner had the plans laid for a nation-wide
campaign. General Johnson's idea was to apply to all
business a temporary blanket code governing hours of
work and minimum wages. The law did not contain the
precise authority for that. The plan had to be used under the President's authority to make voluntary agreements.

The perils of a campaign after the wartime model
were recognized at the White House. Its success depended first on the prestige of the President. If the campaign failed, his influence and the whole recovery program would be irreparably damaged. Inevitably it would
whip up hopes, perhaps stir dangerous emotional be-
havior. Possibly it could not succeed without intensive
promotion of a boycott, but it seemed the only way to
give a quick boost to purchasing power and mobilize public sentiment to expedite the organization of industry
under codes. On a sweltering night, July 24, President
Roosevelt broadcast to the country his appeal for a great

co-operative movement. Three days later postmen began to deliver five million copies of the President's Re-Employment Agreement to employers throughout the country. The postmen were instructed to give them to every person on their routes who employed more than two people, except professional men and farmers. The voluntary agreements were to be effective until December 31. As each employer came under his code, he was to drop the voluntary agreement. The deadline for the submission of codes was set for September 1, after which weeks would be required for hearings and negotiations.

The voluntary agreement prohibited child labor and profiteering. For white-collar workers it established a minimum wage of from $12 to $15 a week, depending on the location, and a maximum forty-hour week. For factory workers it established a thirty-five-hour week and minimum wages of 40 cents an hour, with some exceptions.

The terms of the blanket agreement were too severe a wrench for many employers, and the process of approving modifications began at once. Thus three types of agreements were placed in effect: the permanent codes, the voluntary re-employment agreement, and modifications of the voluntary agreement. The Blue Eagle spread over the country. Chambers of Commerce, civic clubs, state and local administrative bodies, carried forward the campaign with all their ballyhoo, culminating in a series of great metropolitan parades. The country rose to the undertaking with a remarkable enthusiasm that swept along the doubters. The optimism of the NRA outran itself, and the autumn goal for re-employment was carelessly raised to 6 million persons.

Meanwhile General Johnson hammered away at the

big industries. With the naval building program as an
inducement, the shipbuilders were brought to quick agreement. The shipbuilding code, signed on July 26, established minimum wages of from 35 to 45 cents an hour,
and maximums of from thirty-two to forty hours a week,
depending on the type of work. The wool textile code,
signed July 26, was similar to the cotton textile code,
except that the minimum wages were $1 a week higher.
The electrical manufacturers' code, signed August 4, fixed
minimum wages of from 30 to 40 cents an hour for a
week ranging from thirty-six to forty hours, depending
on the type of work. The coat and suit code, also signed
August 4, fixed wages from 47 cents to $1.80 an hour and
hours from thirty-five to forty a week.

The oil, coal, automobile, and steel industries still
balked. The oil and coal men could not agree among
themselves. The automobile industry was worried about
unionization. Steel, the big bankers' industry, was grimly
reserved. Mr. Roosevelt came down from Hyde Park
and in a whirlwind week put direct pressure from the
White House behind the NRA. He authorized General
Johnson to impose a code on the three wrangling groups
in the oil industry. He amended the final draft of the code
himself and announced he would head the enforcing
agency to be set up. The General strode into the room
where three hundred oil men impatiently waited. He
spent three minutes telling them that they had until ten
o'clock the next day to register protests before the code
was sent to the President for signature.

"We will now pass copies of the code," he announced
brusquely. "The meeting is adjourned."

Oil executives saw the stack of copies of the code and
stampeded toward it.

"Please sit down," shouted Johnson. "Sit down or I'll stop it immediately."

The leaders of the oil industry slunk back to their chairs. Johnson left the copies with his secretary, put on his hat, and walked out.

He was snowed under with protests against the code, but the impasse was broken.

The President called the coal operators into the White House, and gave them a discourse on the plight of their industry which astounded them by its accurate detail. He reminded them that they were riding a "dying horse" and that they were furnishing a hothouse to Communism.

Myron C. Taylor, chairman of the board of the United States Steel Corporation, and Charles M. Schwab, chairman of the board of Bethlehem Steel, suddenly appeared at the White House one morning that week. They were in the President's office an hour, and they emerged silently grim. They went to a hotel room where other steel operators were waiting. One morsel from their report escaped into general circulation. Mr. Schwab, it seemed, had explained his duty to look after the stockholders of the Bethlehem Steel Corporation.

Mr. Roosevelt had smiled sweetly at him and inquired, "Were you looking after your stockholders when you paid those million-dollar bonuses to my friend 'Gene Grace?"

Mr. Roosevelt's parting word to Mr. Schwab, it seemed, was to give his warm regards to his friend "Gene," the president of Bethlehem Steel, and tell him that he would never again make a million dollars a year.

Before he left for Hyde Park that Saturday night, August 19, the President signed codes for the lumber, oil, and steel industries.

The lumber code provided a forty-hour week, extensible to forty-eight hours at seasonal peaks, and minimum wages of from 23 to 50 cents an hour. It set up a lumber code authority to estimate consumption, work out production quotas, and set minimum prices to prevent lumber products from being sold below cost. It contained one long-range feature on which the President insisted— a pledge to undertake forest conservation measures according to plans to be worked out in co-operation with the government.

The oil code set a flexible week of from forty hours up, and fixed minimum wages of from 23 to 52 cents an hour. The crux of the dispute in the oil industry was price-fixing. Part of the industry wanted no price-fixing, part of it wanted price-fixing all the way from the well through the refined products to the consumer, and part of it wanted partial price-fixing. As a compromise the fixing of base prices was permitted a ninety-day trial. Withdrawal of oil from storage was limited to 100,000 barrels daily for the remainder of the year. A committee appointed by the President was to recommend a quota to each of the oil-producing states. Interstate shipments in excess of those quotas were to be prohibited.

The steel code provided a maximum forty-hour week (which could be lengthened to forty-eight hours at the seasonal peaks), minimum wages of from 25 to 40 cents an hour, and an eight-hour day effective November 1, if the industry was by then operating at sixty percent or more of capacity. The steel masters had made few concessions. They left no doubt that they would oppose unionization of the industry to the bitter end. The eight-hour day was not to be effective unless production reached sixty percent. And the operators found further solace in the fact that the code was limited to a trial operation of ninety days. Nevertheless, steel had bowed to the government.

One week later all of the automobile industry, except Henry Ford, came under a code. The code stipulated a 43-cent hour in the larger plants and an average work week of thirty-five hours, with a maximum of forty-eight hours at seasonal peaks. The unique feature of the automobile code was an interpretation of the collective bargaining clause of the NRA, which asserted the right of employers to select, retain, and advance employees "on the basis of individual merit, without regard to their membership or non-membership in any organization." Labor protested in vain. Other open-shop code drafters at once began copying the interpretation, or improving on it. Its inclusion was an error, as General Johnson soon afterward admitted.

Coal was the toughest problem of all. Thirty years of competitive warfare leading to anarchy were the history of the bituminous industry. There were at least thirty percent too many mines and too many miners. The marginal properties had for years been the seat of abject poverty and constant disorder. The United Mine Workers of America, which once had most of the Northern mines under union agreements, had lost their grip in 1927 and been broken by the depression. At the beginning of 1933 less than a quarter of the coal in the country was being dug under union contract. When the National Industrial Recovery Act was passed, John L. Lewis, president of the United Mine Workers, saw his opportunity. He flooded the coal fields with organizers. In thirty days he had 150,-000 new members. With this reviving power behind him, Lewis jumped into the code negotiations among the operators. It was a long and angry fight. Strikes broke out.

Blood was shed at the mines of the Frick Coke Company, a U. S. Steel subsidiary. Sympathy strikes spread through the Pittsburgh district. The President sent General Johnson into the coal fields. He urged patience and co-operation with the NRA, but for once he came back beaten and remarked: "I stuck my nose into something that was none of my business and I got what was coming to me." Mr. Roosevelt sent him back into the fray. Johnson commanded the aid of Gerard Swope in talking to the steel executives, and after hours of stiff negotiation came out with a truce. The truce gave the miners their own checkweighmen, which appeared to have been the issue which started the strike. The President named a temporary outside conciliation committee for the coal industry and followed that with the creation of a national labor board under Senator Wagner to assist in the settlement of industrial disputes.

Despite the President's mid-August attempt to get the coal industry under a code, the wrangling continued for another month. Meanwhile coal companies were piling coal above ground at low wages. A series of labor leaders in the stormier districts sought to block the operators' game by organizing "holidays" until the code was in effect. Miners were shot outside the Frick mines. The President called in the coal operators for the last time and gave them twenty-four hours to come to an agreement. An eight-week battle was at last brought to a conclusion. The coal code provided for an eight-hour day, a five-day week, fixed minimum wages from $3.36 a day up; it set up machinery for arbitrating disputes, and provided for a fair price scale. It met the miners' demands concerning company stores and houses, checkweighmen, and other disputed points.

Meanwhile the domain of Lewis had expanded into the South. Two weeks after the coal code was signed, 95 percent of the operators put their names to a union agreement which filled out the code. Only the Alabama and Western Kentucky mine owners refused to subscribe. Lewis emerged as the champion of 700,000 coal miners, forming the largest industrial union in the country. The operators were promised that there would not be another bituminous strike before April 1, 1934. The coal code was a remarkable achievement for a sadly disorganized industry. It left unsolved, however, the problems arising from a huge oversupply of mines and miners and the continuing competition of cheaper fuels.

While the NRA was battering down old forms and traditions, the AAA was stirring the West and the South with its own novelties. As Administrator of the AAA, Mr. Roosevelt appointed George N. Peek, farm implement manufacturer, a scarred and hard-boiled veteran of the McNary-Haugen movement. The spring planting season was over before the enabling legislation was passed and the AAA could be organized. The deceptive speculative rise had encouraged farmers to plant more instead of less, thereby aggravating the problem with which the AAA had to deal. The sudden burst of demand from the cotton mills encouraged the Southern planter to believe that increased consumption was going to solve his problem. The most formidable undertaking which confronted the AAA was to reduce the size of the cotton crop after it had been planted. The world carryover of American cotton in 1932–33 was 13,000,000 bales. The Southern farmers proceeded to plant 40,000,000 acres, which would have produced between sixteen and seventeen million bales of cotton. The AAA undertook the extraordinary task of inducing the cotton planters to turn around and plow under one-quarter of their acreage. The farmer was offered two choices: one was to accept cash payment for plowing under cotton. The other was to accept a lower cash payment plus an option to buy at 6 cents a pound an amount of cotton equal to that which he destroyed. (The old Farm Board stock of cotton had been transferred to the Department of Agriculture for use under the Smith Cotton Option Plan, of which this was a modification.) The payments per acre with the option ranged from $6 to $12, without the option from $7 to $20, depending on the yield per acre in previous years. No payments were offered for destruction of cotton on land yielding less than one hundred pounds to the acre.

Twenty-two thousand AAA agents, mostly volunteers, blanketed the South. The two-week campaign resulted in agreements to take 10,324,000 acres out of production. On August 1 the Secretary of Agriculture placed a tax of 4.2 cents a pound on the processing of cotton to raise $120,000,000 in cash bonuses for the cotton farmers.

Eye-witnesses throughout the South testified to the remarkable alacrity of 1,800,000 cotton planters in carrying out a program which offended their fundamental habits of thought. The Southern mule proved to be the stanchest defender of the old order—if press reports from various parts of the South could be taken literally. Trained to walk between the rows of growing cotton, the mule stubbornly fought to the end the unorthodox and uneconomic practice which compelled him to tread down the growing plants as he pulled the plow.

The second great crop reduction program of the AAA was in wheat. Despite a short American wheat crop in 1932, the carryover was approximately 360,000,000 bushels, nearly three times normal. Wheat exports had dropped from the old level of nearly 200,000,000 bushels annually to about 40,000,000 bushels. Crop failure in certain sections of the country in the spring of 1933 prevented the wheat surplus from piling up still higher. But if the normal acreage were planted in the fall of 1933 and the spring of 1934, approximately 200,000,000 bushels would be added to the carryover. On July 9, a processing tax of 30 cents a bushel on wheat for domestic consumption became effective. That was expected to yield from $130,000,000 to $150,000,000 to reimburse wheat farmers for reducing their output. The fixing of the percentage of reduction was held up until the international wheat pact which had been in negotiation intermittently for three years could be concluded. Until the Roosevelt Administration came into power, the United States was one of the primary obstacles to any international wheat pact. Until the AAA was created, the United States had no mechanism for controlling production and exports. The AAA provided an effective and flexible mechanism. It could control production but it could also subsidize exports so long as there was any remaining open market into which wheat could be dumped. Before the London Conference President Roosevelt sent representatives— Henry Morgenthau and Frederick E. Murphy, publisher of the *Minneapolis Tribune*—to Geneva to participate in the International Wheat Conference. Negotiations moved on to the World Economic Conference and, after an intermission, were resumed in August. Late in August delegates of twenty-one nations came to terms—with the aid of Secretary Wallace's timely threat to dump wheat on a big scale, Mr. Murphy's skill as a negotiator, and the hearty backing of Canada. Under this agreement the four great exporting countries, Canada, Argentina, Australia, and the United States, agreed to limit their exports for the year 1933–34 to 560,000,000 bushels, and in the following year to reduce export fifteen percent below the average exportable production of the years 1931–33. The principal importing nations agreed to apply no further measures to increase their own domestic production. They agreed to reduce their wheat tariffs and quotas whenever the international price of wheat reached 63.08 cents a bushel in gold (the equivalent of about 90 cents in the United States at that time) and remained there for four months. The extraordinary change in the world's wheat-producing map was clearly brought out at the conference. The old importing countries—France, Italy, and Germany—had stimulated their domestic production until France was producing more wheat than Canada, and Germany more wheat than Australia. When the pact was drawn, the world's store of wheat was the largest on record: nearly a billion bushels. This country's share of the world export allotment for 1933–34 was fixed at 45,000,000 bushels. Secretary Wallace determined to seek a fifteen-percent reduction in the American wheat output, which meant taking approximately 9,600,000 acres out of production. The cash bonus offered to the wheat farmers totaled approximately $138,000,000. Of this amount the AAA agreed to distribute approximately $90,000,000 in the fall of 1933 and the remainder in the spring of 1934 when the farmers had proved that they had abided by their agreement. Nearly one million wheat farmers signed agreements under the two-year crop reduction program.

As a crude beginning toward reducing hog production, the AAA spent $50,000,000 in buying pigs and piggy

sows and processing them for distribution to the un.
employed through the Federal Emergency Relief Administration. They offered to buy four million little pigs and
one million sows. They got the pigs but the farmer, with
customary shrewdness, kept his sows, presumably for the
purpose of raising more pigs to sell to the government at
a good price the following year. This plan, as Secretary
Wallace announced, came from the "grass roots" and
was only the forerunner to a broad program in 1934 to
take at least 10,000,000 acres of corn out of production
and reduce the output of hogs by one-quarter. The tremendous waste in the pig purchase program was attested
by scattered reports from the packing centers. Pigs contained little that could be saved and distributed for consumption as food. Many of them were ground up for
fertilizer and, when storage facilities were exhausted,
all but a few parts had to be dumped.

The problem of establishing a fair price for the
farmer for milk was attacked in a different way. Minimum prices to be paid the farmer for milk were established by market agreements in the most important milk
states. Maximum prices for milk to the consumer were
fixed and competition among distributors was left to
work its natural result between that ceiling and the minimum prices established for the farmer. Making this system operate successfully immediately proved exceedingly
difficult. In drafting and enforcing the milk agreement in
Chicago, the AAA was forced to employ its rigorous
licensing power for the first time. Most of the officials of
the AAA were reluctant to bring that power into play
because of its questionable constitutionality. The NRA
did not want the power used for fear that a test case
taken quickly to the Supreme Court would result in an

adverse decision, vitiating the threat inherent in the
NRA's similar licensing power. The AAA tussled with
the forbidding collection of Chicago milk distributors
who descended on Washington to fight over the agreement while Mr. Roosevelt was enjoying his yachting
cruise up the New England coast. When he returned, the
momentous question of using the licensing power was put
up to him. He asked one question: Was there any chance
of obtaining an effective agreement without the use of the
licensing power? He was told No. "Go ahead and license
them," he replied.

The practical difficulties of maintaining a minimum
price for milk, when there was an over-supply and where
competition among distributors was keen, were brought
out in the ensuing months. Throughout the summer and
early fall complaints poured into Washington that the
milk distributing business was being pushed into the hands
of bootleggers who were buying milk below the legal
minimum price and underselling the legitimate distributors. Meanwhile, the rising cost of feed added to
the dairyman's burden. Milk strikes threatened or occurred spasmodically in the principal milk sheds during
the summer and fall. It was evident that the problem of
obtaining fair prices for milk to both the farmer and the
consumer was far from being solved.

The allocation of $30,000,000 to buy surplus butter
was the forerunner of a broader program to control the
production of milk and milk products. The activities of
the AAA expanded rapidly in all directions. Processing
taxes were imposed on tobacco to pay farmers for reducing their tobacco acreage in 1934–35. Marketing agreements were drawn or in prospect to cover rice, fruits,
walnuts, and other products. Perhaps the most ambitious

attempt to control output by agreement was in the case of sugar. Negotiation of a sugar pact, embracing the United States, its insular possessions, and Cuba, continued throughout the summer without reaching a satisfactory conclusion.

In mid-September the AAA announced its intention of subsidizing the export of from 30,000,000 to 35,000,000 bushels of Northwest wheat, at a probable loss of $7,-000,000. Exports of cotton and wheat in small quantities had already been facilitated by the R.F.C. credits of $50,000,000 to the Chinese government and of approximately $4,000,000 to the Amtorg Corporation, the Soviet trading agency in the United States.

A quick glance around the circle of the other undertakings of the Administration revealed uneven performance. The debt reduction program was practically at a standstill. The wave of recovery had rescued the railroads; the vitally important reduction of railroad debt had not materialized. Co-Ordinator Eastman had succeeded in inducing the highest-priced railroad executives to reduce their salaries—the saving was inconsequential but the moral effect great. Recovery and a multitude of legal complications, plus the uncertainty of the investment market, were tying the hands of the Farm Credit Administration in its effort to aid farm debtors. Mortgages directly under government control, through the Federal Land Banks, were being readjusted, but the life insurance companies would not trade mortgages for the new mortgage bonds. In many cases insurance companies and other institutions holding mortgages were blocked by the state laws and regulations governing their investments. With the help of the R.F.C., the F.C.A. was beginning to help reopen closed banks by taking mortgages off their hands. Next to nothing had been done with the refinancing of home-owners' mortgages. The legal complications were even more troublesome than in the case of farm mortgages. Furthermore, the home-owners' loan organization was extremely weak: it had been loaded with political appointees.

The Civilian Conservation Corps was hard at work. Mr. Roosevelt had extended the life of the corps for another six months. Preparations were under way for the opening of new winter camps in the South to replace those above the heavy snowline in the North and West. The membership of the corps was declining as amateur foresters found jobs, took to the road, or were dismissed. Most of the vacancies were left unfilled. The experiment was being continued on a slightly diminishing scale.

The $500,000,000 Emergency Relief Fund was being parceled out. Approximately one million families had been taken off relief rolls since March, but the indications were that the winter months would bring relief requirements to a new high level because of diminished private resources.

The federal budget was doing well. In one year the public debt had risen by three billion dollars, but revenues were running well ahead of 1932 while expenditures were lower. The new combination of regular and extraordinary budgets made the exact state of affairs hard to determine. Indications were that revenues for the fiscal year would more than cover the regular budget and carrying charges on the extraordinary budget.

Repeal of the Eighteenth Amendment was sweeping the country with revolutionary speed and thoroughness. Formerly dry strongholds in the South such as Alabama, Arkansas, and Tennessee had fallen into line, and Maine,

mother of prohibition, had come over to repeal. Ratifica-
tion of the repeal amendment by the necessary thirty-six
states before Christmas was assured. The recovery of revenue sources to the federal, state, and municipal governments, the revival of a substantial business, with attendant capital expenditures, new outlets for grain and grapes
—all would be stimulants to general recovery. Meanwhile beer was enlarging its sway as the modification of
state prohibition laws continued.

Mr. Roosevelt took another step away from the old
gold standard and gave general recovery a light push by
enabling gold producers to obtain the world price for
gold by sales through the Treasury. This was one step
short of a free gold market in the United States. Several
reasons were suggested for letting newly mined gold go
abroad: the United States did not need it, other countries did need it, and an increase in the floating supply of
gold was expected to help to increase prices. At the same
time Mr. Roosevelt issued revised orders governing gold
hoarding, by which possessors of gold were required to
report their holdings through special forms. Thereafter
they could retain their gold only under special licenses.
The Attorney General had refrained from acting on his
repeated threats to prosecute hoarders. Meanwhile, most
of the known hoarded gold which could be located had
been rounded up by personal solicitation. The new order
was destined to reach theretofore unidentified hoarders
and to facilitate prosecutions.

The Tennessee Valley Authority was beginning preliminary work on the Cove Creek dam. It also announced
a proposed schedule of electrical rates to farm and urban
householders for power from Muscle Shoals. For the
typical general consumer the rate averaged about 2 cents

a kilowatt hour. For 50 kilowatt-hours per month the rate was less than half that in New York City; for 450 kilowatt-hours per month, it was only a little more than one-third the New York City rate. The electrical utilities groaned, but the T.V.A. insisted that in the making of the rate schedule allowance had been made for such items as taxes and interest, which the T.V.A. did not have to pay, in order to furnish a fair comparison with the rates of private utilities.

About the first week in September, the high hopes of the country began to droop a little. Business was slacking off gradually. The NRA had failed to reach its early-summer objective of putting from four to six million people back to work. Wage and salary earners were complaining about the increased cost of living. Agricultural commodities hung far below the dizzy peaks of the July speculative mirage, and farmers were grousing about the prices of overalls and tools. Business became infected with the bankers' concern over the monetary policy of the government. Strikes were popping up everywhere. The uncomfortable feeling began to spread that the New Deal was breaking down.

The diminution of confidence was the inevitable result of too much ballyhoo. It was popular to blame the management of the NRA for the ballyhoo. It is difficult to see how the NRA could have got as far as it did without the publicity methods and other trimmings of a wartime drive. The blanket agreement campaign, the parades, the state and local publicity campaigns had an educational value, hastened the codification of some lines of industry, and yielded a net benefit all around. On the other hand, an error was made in publicly announcing a goal which could not be reached by the NRA alone. The blanket campaign diverted the attention of some of the most important members of the meager staff of the NRA from the terrific job of making the infinite number of detailed decisions needed to facilitate the adoption of codes. And it diverted the attention of the Roosevelt Administration as a whole from other undertakings which were vital. All activity except under the NRA seemed to lag, though this was in part an optical illusion created by the forward surge of the dramatic General Johnson.

When all is said, the NRA ballyhoo only prolonged the excessive optimism aroused by the sharp stock and commodity rise of the spring. Speculation was again the American will-o'-the-wisp of prosperity. The speculative market rise far outran the actual fall of the dollar in ratio to gold and the reasonable expectations of increased business. Some of the very men who denounced most heartily the NRA publicity when they began to feel a sinking feeling in September had been most extravagant in their own ballyhooing of a returned prosperity during the early summer speculative boom.

As a short-term mechanism for lifting the country out of the depression, the NRA was highly overestimated from the beginning. The lifting power of the NRA alone was very limited. As it happened, the NRA rested on a gradually subsiding base. It had to take up the slack of the recession from the speculative height before it could show a net gain.

The NRA had insufficient leverage for a mighty jacking-up of wages and salaries. By the co-operative method, impelled by public opinion, it could make employers agree to abolish child labor and to establish minimum wages and somewhat shorter hours. But it could not go too far without losing the public opinion behind

the co-operative tendencies. It could not afford to whittle
the majority down into minority by making extreme demands. A partial alternative was to spur public sentiment farther toward mass action. The consumers' boycott was encouraged mildly and euphemistically by the
cry to "Buy under the Blue Eagle." The boycott had
dangers and distinct limitations. Its effective use was
largely confined to pressure on merchants with whom the
public came in direct contact. The public quickly realized
that a Blue Eagle in the window was not an infallible
sign. The proprietor might be violating the terms of his
agreement or code while his more honest competitor who
felt unable to meet the terms did not display the Blue
Eagle. Even if the terms of the agreement or code were
met technically, there were too many loopholes for chiseling and evasion. Restaurant owners in many instances
reimbursed themselves for higher wages to their employees by charging them for meals which theretofore
they had furnished free. A list of the types of evasions
under the blanket agreement and codes of the NRA
would fill a volume. Like the Eighteenth Amendment, the
NRA agreements and codes were hard to enforce. There
were three approaches to the solution of the enforcement
problem. One was the administrative agency representative of employers and employees set up in each code. In
the comparatively few industries with strong and inclusive trade associations, a large measure of industrial self-
enforcement of the codes seemed to be eventually practicable. The great mass of individual businesses and small
industries seemed to require state and local directors of
compliance. In September, the NRA began to set up a
nationwide organization to regularize NRA practices
and enforce compliance with the voluntary agreements.

Such an organization had to be voluntary and therefore temporary. A wartime army would have been necessary to enforce compliance against widespread evasion. The vital interest of employers who were living up to the codes in seeing that their competitors also lived up to them was the potential backing for rigid enforcement.

The third approach to the solution of the enforcement problem was the unionization of employees. And that was also the only way in which the leverage of the NRA on industry could be effectively supplemented. The only industries in which the labor provisions of the codes went much beyond the abolition of child labor, a very minimum wage, and a rather high maximum week were those in which labor was organized for collective bargaining. The only major industry with a vertical union was bituminous coal. The rapid reunionization of the coal industry by the United Mine Workers produced a codified wage agreement from top to bottom. The highly organized apparel industries and a few specialized and concentrated lines of work in which the old craft unions were strong and aggressive were the only others in which general wage agreements were achieved.

Henry Ford challenged the authority of the NRA in a firm manner by refusing to sign the automobile code. Determination not to let his plant be unionized, the long-standing feud between him and his competitors, a fundamental attachment to "individualism"—whatever his reasons, he presented the government with a dilemma. Mr. Ford had been one of the pioneers of high wages. He apparently intended to meet the wage and hour provisions of the code or to improve on them. The NRA had the choices of testing its licensing power on Mr. Ford, of taking milder disciplinary measures through the courts, of encouraging a boycott of Ford cars, or of ignoring his defiance.

Mr. Ford was too big to be ignored. An irregular boycott of Ford cars was begun on the part of a few state governments and perhaps a good many individuals. The use of Mr. Ford for the first test of the major disciplinary power of the NRA was open to many objections, when so many other manufacturers who had subscribed to codes were known to be violating them. Mr. Ford shook confidence in the power of the government to carry through. As a real menace to the NRA experiment he was no competitor with the thousands of chiselers. The broader public interest dictated that the NRA first reach down and discipline the manufacturers who were evading, let us say, the cotton textile code, or who had refused to subscribe to it. The power to discipline was the key to the whole experiment. Industry's own lack of power to make and enforce agreements impelled the request for governmental assistance which made the experiment practicable. Unless the codes were enforced rigidly, the whole undertaking was bound to break down.

The immediate results of the NRA were uneven, and that unevenness retarded progress. When the wage bills in certain industries were jacked up, they were reflected in higher living costs and diminished consuming power to workers whose incomes were not correspondingly increased.

The relentless quest of the consumer for low prices further hampered the effort to encourage a polite boycott. It looked as if an actual consumers' strike were developing to some extent.

All these inequalities and weaknesses in the first great drive of the NRA were secondary to the fundamental fact

that the country could not be lifted out of the depression
through the consumers' goods industries. The gap between
the wage bill and the price list could be narrowed but it
could not be closed. The only way in which the consumers'
goods industries alone could draw the country out of the
depression was by steadily expanding the demand for
consumers' goods more rapidly than production. Roughly
speaking, without taking account of all the modifying elements, including the time lags, that meant that the factory
owner would have to pay more for his materials and in
wages than he received for his finished output. Or, suppose that all the consumers' goods industries were mobilized and all the available jobs in them parceled out among
the unemployed on the basis of a fifteen-hour week. The
inability of the employees to buy the full output would instantly leave a surplus of goods. Production would be
curtailed, men would be thrown out of work, and the
process would continue until the whole thing had run
down hill again. All this was widely overlooked. Circumstances combined to make the first drive of the NRA an
effort to lift the country out of the depression through the
consumers' goods industries. No one was more acutely
aware of this fatal flaw than General Johnson, the chief
exponent of the short-term uses of the NRA. While he
was cajoling and bludgeoning employers and labor, ex-
horting the public to wartime spirit—in short, driving
ahead on all fronts—his constant effort behind the scenes
in Washington was to impress the need for getting the
capital goods industries moving. The apparatus (what
there was of it) for stimulating the capital goods industries was not under his control.

"If we don't get heavy industry moving, we're sunk,"
Johnson preached from the first of August. He had no

difficulty in obtaining verbal agreement with that assertion. The Executive Council meetings devoted a good deal
of time to settling minor questions of jurisdiction and to
sundry problems of administration. Johnson, who was
geared to the pace of the NRA, fretted and fumed. He
let his secretaries handle matters of detail or he ignored
them. He had no time to waste sewing on buttons or tidy-
ing up the mess hall while the battle was on. Yet on one
or more occasions that group of individuals highly publicized as the "super-Cabinet," whose colossal task was to
manage the American experiment, spent considerable time
in settling which department was to have this little job and
which was to have that man and at what salary. Johnson
and many others fretted in vain. Nothing happened to
stimulate construction and the heavy industries.

All the NRA could have been expected to do in three
months was to fill in the wage wash-outs, establish a minimum level below which competition at the expense of
labor could not go, thus forming a steady base for the
operation of other forces, distribute work a little, narrow
the gap between production and consuming power, and
make the first rude beginnings on the reorganization and
stabilizing of American business life. The NRA did all
that with extraordinary success, when the magnitude and
novelty of the undertaking are kept in mind. The first
drive of the NRA was merely the first shock of a guided
industrial revolution. From the beginning the great potentialities of the NRA were long-range. By long-range I
do not mean the one year to which the licensing power was
limited or the two-year life of the original National Industrial Recovery Act. The weaknesses in the economic
system which led up to the NRA had long been developing. They were primary causes of the depression, which in

turn aggravated them. The NRA is a planned economy in embryonic form. One of its indispensable virtues is its flexibility, which affords the widest latitude for experiment and continual revision in the light of experience. In late September and early October the NRA entered its second phase: one of consolidation of gains, of systematizing of administration, of preparation for a second drive at a later date. The first brief experience emphasized the need for flexibility and differentiation in the methods of industrial government. A few of the better-organized industries with strong trade associations probably were ready to assume the major responsibility for industrial self-government under NRA supervision if the government would help them discipline recalcitrants. For the great mass of miscellaneous manufacturing, commerce, and business, rather simple requirements for maximum hours and minimum wages appeared to be all that was feasible or desirable for the present. To what extent the code system could be made effective, outside the major industries and certain types of business concentrated in the large cities, remained to be revealed by experience. There were persuasive signs that a national maximum-hour and minimum-wage law—with the minimum-wage levels subject to upward or downward readjustment by the government in accordance with changes in the cost of living or with the increase in efficiency in production —was necessary to supplement the code system. A national thirty-hour and five-day week for everybody appeared to be the very minimum requirement within the realm of fairly quick practicable attainment. In making the concessions necessary to preserve the co-operative atmosphere of the movement, the NRA gave way on the question of maximum hours of work. Tactically that was perhaps justifiable. As one high official in the government expressed it: "The first thing to do is to get the bear's claw in the trap."

General Johnson's concern about the capital goods industries was well founded. While the boom was going on in the consumers' goods industries, capital goods stood still. The main source of stimulation within the Administration's direct power was the public works program. The tremendous size of that program was partly illusory. A large part of the $3,300,000,000 consisted of items which had been transferred from the regular federal budget; some of them could be classified as public works only by stretching the definition. Of the $1,500,000,000 which was immediately allocated, two-thirds had already been allocated by Congress; in this sum were $400,000,000 in loans to states for road building, $100,000,000 for farm credit, and a number of miscellaneous projects. The only big project of the public works program which immediately got under way was naval construction, for which the President set aside $238,000,000. Even the road building money was distributed slowly. With the remaining money at its disposal, the Public Works Administration had to take up the slack not only in still diminishing private construction, but in declining expenditures on public projects by states, counties, and municipalities. Total building expenditures in the summer months of 1933 were less than in the corresponding period of 1932. When the production of consumers' goods in mid-summer reached 92 percent of normal (1923–5 average) the building industry stood at 25 percent. The distribution of the federal public works money for local projects was necessarily very slow; each separate project had to bear the approval of a state authority and was then subjected to a thorough investi-

gation by the Public Works Administration before the
details of financing the project could even be discussed.
After preliminary approval was given, a long period necessarily elapsed before the final contracts between localities and the government could be signed and before bids
could be obtained and work begun. This whole process
was at best time-consuming, but, without question, was
also retarded by the determination of Secretary Ickes to
avoid any chance of scandal. Each undertaking was fine-
combed for every fragment of potential graft.

In mid-September only a few thousand men had been
put to work by the huge public works fund. Undoubtedly
more would have been put to work if the public works program had been begun earlier in the spring, if red tape and
safeguards had been thrown to the winds, and the money
poured out with wartime abandon. Even under these circumstances, the capacity of public works to give a quick
impetus to recovery was limited. Whenever the distribution of money began, it necessarily had to be spread over
a period of months and years.

Private investment in new enterprises was practically
inert. Capital issues for the first half of 1933 totaled only
$81,000,000, which was only a third of the total for the
first half of 1932, only four percent of the total for the
first half of 1931, and only a little more than two percent
of the total for the first half of 1930. In August 1933,
capital issues totaled only $14,000,000, mostly for brew-
ery construction.

For this stagnation of private investment, the bankers
blamed chiefly the Administration's uncertain money policy and the Securities Act. Both were deterrents to the
marketing of new securities. The personal liability clauses
of the Securities Act frightened the investment banking

houses and, as long as the threat of monetary inflation overhung the country, the private investor naturally was reluctant to put his money in bonds. There were many indications, however, that big investment banks were overstressing these two obstacles. They did not like the Securities Act, they most violently disliked the Banking Act and the major experiments of the Roosevelt Revolution viewed as a whole. It was reasonable to suspect that they were engaged in a program of sabotage. The whole position of organized finance was at stake. It was easy to foresee that, if the Securities Act were modified and the dollar stabilized, and still no great volume of investment for new enterprises ensued, the bankers would then lay the blame on the uncertainties surrounding the NRA, the AAA, or any other venture of a régime which challenged bankers' rule. Very likely a reasonable amount of investment was bottled up by the Securities Act and monetary uncertainty. Possibly there was some lusty new ladder industry waiting to spring forth from the loins of investment banking. But if the bankers knew what it was, they did not tell. The country had plenty of productive plant already built and impatiently waiting use. Some of the hardiest advocates of the necessity for reassuring investors were primarily interested in the resumption of foreign lending. The difficulty of finding large pent-up needs for maintenance and new equipment was illustrated by the experience of the Administration when it decided to help the railroads buy steel rails. Some of Mr. Roosevelt's advisers decided that the railroads of the country could use approximately two million tons of steel rails. The President asked Mr. Eastman, the Federal Railroad Co-Ordinator, to make a careful survey and find out how many tons of new rails the railroads could use if they could get them at a low price and on easy credit terms. After a preliminary survey, Mr. Eastman estimated one million tons. After further investigation, he reduced the figure to about 700,000 tons. Possibly the railroads could have used more rails than they were willing to take, but the incident illustrated the ease with which the potential demand for capital goods could be overestimated.

While the bankers were marshaling the forces of sound money, the disappointment of the farm belt expressed itself in a renewed demand for currency inflation. Near the end of September the dollar hit a new low of 63.7 cents in gold on the international exchange. Mr. Roosevelt disregarded both extremes and quickly moved to pick up the faltering recovery movement with a vast campaign of credit expansion. Jesse H. Jones, chairman of the Reconstruction Finance Corporation, went before the American Bankers' Association. In a browbeating speech, he practically ordered the commercial bankers to liberalize their lending policies, and urged them all to put themselves in a position to lend more by selling preferred stock to the R.F.C. Smarting from these lashings, the bankers heatedly pointed out that they could not find good borrowers, that their funds belonged to their depositors, and that, while Mr. Jones was urging them to lend freely, bank examiners were tightening up their requirements in preparation for the launching of the federal deposit-guarantee plan. The Roosevelt Administration was up against the nature of the banking profession, which tends to make its practitioners cautious when they should be bold, and bold when they should be cautious. The depression had weeded out a good many of the more daring bankers and severely chastened the survivors. The banking idol was Confidence, yet the bankers did more to destroy Confidence and to undermine it when it began to return than any other group in the country. They could not be relied on for much driving power to push the country out of the depression. The resuscitating forces in the hands of the commercial bankers were incomplete. The bankers as a group were emotionally aflutter, if not completely lost in the presence of revolutionary changes. They had to be pushed into action.

The main points in the Administration's broad credit expansion drive which began in September were these:

A continuation of the Federal Reserve Board's open market operations which already had drowned the stronger banks in enough credit to support a business loan expansion of more than $7,000,000,000;

R.F.C. loans up to $1,000,000,000 to bankers at 3 percent to be relent at 5 percent to help NRA members carry larger payrolls. It seemed unlikely that much of this would be used;

R.F.C. loans for the organization of local mortgage companies;

The purchase of $1,000,000,000 in preferred stock of banks by the R.F.C.—if the banks would sell it. This was largely a smokescreen thrown out to conceal from the public the identity of the banks which really needed to sell preferred stock to the R.F.C. in order to qualify for deposit insurance. Other banks were urged to sell preferred stock to generalize the whole undertaking;

A reduction of the base lending rate of the R.F.C. from 4½ to 4 percent;

R.F.C. advances through the Farm Credit Administration to facilitate farm mortgage refinancing. Liberalization of rediscounting by the Federal Reserve Banks and of lending by the R.F.C. on the new farm mortgage and home-owners' loan bonds;

An intensive campaign to thaw out and reopen frozen banks, with the help of the R.F.C. By mid-July approximately $1,500,000,000 in bank deposits tied up in the March debacle had been released. By mid-September, approximately $2,000,000,000 in deposits remained in closed or restricted banks under conservators;

The energizing of the capital goods industries by speeding up the public works program and through government loans to industry for new equipment. The financing of the purchase of steel rails was the only plan in the latter category which was quickly developed. An impediment was the price of steel, which had been held up during the depression by a virtually monopolistic contraction of production in the steel industry. Mr. Roosevelt called in the steel masters, dangled the 700,000-ton steel rail order in front of them, and announced the government's readiness to lend the railroads the money for the purchase if the price were cut down below forty dollars a ton. The contracts were to be let to competitive bidders below the forty dollar a ton maximum;

The advance to cotton growers of 10 cents a pound, a trifle more than the New York cash price at the time, on cotton withheld from the market, if the growers signed up for the 1934–35 crop reduction programs. This plan promised to serve: first, to support the price of cotton; second, to give the crop reduction program for the ensuing years a running start; third, to enable farmers to pay their current obligations and perhaps leave them a balance of purchasing power; fourth, to allay the rising demand for the issue of greenbacks;

The possibility of a further loan to Soviet Russia to remove part of the surplus of copper, cotton, and various farm products.

Three parts of this vast credit expansion program were of primary importance: the energizing of the capital goods industry, the recapture of purchasing power frozen in closed banks, and the extension of loans to cotton growers against future production. The cotton loan plan was, among other things, a form of consumer credit. During the summer and fall months some of the most inventive minds in the Administration devoted themselves to consumer credit schemes, including the revival of installment buying. It seemed probable that before the winter was over the Administration would give an experimental trial to several devices for the financing of consumption. The most that could be done with the public works program during the winter was to complete the allocation of funds and get contracts with municipalities drawn in preparation for a spring drive in the building field.

One other project which illustrated the scope of the powers at the disposal of the Administration began to get under way in early October. That was the organization of a $350,000,000 corporation to buy surplus farm products of all kinds for distribution to the unemployed. The government was about to establish a gigantic commissary, financed probably by the Federal Emergency Relief Administration, the AAA, the R.F.C., and the various states.

The future of the money system remained a secret between Mr. Roosevelt and powerful political forces that could not be gauged with certainty. Beneath the conflict between the sound money people, who included labor, and the farm belt inflationists, there had been a greater convergence of point of view than either group realized. In the spring the conservatives had shrieked when the dollar was taken off its gold base. By October, most of them were clamoring for a return to gold and they were willing to see the dollar at sixty-five cents in terms of its old gold content if it could be held there. Their grave concern was to head off printing press inflation.

In the spring a thirty-five or forty percent reduction in the gold content of the dollar with a little supplementary aid for silver would have satisfied most of the inflationists. Even in the autumn, behind all the blood-curdling cries for greenbacks, the spring formula probably would still have satisfied most of them. Mr. Roosevelt had many good reasons for ignoring the demand of the sound money people that he stabilize the dollar in ratio to gold and make a statement that there would be no further tinkering with the currency. At home, political management dictated that he leave the question open as long as possible, reserving his powers over the currency to appease the most rabid inflationists if they should attempt to override him with mandatory inflation. The whole problem of fixing the new dollar with reference to the gold was complicated by the franc and the pound. If the French franc should be forced off gold, as some observers thought it would be before the end of October, unpredictable disturbances would result. At least there was great diversity of opinion among economists concerning the effects of such an occurrence on the price of gold. The future course of the pound was another imponderable. The British had officially evinced no interest in a hasty return to gold. Presumably they would have been delighted to have the dollar take a fixed place on the gold yardstick, so that they could survey the effects, particularly on the British export market, at their leisure before determining the level at which they wished to hold the pound. The debt discussions with the British were resumed in October amid rumors of renewed negotiations concerning the ratios between the pound and the dollar and gold. However, the management of the dollar, unlike the management of the pound, had to be conducted primarily with the internal price level in mind. Foreign trade was too small a factor in American economy to be given much consideration. While Mr. Roosevelt kept his monetary thoughts strictly to himself, there was no reason to think that he had abandoned his interest in the commodity dollar. The commodity dollar demanded a fluctuating gold content, although the changes perhaps did not need to be made daily or weekly or even monthly. It seemed reasonably certain at least that the old free gold standard under which a citizen could obtain gold for currency was gone. Small amounts of gold could be used to settle international balances. The bulk of the gold supply seemed doomed to reimprisonment in the vaults of the Treasury, there to receive the distant homage of money-conscious men who could not see it but would perhaps feel security in the knowledge that it existed.

The Roosevelt Administration entered October, its eighth month, amid uncertainties and doubts. The September spell of despondency, which inevitably followed the mid-summer emotional jag, was giving away to a more realistic appraisal of results. Business activity had lost approximately one-third of the ground it had gained between March and July. Industrial shares on the stock market had lost about twenty percent of their gains, and rail shares about forty-three percent. Wheat had sunk back from its speculative peak but it stood at 90 cents, more than double its depression low. Cotton had dropped back about 2½ cents a pound, but it also was selling for more than double its depression low, and was pegged in the neighborhood of 10 cents by the new loan plan. Other im-

portant agricultural commodities stood below their summer speculative peaks but, with one or two exceptions, far
above the prices of 1932.

Department store and chain store sales were picking
up after a slight September slump. After a gradual recession from the height of activity induced by the boom in
automobile production, steel output stood at about forty
percent of capacity. Automobile sales for the first nine
months of 1933 had exceeded by fifty percent sales in the
corresponding period of 1932. The industrial chart was
irregular but a substantial net gain had been recorded.

Behind a multitude of statistics stood significant basic
accomplishments. The disparities indicating the breakdown of the whole economic system had been markedly
decreased. The work of the NRA, supplemented by voluntary or forced wage increases, was revealed in this set
of figures from one index based on 1923–25 production:
In July industrial production stood at 100 by this index.
At the same time factory employment was 70.1 percent of
normal and payrolls were 49.9 percent of normal. In
August, industrial production was down to 92 percent of
normal, but factory employment was up to 73.3 percent
and payrolls up to 55.7 percent. In September industrial
production fell a little farther, to about 85 percent, but
factory employment and payrolls gained a little more.

The long strides taken toward correcting the disparity
between the price level and the old debt level were revealed in the Department of Labor's index of 784 commodities. This index uses 1926 as par. Between March
and October the index of manufactured products rose
from about 65 to about 73, and the index of farm prices
rose from about 40 to about 58. Farm prices were still
far short of the ultimate goal but, notwithstanding com-

plaints from the farm belt about the increased cost of living, they had made substantial gains on the prices of finished products.

The correction of disparities was the primary problem of recovery. The deflationists could point out that the burden of debt was unevenly distributed and could preach the doctrine of greater activity at a lower price level. The fact remained that important sectors in the economic system were loaded with debt and required both greater activity and a higher price level. The peaks of debt on farms, railroads, and homes had to be leveled off, but that did not remove the necessity for bringing prices up still farther. So long as the price-lifting process was kept under control, farm commodity prices would continue to overtake the prices of finished products until both reached a workable relationship with debt. Preserving the equilibrium, once it was reached, was a more complicated problem. The goal had to be approached gradually in order to keep farm purchasing power and labor's purchasing power advancing together. Too rapid a rise in prices meant the canceling of labor's gains. Too slow a rise would leave the farmer incapacitated as a consumer. The balancing of the advance presented complex difficulties in the realms of politics as well as of economic management.

Two figures summarized the really prodigious progress toward recovery which had been made in seven months. The estimate of the Bureau of Agricultural Economics placed the farm income for 1933 at $6,360,000,000 as compared with $5,143,000,000 in 1932. Part of this estimated increase of $1,213,000,000 was canceled by the rising cost of living; there remained a substantial net gain. The other most significant index was the gain in employment. At the end of seven months, approximately

2,200,000 (an average of several estimates) more people were at work than at the beginning of March. And in the interim probably a great many others had had some work. A long road lay ahead, but in the dark days of March few persons would have ventured to predict that so much of the distance could be covered in the next seven months.

VIII

People in the White House

THE personality of the President is a factor in recovery which every person must weigh for himself. His vitality, effortless self-confidence, enthusiasm, and joyousness have been the main driving force of his Administration. Good humor and gayety probably are as important as Mr. Roosevelt's more solid qualities. Another man might have made some of Mr. Roosevelt's decisions, but they would not have had the same effect. He has the ability to warm and stimulate all who come in contact with him.

The stream of callers at the White House is an absorbing "before and after" study. Men go into his office haggard and gray-faced from worry or overwork and come out looking as if they had just returned from their vacations. Even if they have not got what they wanted, they feel better. The terrific strain of the days that began on March 4 took a heavy toll in the Administration. Douglas, Cummings, Woodin, Moley, Johnson, and a hundred other men drove themselves to the verge of collapse. The President, who bore a heavier responsibility than any of them and was second to none in long hours of work, always appeared to be enjoying himself hugely. Probably no man was ever better equipped temperamentally to carry the burden of high office. The Presidency has aged or broken men in simpler and easier days. Mr. Roosevelt thrives on his job. The thicker and more complicated the action, the more he seems to like it. It is a common saying among the members of Mr. Roosevelt's family and his secretaries that the quickest way to locate him is to wait for the sound of a hearty laugh. Mr. Roosevelt's ability to laugh is his almost never-failing escape from tension. While others wind themselves up in mental and emotional knots, he keeps his mental faculties at the maximum level by refusing to brood or worry. It is curious to recall that before he became President Mr. Roosevelt's lighter notes were frequently spoken of as indicative of a man who lacked the depth and resolution essential for the highest office in the land.

It was a piece of good fortune for the country and Mr. Roosevelt that he entered the White House a grossly underrated man in the public mind. His sure and rapid actions thrilled and spurred the country more than they would have done if he had been heralded as a Messiah. His performance satisfied even his closest friends, which is saying a great deal, as their opinion of his ability was high. Mr. Roosevelt is an extremely complex person. Strip his high office from him, and he would remain one of those rare people who reminds you of no one else. The nation has never had a President with his blend of pronounced qualities.

Mr. Roosevelt is probably the most radical man in Washington, and yet a very conservative man. He is both daring and cautious. He can seize a new idea or make a decision with breath-taking speed, yet he can temporize until the last possible second for reaching a decision. He is extremely mobile and flexible, yet underneath he has a steel-like vein of stubbornness.

It is not always possible to forecast in which combination Mr. Roosevelt's qualities are going to assert themselves. He has an extremely agile mind and the ability to

skip around over a dozen subjects in as many minutes
without losing track of any of them. Every newspaperman who has attended his press conferences knows his
gift for simple and logical analysis. He accumulates
masses of detail but he can cut through them to the heart
of the problem. Yet Mr. Roosevelt's actions are not always logical. Cool assessment of political realities plays
its part in guiding him. Beyond that he has an acute sen-
sitiveness to intangibles. Since no one around him can analyze this faculty, it must be put down as political intuition.
It is, of course, not infallible. But in any complex situation, Mr. Roosevelt's judgment is likely to be better than
that of anybody around him. He has often acted with
abrupt disregard of all the counsel that he has sought or
received. His closest associates have shaken their heads
mournfully or held their breath—only to find that "the
chief," for uncanny reasons that even he could not explain,
was right again.

The Roosevelt Administration is highly centralized.
Mr. Roosevelt holds in his own hands all the strings of
the executive department of the government. The country
has had other strong executives who dominated their Administrations. President Wilson was one of them. More
often perhaps it has had decentralizing Presidents. When
President Harding made Charles E. Hughes Secretary of
State and Andrew W. Mellon Secretary of the Treasury,
he practically divested himself of active responsibility for
the two most important departments of the government.
Mr. Coolidge retained Mr. Mellon and in general distributed the main burden of responsibility among the
members of his Cabinet. Mr. Hoover took a much larger
share of responsibility on himself.

Mr. Roosevelt has almost a monopoly on the responsibility in his Administration. It is not strong enough to say that no important matter of policy in any department is settled without his approval. Many branches of the Administration have little idea what their policy is until Mr. Roosevelt has told them. His methods of action vary. He may accept the proposal of one of his advisers without a change. Naturally he must rely to some extent on his appointed deputies. Again, he may restate the policy and leave his deputy to work out the details. Or, he may approve the policy but promptly dictate new details. Throughout the first phase of the Administration Mr. Roosevelt was, for all practical purposes, his own Secretary of State, his own Secretary of the Treasury, as well as the general overseer of the routine departments and of the extraordinary experiments which put much of the economic life of the nation under his control. His interest in details was shown, for example, during the organization of the Civilian Conservation Corps. The various departments which collaborated in that undertaking drew up plans and maps for the location of some 1400 camps. One might suppose that the President, then overloaded with problems which would have sunk a dozen ordinary men, would have been content with the knowledge that competent officials had picked suitable sites for these camps and that his trusty lieutenant, Louis McHenry Howe, had tentatively approved their choices. Not at all. The camp locations were not approved until Mr. Roosevelt had looked at the map and the data concerning the possible uses of each camp and made up his own mind. The example is not quite typical because Mr. Roosevelt had a special personal interest in the Civilian Conservation Corps, but it is indicative of his extraordinary capacity for detail. Fortunately, he works with rapidity and with economy of energy.

Mr. Roosevelt's highly centralized type of administration has its weaknesses. During the early months his Cabinet members and the heads of the new agencies formed the habit of unloading unnecessary work on him. One suspects that one of his major purposes in spending part of his summer away from Washington was to encourage his ministers to rely on themselves to a larger extent. At the same time, in a time of revolutionary movement when so much is at stake, the responsibility must rest in the President. One man must keep the lines of action correlated.

All the qualities which have impressed themselves on the nation since Mr. Roosevelt's inauguration may be found emphatically revealed in his previous career. His entry into public life as a green member of the New York Legislature was as dramatic on a smaller stage as his entry into the Presidency. In a spectacular, obstinate fight, against overwhelming odds, he defied and defeated Tammany Hall and the bosses of his party. During that political battle his warming personality, infectious enthusiasm, and stubbornness held together a minority of legislators who had little in common. In his days as Assistant Secretary of the Navy, Mr. Roosevelt's imagination caught the idea of bottling submarines in the North Sea by stretching a mine barrage from Scotland to Norway. The great bulk of expert opinion considered the idea an impracticable dream. Mr. Roosevelt had to overcome the strong opposition of the General Board of the Navy and of the British Admiralty before he put the plan across. As Governor of New York, Mr. Roosevelt revealed his adroitness as a politician. He was a man without a party.

The Legislature was controlled by conservative Republicans. Most of the legislators of his own party were controlled by Tammany Hall. Yet he was able to establish an enviable record for progressive legislation.

The frigidity of the White House and the impersonality of the Presidency melted when Mr. Roosevelt and his family arrived. The nation has had many Presidents who have worn their high office with simplicity, but few who have been able to wear it informally without loss of dignity. The first day that Mr. Roosevelt went to his White House office, Patrick McKenna, the official doorkeeper for every President since the first Roosevelt, responded to the summons of the presidential buzzer. He put his head in the door and was cordially greeted as "Pat." He nearly collapsed. A great many people called him "Pat," but no President had ever before called him "Pat."

Within a week Mr. Roosevelt was calling everybody on the White House staff by the first name or nickname. He calls his Cabinet officials and other aides by their first names. He calls most of the members of the Senate, including the venerable Senator Glass, by their first names, and he quickly learned and uses the first names of the newspaper correspondents who attend his press conferences.

It is conceivable that in his early days in politics Mr. Roosevelt cultivated the art of first names in the effort to break down the barriers between his aristocratic background and the politicians of more plebeian birth with whom he had to associate. If the practice was originally deliberate, it has long since become a habit which goes naturally with Mr. Roosevelt's geniality. Few persons, except in his immediate family, call Mr. Roosevelt "Franklin" to his face. Some of his old associates in Al-

bany address him as "Governor." To everybody else he is
"Mr. President," but this salutation, which traditionally
goes with the dignity of the office, does not have a stilted
sound when addressed to Mr. Roosevelt.

The use of first names is only one index of Mr. Roosevelt's democratic informality. The simple and personal
touch can be seen in almost everything he does. He uses
"We" and "I" and "Me" instead of "the Administration" in his public utterances. He conveys no implication
of kingship. On the contrary, it is an acknowledgment
that the President of the United States is a human being.

Newspapermen grew tired of listing the precedents
that Mr. and Mrs. Roosevelt shattered during their first
months in Washington. Mr. Roosevelt has revealed in
many ways his respect for the experience of the past; he
has very little respect for the hollow artificialities of social tradition. There was an old tradition that the President never left the White House to pay a call. Mr. Roosevelt promptly broke it by driving over to see former
Justice Oliver Wendell Holmes on his birthday. The
State Department has been accustomed to lending one of
its best-versed diplomatists to advise the occupants of the
White House on the fine points of White House and diplomatic social tradition. The forms were sacredly guarded.
The President stood here, the wife of the President
there. They received the guests in one room and marched
them into another. The reception of official guests was
a very precise thing suggesting a military ceremony.
The Roosevelt family abolished that. At official dinners
the guests are still seated according to their rank. Beyond
that, not much remains of the protocol in the White
House. When Mr. Roosevelt received the diplomatic
corps for the first time it was in the informal Oval Room

on the second floor. They sat about and chatted and had a pleasant time. When Mr. Roosevelt received Prime Minister MacDonald and the succeeding line of special foreign emissaries in the spring, he went out on the front portico to welcome them. That broke another tradition.

A few evenings after Mr. Roosevelt took office, one of his secretaries, Marvin H. McIntyre, and several newspapermen who were waiting on the portico for a meeting to break up, decided to pass the time by singing. Somewhat uncertain harmonies from "Home on the Range," filtered through the White House doors. Nobody could recall a precedent for that occurrence.

The White House has ceased to be a castle and has become a home with the open-handed hospitality usually associated with the manor houses of the old South. The atmosphere is rather Jacksonian, or as near as a democratic family with the background of the Hudson River aristocracy can come to it.

Nothing exemplifies Mr. Roosevelt's truly democratic conceptions better than his press conferences. He abolished the system of written questions which had been in use during most of three Administrations. He determined to hold conferences at which newspapermen could ask questions freely and receive answers. President Harding had tried that system for a short time and abandoned it after he crossed his wires with Secretary Hughes on an important international matter. Since then it had been more or less accepted that no President should be expected to submit as a regular practice to an open bombardment of questions. When Mr. Roosevelt first told a few of the veteran Washington correspondents what he would like to do, they cautioned him against it. They considered the aspiration noble but they thought it impracticable with a group of correspondents that might number one hundred or more. Mr. Roosevelt was determined to give the plan a trial. It worked successfully the first time and it has continued to work since. Twice weekly the doors of the President's office are opened to the press, and for a half to three-quarters of an hour he handles all questions as they are flung at him. He may parry or ignore a question—as it is often necessary that he do, especially when delicate international problems are involved —but in a great majority of instances his answers are direct and illuminating. He may not be quoted directly, but the substance of what he says may be used unless the "off the record" rule is applied. Occasionally the President imparts information with the provision that it not be published in any way. Very often such "off the record" information is an explanation of why he cannot discuss a particular subject. It is frequently useful in enabling newspapermen to check the authenticity of information which they have obtained elsewhere. The general rule of open publicity and free discussion has been extended through all the divisions of the executive department of the government. The public probably knows through the press much more about the real "inside" of the Roosevelt Administration than it has ever known about any Administration before.

Mr. Roosevelt's success in maintaining a new type of relationship with the press is partly due to his exceptionally competent press secretary, Stephen T. Early. Mr. Early knows the mechanics of news-gathering and is popular with the correspondents. He carries out efficiently the Administration's policy of making information available quickly and in full.

The experience of the transition is not new to Mrs. Franklin D. Roosevelt. Her own life reflects a series of thoughtful transitions or adjustments to the changes in the American environment. As a young wife, she followed the prescribed routines of the capable "woman in the home"—making proper calls on proper days, having six attractive children in ten years, managing a comfortable and efficient household, and making obeisance to the canonized tenets of the older generations. Then the feminist movement brought its chaotic upheavals in the conceptions of a "woman's place." Mrs. Roosevelt emerged as perhaps a type of the best product of this virile influence: a woman who retained the intrinsic values of tradition and gained the advantages of the wider life of the new freedom.

As wife of the Governor of New York State, she went her energetic way with little microscopic attention from the public; she wrote for magazines, engaged in a furniture handicraft venture, directed and taught in a school, gave occasional radio talks, and served on numerous social service committees.

The transition to the position of "First Lady" impressed everyone else more than it did Mrs. Roosevelt. When asked how she intended to conduct herself in the goldfish bowl of this position, she frankly and directly answered: "I'll do as I always have done and then there won't be any difficulties."

And doing as she always had done included taking her responsibilities seriously and executing them successfully. As the wife of the President and as the first hostess of the nation, she is gracious, meticulously thoughtful, and very popular with all who come in contact with her. But she is not only the "shadow"—the helpmeet—the retiring "seen but not heard" First Lady to which America has been accustomed.

Perhaps it is her dynamic energy which will not permit her to confine herself to the narrowly prescribed routines of the mistress of the White House. In one day alone she exerts herself with ease more than most active women do in a week. The day may start with a horseback ride at seven-thirty in the morning. Writing and scrupulous attention to correspondence may occupy the rest of the morning. She will undoubtedly receive delegations and individuals with claims for White House attention at frequent intervals during the day. She will jump into her blue roadster and make a call, for example, on a Congressman's wife in a hospital. Those who are familiar with one of her typical days fail to understand how she can, not only conceive, but execute so many sincerely meant acts of thoughtfulness toward her friends and acquaintances. The threads of the domestic management of the White House pass through her hands. She travels extensively and receptively. Indeed, she is a valuable thermometer of the public temperature for the President. If she visits a coalfield district, for example, she is not the "Lady Bountiful" distributing smiles and wash cloths; she goes humbly, seeking to understand the people and conditions which she sees. Some miner's child will receive glasses which he needs, but no one will ever know that they came from Mrs. Roosevelt. While she has not the formal education of the scholar, she has the greater gift of ability to learn and to change; there is no "hardening of the arteries" of her versatile mind.

Eleanor Roosevelt is moral without being a moralist. Her personal code for the conduct of her own life is

Spartan; she never tries or wants to impose her standards on others.

She has an almost incredulous "will to believe" which has occasionally led her into embarrassing difficulties. A petitioner who comes to her with a seemingly sincere proposition is likely to engage, not only her sympathy, but her active enthusiasm. Thus she has sometimes been guilty of the very human and lovable sin of gullibility. And she is extremely accessible!

Her impulsive, warm spontaneity is safeguarded by her most dominant characteristic—her self-discipline.

A survey of Mrs. Roosevelt's friends is a key to her character. This group is varied and cosmopolitan. It includes social workers, Cabinet wives, individuals with whom she has professional interests, and a large number of individuals who cannot be pigeon-holed, but who find in her a rare capacity for fundamental intimacy.

In the Roosevelt family life, individual freedom is the accepted privilege. The five children of the chief exponent of a regulated economic system have courageous opportunities to make their own failures and successes. Mrs. Roosevelt prefers the frank friendship of her children to their sense of filial duty. She is not a matriarch. She is ambitious for her children to achieve the maturity of independence.

Because of her fine honesty and human emotional make-up, devoid of sentimentality, Mrs. Roosevelt arouses in those who know her a fierce, lasting loyalty.

IX

The Official Family

THE liberals have come to the front in Mr. Roosevelt's official family. He went into office with a balanced Cabinet. In the first days of crisis, the conservatives had their triumphs. As the Administration pushed into unexplored fields, their influence gradually waned. New experiments demanded new faces. In manning the great recovery agencies Mr. Roosevelt inevitably turned to men whose points of view were compatible with the undertakings they were supposed to administer.

In July 1933, the President brought his enlarged official family together in an Executive Council for National Recovery. Its Tuesday meetings thereafter supplanted one of the regular weekly Cabinet meetings. Twenty-one executives formed the Executive Council. It is a significant sidelight on the New Deal that of those twenty-one individuals only six had ever been elected to a public office of any consequence, not more than ten had been active in Democratic politics, and a good many of them had been practically unknown to the country at large until 1932 and 1933. Old reputations waned and new ones were made. In the flux of the New Deal, the nation, and Mr. Roosevelt, began to find some of the "big men" they had been looking for.

The personality and background of the men—and woman—who have made notable impressions in the

Roosevelt Administration are one index to the temper of the New Deal.

William H. Woodin was the man of a very important hour. The moment that Mr. Woodin slipped quietly out of the pandemonium caused by the jangling nerves and clashing ideas of some of the country's premier bankers and financial authorities and went to his hotel room to think, the problem of reopening the nation's banking system began to be solved. Mr. Woodin was not a banker, although until a few days before then he had been a director of one or two banks and of the Federal Reserve Bank of New York. His career as an industrialist, however, had brought him in very close contact with the nation's biggest bankers and he knew them well. At a critical moment in history, Mr. Woodin, very much to his surprise, found that he was Secretary of the Treasury in the United States Government. He had lived sixty-four years without holding a public office and he knew very little about the organization of the Treasury Department. Mr. Woodin naturally sought the aid of all the best minds in the government and in the big banking world. He listened to them for two days. Then his calm perception told him that he was not getting very far by that method. The big bankers were talking about a nation-wide scrip issue, and this and that. They could not agree among themselves. Mr. Woodin went off by himself and decided on the simplest of means for reopening the banks. He went back and informed the bankers and Treasury officials what he proposed to do. The atmosphere clarified, and the drafting of an emergency banking act proceeded. Throughout those hectic days in which the nation's banks were closed and gradually reopened, Mr. Woodin remained as serene as if he were listening to a sonata. In an unprecedented situation Mr. Woodin turned to a simple old-fashioned remedy—the provision of plenty of currency. There perhaps were better remedies. Mr. Woodin's worked with reasonable success.

Mr. Woodin's whole background is conservative, but he is no theorist. He apparently suffered no emotional or intellectual pangs in following Mr. Roosevelt into the realm of a managed currency. He smilingly admitted that he now favored many things that he had never imagined he would favor. This was not a politician's shift. Mr. Woodin merely has a great measure of common sense.

Illness kept Mr. Woodin away from Washington during most of the late spring and summer. He continued to keep in touch with the Treasury by telephone. His resignation had been forecast for months, but Mr. Roosevelt made it plain that he would not let Mr. Woodin go unless his doctors insisted. So long as his health would permit, Mr. Woodin seemed destined to be Secretary of the Treasury. All he really needed in his department was a few liberal subordinates to leaven the stiff orthodoxy with which the Treasury is afflicted.

Lewis W. Douglas's hour swiftly followed Mr. Woodin's. The slashing of the budget was Mr. Douglas's triumph, and his only triumph in the first phase of the Roosevelt Revolution. The New Deal moved rapidly away from him; he tugged hard to hold it back and in that negative capacity he probably had a modicum of success. For several months Mr. Douglas was a regular attendant at the President's so-called "bedside Cabinet" meetings at which Louis McHenry Howe and Raymond Moley were his only regular colleagues. For a time, he seemed to fall from favor. Then in the autumn of 1933 he bobbed up again still in a good humor and still fight-

ing to keep the dollar sound and to get the budget really
in balance.

Mr. Douglas practices the economy which Calvin Coolidge preached but had too much political sagacity to apply, except perhaps to his personal budget. Mr. Douglas
made a swift reputation in Congress by his defiance of the
veterans' lobby. In the Administration he has continued
to add to his reputation by his calm refusal to compromise. Mr. Douglas has political courage of the first order.
Nor is his interest by any means confined to figures; the
balancing of the budget and the formulation of detailed
plans for reorganizing the federal administration merely
constitute his job at the moment. Mentally he is one of
the best-equipped men in the Administration. (Like some
of the other New Deal leaders he has been a college professor.) Furthermore, he is only thirty-nine. If the Democratic party goes conservative and Mr. Douglas's stern
loyalty to his principles doesn't make too many enemies
for him in the meantime, he is likely to have a political
future.

About the time that the country first began to notice
Mr. Douglas in Congress it also became aware of the
huge and genial James A. Farley hastening over the land
rounding up delegates to the Democratic National Convention for Franklin D. Roosevelt. Mr. Farley had
worked his way up from the small-time politics of Rock-
land County, New York, to membership on the State Box-
ing Commission and the Secretaryship of the Democratic
State Committee when Mr. Roosevelt found him. Under
Mr. Roosevelt he became Chairman of the State Committee, then Mr. Roosevelt's national campaign manager.
In 1932, the old hands of the Democratic party still
looked on him as a political neophyte. By the middle of

1933 they began to talk about him as a man with a future. He was already Postmaster General, Chairman of the Democratic National Committee, and Chairman of the New York State Democratic Committee. Mr. Farley never turns loose a job until he has two more in hand. Mr. Farley cannot be classified as either a liberal or a conservative. By background he is the latter, but he has sagaciously refused to become involved in economic issues. For the time being Mr. Farley has made himself a specialist in the purely political problems of the Administration. The job of repulsing hungry Democrats has taxed his endurance, but he is slowly building up a very powerful political machine. He presumably has no doubt that the American experiment will succeed and that the United States will continue to hold elections regularly. Mr. Farley is strengthening the Democratic party to help Mr. Roosevelt; it is also impossible to overlook the fact that Mr. Farley himself is a rising figure. He is only 45. He has an exceedingly attractive personality and abounding energy. Furthermore, he is an excellent executive. Give him a little longer exposure to the problems of government as a member of Mr. Roosevelt's Cabinet, and he is likely to be heard from.

Miss Frances Perkins is the first woman to sit in the Cabinet, but when Mr. Roosevelt announced that he had selected her as his Secretary of Labor he refused to admit that it was because he wanted a woman in the Cabinet. The merit in Mr. Roosevelt's implied compliment to her superior ability was quickly proved to the public satisfaction. In a few weeks she had overhauled the personnel of the Labor Department, which notoriously was the worst in the government. She reorganized the Department's

statistical service, the inaccuracy of which she had exposed
while she was Commissioner of Labor under Mr. Roosevelt in New York. She made the country sit up by inform-
ing a Congressman at a committee hearing that his question did not make sense. She visited steel mills, talked
with the workers, and from what she learned was able to
state some unpleasant but irrefutable conclusions to the
steel industry at the NRA hearing on the steel code. Perhaps her greatest conquest was the American Federation
of Labor. The leaders of that organization publicly asserted their intention of having nothing to do with her.
The boycott did not last long. By the time the NRA began
to function, William Green and his confreres considered
Miss Perkins their warmest ally and wisest counselor.

Back of Miss Perkins is a New England heritage and
long experience in social welfare work and industrial relations. She is a new type in the American Cabinet—and
would be none the less so if she were a man. Her ability
and the nature of the Roosevelt experiments have combined to lift the Secretaryship of Labor from its customary place at the bottom of the list of ten Cabinet portfolios to a position very near the top.

Harold L. Ickes spent thirty years fighting for the
cause of reform and progress before he picked a winning
candidate. His luck changed when Anton J. Cermak was
elected Mayor of Chicago in 1930. In 1932 Mr. Ickes
joined his old progressive colleagues in supporting Mr.
Roosevelt. Outside Chicago and Illinois he was not well
known. He needed only a few months in Mr. Roosevelt's
Cabinet to establish himself as one of the strong men of
the Administration. A prodigious worker, he soon found
himself in charge, not only of the Department of Interior,

but also of the oil industry and a $3,300,000,000 public works program. He managed, nevertheless, to keep his sense of humor and establish himself as the Cabinet wit.

Mr. Ickes brought a number of genuine conservationists into the Department of Interior. His ability to select the right man for the right place before anybody else could make a suggestion resulted in his getting non-political lieutenants of his own choice. Mr. Ickes talks freely and pleasantly, but he is a tenacious fighter. Furthermore, he usually wins his fights. His summonses to the White House have become more and more frequent. Mr. Roosevelt apparently likes "the cut of his jib," even better than he did the first time he saw him and offered him a Cabinet portfolio. Political speculators have already begun to talk about him as a suitable nominee for the Vice-Presidency in 1936.

The first phase of the Roosevelt Revolution produced a mystery and left it unsolved. It was why Hugh S. Johnson had not become a national figure before 1933. In saltiness, picturesqueness, and sheer versatility, General Johnson was the discovery of the period. West Point graduate, experienced soldier, author of boys' books, lawyer, manufacturer, economist, philosopher, administrator —his vitality and range of capacities had taken him through a varied career before he became a member of the brains trust in 1932. During the war he evolved and organized the draft system. He then went on the War Industries Board, where he became acquainted with Bernard M. Baruch and George N. Peek. After the war he went into the farm implement business with Peek, and in that experience he learned about the declining purchasing power of the farmer. Later he became Mr. Baruch's personal associate. As Administrator of the National Recovery Act he bullied, roared, cajoled, laughed, dashed dramatically here and there, shrank into a model of reserve, quoted the Scripture and swore like a trooper, outdid our best-known light columnists in the contrivance of striking phrases, fought grimly, and compromised like a politician. Furthermore, he got results.

The first drive of the NRA was Johnson. If Mr. Roosevelt had had half a dozen Hugh S. Johnsons to throw in as shock troops, the whole recovery program on a broad front probably would have moved faster than it did. A small army would have been needed to mop up after them. Another type of man may be more useful for detailed organization and the consolidation of gains, but the gain has to be made before it can be consolidated.

Louis McHenry Howe's place in the new régime is hard to assess. He remains, where he has been for twenty years, at the side of Franklin D. Roosevelt. He lives at the White House. The field of action has become too broad, the chief performers have become too numerous, for Colonel Howe to keep track of everything in the manner to which he was habituated when Mr. Roosevelt's work was simpler. His hand will appear for an instant, almost haphazardly, in the most unexpected situation. He seems to roam at random. He alludes to himself as "the dirty job man." He takes onto his shoulders troublesome affairs which fit in no one's else department. One of his jobs was to get the Civilian Conservation Corps launched. It was the first venture of the New Deal on untried ground, and Mr. Roosevelt wanted 25,000 men in camps in ten days. Colonel Howe had to mix sharp proddings with an infinite amount of tact. He got the undertaking started and kept it moving with extraordinary success. He was therefore doubly upset by the toilet kit episode and was by no means appeased by the reassurance of some editorial writers that they knew it was only the result of amateurishness.

Colonel Howe scored a diplomatic triumph in his handling of the second bonus army. He is extremely effective in the reception of protesting delegations, which is one of his main jobs as Secretary to the President.

Few men have ever attained an important position under Mr. Roosevelt until they have been submitted to the searching scrutiny of Colonel Howe. When he has given a firm veto, it seldom has been overridden. Colonel Howe has a long nose for ulterior motives and it is especially sensitive when it is turned on a man who has connections with Wall Street. For twenty years Colonel Howe's only ambition was to see Franklin D. Roosevelt elected to the Presidency. His own views on fundamental social questions, if he had any, were rigorously subordinated to his political purposes. Occasionally he gave voice to a vague and diluted 1912 Progressivism. During the pre-convention period he was smitten with alarm when Mr. Roosevelt was so indiscreet as to hint publicly at his true liberalism. Without question, he would have salaamed daily to J.P. Morgan if it would have helped to elect Franklin D. Roosevelt. Now that his great aspiration has been achieved, Colonel Howe has begun to divest himself of the air of mystery. Definite conclusions concerning the cause of the nation's distress begin to escape from him. He has begun to use phrases familiar to the left wing of the brains trust. One suspects that he derives a sharp satanic pleasure from the consternation caused in the counting houses by the Administration's monetary policy.

For twenty years Colonel Howe has been the zealous watchdog of Franklin D. Roosevelt's interests. For years it was a lonely job. He now has difficulty in becoming emotionally adjusted to the frequent intrusion of others on the presence of his idol. One suspects that no man in Washington felt a greater sense of relief than Colonel Howe when Raymond Moley left Washington.

George N. Peek, the administrator of the vast agricultural experiment, was an Illinois farm implement manufacturer when the post-war agricultural deflation came along to remind business men that the farmer not only sells but buys. Mr. Peek was constitutionally unable to accept supinely the plight of the agricultural belt. He plunged into the effort to find a way to put agriculture on a basis of equality with industry. He was one of the chief organizers of the farm revolt of the early twenties. He lobbied the McNary-Haugen bill through Congress, but failed to draw Mr. Coolidge from the path of orthodox economics. In 1928 he converted John J. Raskob and Alfred E. Smith to the equalization fee. A life-long Republican, he bolted his party to direct Mr. Smith's vain campaign among the farmers. Undismayed, he returned to the fight in Mr. Roosevelt's behalf in 1932. Still fondly attached to the equalization fee, he doubted the practicability of the crop reduction features of the domestic allotment plan. He would have dumped the American farm surplus abroad—so long as there was any place to dump it. However, the Administration needed his practical experience and his ability to talk the language of both farmers and business men. At 60 Mr. Peek took over a job of revolutionary proportions. He is rugged and blunt and he can swing "the big sticks" with effect.

Henry A. Wallace, Secretary of Agriculture, represents the highest civilization of the corn belt. At 45, he is the third generation of his family to publish the same farm journal. He has conducted original and successful experiments in corn growing. He is well read in literature and philosophy and he likes poetry and solitude. He is a good theoretical and practical economist. He is a straightforward realist who refuses to be blinded to the fact that American agriculture is faced with a long-term problem in readjustment. He looks and acts more like the popular conception of a college professor than does any professor in the brains trust.

Quiet, studious, and business-like, Henry Morgenthau, Governor of the Farm Credit Administration, is one of the less spectacular and more effective members of the Administration. Like Mr. Wallace he is a farm journal publisher. In Dutchess County, New York—Mr. Roosevelt's county—he is a practical farmer. For four years he was Mr. Roosevelt's chief aide in agricultural and conservation work in New York. He wears his job as the biggest banker in the country with unaffected simplicity.

Robert Fechner, director of the Civilian Conservation Corps, did not complete his grammar school education as a boy, and he has spent his life as a working man and labor leader. Mr. Fechner substitutes common sense for high-spun economic theory.

Harry L. Hopkins, director of the Federal Emergency Relief Administration, was a social worker of high repute before Mr. Roosevelt made him chairman of the newly formed Temporary Emergency Relief Administration in New York State. Mr. Hopkins thus became one of the pioneers in this country in the exploration of the problems of government relief. He has none of the smugness frequently associated with the social service worker. He is direct, shrewd, open-minded. He lays all his cards on the table and sees to it that those with whom he deals have no aces up their sleeves. His attack and problem is direct; when he means "lousy," he says "lousy." There is nothing of the pussyfooter in his methods. Sentiment touches him; the under-dog to him is a reality and not a political phrase. He insists upon accurate statistics; one of his first undertakings in Washington was to try to ascertain for the first time how many families were on relief rolls. He is not limited by statistics; he wants the qualifying human aspects of each situation. Someone has aptly called him a "direct-speaking humanist."

Joseph B. Eastman, Federal Co-Ordinator of Railroads, was for years the sharp, unrelenting dissenter of the Interstate Commerce Commission. He plainly marked himself as the man whom a liberal government would call on to attack the tremendous problems of readjusting the transportation system. He has long expressed the conviction that government should assume "complete responsibility" for the rail carriers. Ironically enough the railroad industry did not seem to be frightened when it found that Mr. Eastman was to be the railroad specialist of the Roosevelt Administration. The railroad men knew he was exacting but also that he was thoroughly conversant with their complicated problems. Possibly a distraught industry subconsciously welcomed his very superior intellect.

In seven months, the New Deal has turned up many new faces, conservative and liberal in mien. Some are old insurgents who at last are having their chances; others prove the existence of a rich store of potential leadership hitherto untapped in America.

X

The Brains Trust

RAYMOND MOLEY's resignation as Assistant Secretary of State in September 1933 provoked speculative furore of an intensity theretofore reserved for such notable disruptions in the government as William Jennings Bryan's retirement from President Wilson's Cabinet. Conservatives of various stripes gleefully proclaimed the disintegration of the celebrated brains trust and hopefully forecast a retreat from the innovations of the New Deal toward the traditional thought of the Democratic party. Liberals tried to reassure themselves that Mr. Moley's resignation portended no change in the major trends of President Roosevelt's policies. In the excitement one significant occurrence was generally overlooked. The day before Mr. Moley's resignation was announced, Mr. Roosevelt made a speech in Poughkeepsie in which he reiterated that the major objectives of the experimental ventures of the New Deal were the permanent objectives of his Administration.

No aspect of the New Deal has been subjected to hotter attack and defense than the brains trust. As hammer blows rained on the old régime, conservatives in Congress and the press railed against "theorists" in government and professorial advisers. That was politer and safer than railing against an extremely popular President, and it was undoubtedly true that college professors and other intellectuals had an important hand in the drafting and directing of most of the revolutionary undertakings of the new régime. The renown of the brains trust and of Moley, Tugwell, and Berle spread round the world. Newspaper correspondents began to examine sedulously each new arrival in Washington to discover if he had ever taught in a university, possessed a Ph.D. degree, or, by aptitude for making charts or writing treatises, could qualify as a person of unusual academic attainment. Within a few weeks they had rounded up thirty or more persons who had one or more of the proper credentials. But they could never agree on which of them really belonged to the brains trust. Some preferred to include only those who had taught in universities. Some preferred to include only the men who saw Mr. Roosevelt frequently, which greatly shortened the list. Others preferred to list all economists. Still others preferred to make youth the test. Some discriminatingly limited the brains trust to the key people of marked intellectual capacity and advanced social point of view, a procedure which enabled them to include a few members of the Cabinet. All of this hubbub and the position of Professor Moley as one of Mr. Roosevelt's chief advisers and lieutenants undoubtedly created the picture of a government run by college professors and economists. To conservatives and liberals alike the brains trust became the symbol of the economic philosophy embodied in the experiments of the New Deal. As a matter of fact, by the time the brains trust received wide publicity it had ceased to exist as an institution.

In the pre-convention campaign of 1932, the brains trust was a definite group. It remained more or less cohesive up to the time of Mr. Roosevelt's inauguration. Then, in the popular mind, the experts for the international economic conversations began to be identified as members of the brains trust. They included three members of the original brains trust—Moley, Tugwell, and Taussig—and a few of the newer recruits had access to the President, but there was no longer a definite body which could be called the brains trust. There were, instead, various subsidiary brains trusts and many scattered men doing their own particular jobs. Mr. Moley remained at the President's hand, but the old round-table discussions practically disappeared. Nevertheless, the original brains trust was in many respects a unique institution. And, accepting the brains trust in its general popular sense, the large number of social scientists that Mr. Roosevelt brought into the government was a remarkable phenomenon.

In the waves of attack which fell on Raymond Moley during his meteoric career in public life, he was accused in one breath of being a dangerous theorist and in the next of being a mediocre man who had made no mark in the academic world by original contribution to thought. Mr. Moley has an ingenious mind but he probably never will create a doctrine, for he is as hardhearted a realist as Mr. Roosevelt himself.

His early career gave no indication that, when the United States embarked on an audacious experiment at a critical point in the world's history, he would be identified as "the second strongest man in Washington." Of French and Irish descent, he was born in an ordinary American home in Berea, Ohio, near Cleveland, in 1887. He was precocious: at 7 he was reading *Ivanhoe*. At 19 he graduated from obscure Baldwin-Wallace College in Berea and went to the neighboring village of Olmstead Falls as Superintendent of Schools. At 21 he was elected mayor of the village. Bad health sent him West for two years. He returned to teach history in a Cleveland high school and obtain his master's degree from Oberlin. He moved up to Western Reserve University, where he attracted attention locally by requiring his classes to read *The New Republic*. In 1919 he resigned his professorship to take charge of the Cleveland Foundation and make a survey of the causes of organized crime and the breakdown of law enforcement. His findings led to reforms in Cleveland and won discerning praise. He was called upon for similar surveys in Missouri, Illinois, Virginia, Pennsylvania, Connecticut, California, and Indiana. In 1923 he moved to Columbia, where he had received his Ph.D. degree five years earlier, as Associate Professor of Government. The New York State Crime Commission engaged him as an assistant. In 1928 Columbia made him a full Professor of Public Law. He acquired the unusual distinction of being a member of three faculties: the graduate school, the school of law, and Barnard College. At Barnard, his informal lectures and tea-parties became popular.

As literary secretary and dean of the brains trust, Professor Moley was with Mr. Roosevelt during most of the presidential campaign. When Mr. Roosevelt made a trip, Mr. Moley went along with suitcases filled with books and memoranda. After election he went back to his classes at Columbia. Then suddenly in mid-November, newspaper editors began searching furiously for information about him. Mr. Roosevelt had just announced that Mr. Moley would be his sole companion on his visit to the White House to discuss war debts and other world affairs with President Hoover. The announcement fell like a bombshell on important institutions in Wall Street. Private investigation confirmed their worst fears. As a realist he might (and did) realize that the war debt problem had to be dealt with, but his understanding of economics did not coincide with that of our best advertised thinkers. About that time a prominent lady telephoned Mr. Moley to congratulate him on his sudden accession to fame and influence and to rejoice with him that the war debts were about to be canceled. She had an idea for making the process of cancellation so complicated that it would be invisible to the great masses of the people. After talking to her awhile, Professor Moley had one of his periodical explosions. "Madam, I don't know what you are, but I am an American citizen," he said, and hung up the receiver.

With the return from Europe of Norman H. Davis and the drive from Wall Street to wedge him into Mr. Roosevelt's inner circle the attacks on Moley were redoubled. In some of the journals responsive to the financial center one read repeatedly that Mr. Davis had replaced Mr. Moley as Mr. Roosevelt's chief consultant. The record of Mr. Moley's writings and verbal utterances was raked for damaging material, but with very little result. He had never said anything very radical or very startling. Mr. Davis's reports on the current state of Europe and especially his knowledge of the disarmament problem were welcomed by Mr. Roosevelt. But Professor Moley, ably abetted by Dr. Tugwell, remained in full charge of the preparations for the economic conference, and the war debt problem remained securely in the control of Mr. Roosevelt and Mr. Moley.

During the interregnum nobody was busier than Professor Moley in preparing for the launching of the new régime. When the new administration moved in, he was established in the State Department, in quarters conveniently near the White House executive offices. Early every

morning he was at the White House for a bedside conference with the President. During the day he was back and
forth between the White House and State Department
half a dozen times. At night his quarters in the Carlton
Hotel were besieged. There were few important laws,
few important policies adopted, to which he did not contribute a hand or a word. Meanwhile he bore the main
brunt of the work of preparing for the conversations with
visiting statesmen and the World Economic Conference.
Yet, throughout the exhausting turmoil of those spring
months, he continued to return to New York every Thursday to lecture to his classes at Barnard. A visiting British
statesman, a firm believer in the virtues of the long British
week-end, was aghast at Moley's pace. Mr. Moley explained: "I know of no scientific proof that all work and
no play makes Jack a dull boy."

In Washington, Mr. Moley sought the companionship
of practical politicians as much as of his old friends in
the brains trust. He did not like to be called "Professor"
and he was quick to insist that there was no longer a
brains trust. "I have a job and am trying to do it," he
asserted stoutly. To accusations that he was a theorist
he could reply: "I am essentially a conservative fellow,"
or "I tilt at no windmills." He professed keen admiration
for such practical politicians as James A. Farley, Edward
J. Flynn, and Senator Joseph T. Robinson.

"Practical politics is dependent upon ability to guess
accurately which way to act," Mr. Moley once said. And
it was easy to see in Washington that he was attempting
to assess the intangibles of practical politics as accurately
as the cold facts of economics. Mr. Moley, however, was
no match for the incomparable Mr. Roosevelt as a politician and divining rod of public psychology. And while

Mr. Roosevelt's temperamental equipment for the strain of public life is miraculously good, Mr. Moley's is extraordinarily bad. Mr. Moley's quiet drawl and dry humor hint at a serene person. At many critical moments he was a firm sedative for excited colleagues. In his earlier days he said that social workers made him weary "because they have no sense of humor." But Moley's usually calm exterior is only a thin crust over a volcano. He explodes frequently. In his Cleveland days two hold-up men pointing revolvers at him made him so angry that he beat them up. In Washington he often seemed on the verge of meting out the same treatment to his adversaries in argument. When he had several days without a face-to-face explosion, he exploded in the privacy of his office to his secretaries. Sensitive and intense, he became extremely unhappy under a fierce critical battering. Lacking the craftiness of men more skilled in political warfare, he plunged along boldly, even recklessly, to the July morning that he found himself hailed as "the first casualty" of the new régime.

An explosion in the State Department seemed inevitable from the moment that Cordell Hull and Raymond Moley were put under the same roof. The career diplomats and the political appointees normally keep that department split into two camps. Into that hotbed was thrust Mr. Moley, who was neither a diplomat nor a politician. He might have been put on the payroll of the Treasury Department or almost anywhere else within easy distance of the White House. His job was to assist the President. The State Department was conveniently located and it was an appropriate place for him because he was in charge of preparations for the war debt discussions and the World Economic Conference. Mr. Moley sensed that his position would be embarrassing. He asked that his appointment as Assistant Secretary of State be announced as only temporary. When he was overruled, he asked newspapermen as a personal favor to say that he was to occupy the office only a few weeks.

If Raymond Moley had been possessed of any political wiles, he would have found a way to avoid going to the London Conference. The spectacle was much more amusing at a distance. It was zeal rather than ambition or vanity which took him to London. It was zeal for the Roosevelt Revolution and the policies which Mr. Roosevelt wanted to have advanced at London and too much faith in his enemies—which led him to the unpardonable indiscretion of committing to a cablegram a frank analysis of the delegation.

When he returned, the idea that he was in disgrace was enthusiastically exploited by all who were looking for his scalp. And that was an astonishingly large group of people, including several persons who had close contacts with the President, a large number of conservative Democrats, various miscellaneous individuals, and most of the vested interests in the country. At first there were some external signs of coolness around the White House. But Mr. Moley was soon a daily visitor again. There was plenty of important work for him to do outside the State Department, where he had never handled anything outside the economic field.

Then the plans for a weekly liberal magazine of popular appeal which Mr. Roosevelt and some of his friends had long been brewing suddenly came to a head. As the most publicized intellectual of the New Deal, Mr. Moley was the obvious man to edit this publication. And Vincent Astor, and his co-backers, W. Averell Harriman and

Mrs. Mary Rumsey, were willing to pay him a fat salary
to do it.

The Administration lost a modern Jacksonian liberal,
a sturdy nationalist, and a man who never forgot the
public interest. Mr. Moley, one suspects, was inwardly
relieved to get out of a maelstrom of intrigue and assault
and into a position in which he could express his honest
views without worrying about the personal or political
consequences.

Rexford G. Tugwell is the philosopher, the sociologist,
and the prophet of the Roosevelt Revolution, as well as
one of its boldest practitioners. He has provided the
movement with much of its rationale (to use one of his
favorite words). His broad picture of the whole scope of
the American experiment is unmarred by the tough realities of politics. He knows it and it does not perturb him.
He makes no pretense of being a practical politician, and
one senses that he would prefer never to be known as a
politician. While his more sensitive colleague, Mr. Moley,
strove to dissipate the idea that there was a brains trust,
Dr. Tugwell was obviously glad that there had been a
brains trust and was sorry that it was not a permanent
institution. While Mr. Moley's secretaries spoke of
"Mr." Moley, Dr. Tugwell's speak of "Dr." Tugwell.
The degree in both cases is Ph.D. Dr. Tugwell believes
that economists are needed to plot the course of the modern world and that the politicians' highest duty is to put
their ideas into effect. Dr. Tugwell is usually quite a distance ahead of Mr. Roosevelt in his exploration of the
potentialities of the new régime. In the vicinity of the
White House he is affectionately known as a "Bolshevik."
In 1932 it seemed very unlikely that the United States
would ever be anything like what Dr. Tugwell thought

it should be, but the rapid movements of 1933 began to
establish his place as a prophet. The country will probably never catch up with him, for as soon as Dr. Tugwell
gets his bearings on a new set of realities he projects
lines farther into the future. Forty-two, handsome, poised,
he has enjoyed himself to the utmost in Washington, for
even in the thick of action he has never lost the calm
aloofness of an observer.

Dr. Tugwell was born in Sinclairville in the fruit-raising
district of western New York. His father owned a cannery and a farm, but Dr. Tugwell has never been known
to claim practical experience as a farmer on the basis of
his boyhood practice in picking apples and watching cows.
Chosen to be a director of an unprecedented experiment
in controlling the production of cotton, wheat, and hogs,
his own preference in foods is for delicacies. He is a
gourmet and accomplished in the concoction of rare
salads. Dr. Tugwell attended high school in Buffalo and
the Wharton School of Finance and Commerce at the
University of Pennsylvania, where he remained until he
had three degrees. He taught economics at Pennsylvania
and Washington for brief periods before going to Columbia. He thought the orthodox textbooks on economics
boring and unreal. In 1924, he and two of his colleagues,
Messrs. Munro and Stryker, published a symposium entitled *American Economic Life*. For dull tables of statistics they substituted pictures of the contemporary world
in its economic aspects: of a striker being beaten by police
for coal and iron companies, and of Douglas Fairbanks
labeled a member of "the higher income class." Two
years later Dr. Tugwell published *Industry's Coming of
Age*, with a prefatory indictment of the teaching of orthodox economics for continuing to "concentrate largely on

the conceptual statements of a theory inherited from an old tradition."

Dr. Tugwell mingled freely with Socialists of the League of Industrial Democracy and the Civil Liberties Union. In the summer of 1927 he spent two months in Soviet Russia with a delegation of American trade unionists and intellectuals. He wrote the chapter on Russian agriculture for the symposium that came out of that expedition. The discovery that Dr. Tugwell had visited Russia was exploited to the utmost by the die-hards in Congress when they first saw the revolutionary farm bill at the special session of 1933. It happened that Dr. Tugwell's chapter on Russian agriculture had been realistic and rather critical of the agricultural policies of the Soviet régime. The audacity and determination behind the great Russian experiment stirred him. But he became neither a Socialist nor a Communist. Instead, he wrote for *The New Republic*.

Dr. Tugwell was convinced that the great American economic machine needed thorough remodeling but he was no less convinced that the plans for the new machine could not be found in imported creeds. Neither did he believe in forcible revolution. In his book *The Industrial Discipline*, he wrote: "I have never found myself greatly in sympathy with the revolutionary tactic. 'Force never settles anything' has always seemed to me a sufficient axiom. It is my reading of history that reconstruction is about as difficult after a revolutionary debacle as it would have been in a process of gradual substitution."

To Dr. Tugwell we owe the useful differentiation of a modern liberal from a radical: "Liberals would like to rebuild the station while the trains are running; radicals

prefer to blow up the station and forgo service until the
new structure is built."

Dr. Tugwell's winter experience in trying to get the
farm bill through the lame duck Congress reinforced his
conviction that he was not cut out to be a politician, and
until about a week before March 4 he stubbornly refused
to take the post of Assistant Secretary of Agriculture. He
finally consented to go to Washington temporarily until
the farm experiment had been launched. He was delighted
to put on Mr. Wallace's shoulders the wearing task of
handling Congressmen and farm leaders. Dr. Tugwell's
activities were by no means confined to the farm experiment and preparations for the World Economic Conference. He was summoned to such varied services as explaining the banking bill to Congressmen, assisting in drafting
the National Recovery Act, and preparing a plan for a
stable dollar.

In nearly every situation, Dr. Tugwell is the advocate
of bold and drastic action. The public works program was
far too small to please him. When speculators went on
their spring spree, he would have closed the stock and
commodity exchanges. He demonstrated what he meant
by thoroughness by having two professors draft a Pure
Foods and Drugs bill which paralyzed with fright every
food and drug lobbyist in Washington.

While his colleague, Professor Berle, pleads for a new
order of business men inspired by higher ethics, Dr. Tugwell does not expect business men to be different from
what they are until the system in which they operate is
changed. When others have seen repentant industrialists
and financiers eagerly co-operating in the creation of a
new era, Dr. Tugwell has seen only a lot of badly scared

men who will return to their old habits as soon as they dare. At the conference table, Dr. Tugwell is a tenacious fighter, but he emerges apparently unruffled. While men around him have dropped from fatigue and let their nervous systems be frazzled to the breaking point, Dr. Tugwell, cool and philosophical, has enjoyed himself hugely.

When the name of Professor Adolf Augustus Berle, Jr., first appeared on the roll of the brains trust, many people thought he was his father, whose career as a Congregational minister and scholar is traceable in *Who's Who in America*. The younger Berle had not attained sufficient fame to be listed among the thousands of learned men in that volume. However, his remarkable intellect and his ability as a lawyer and economist were known and freely acknowledged in discriminating circles. Before the end of 1932, his book, written with Gardiner C. Means, *The Modern Corporation and Private Property*, established him in the front rank of contemporary analysts and thinkers.

At 38, Mr. Berle is a former "infant prodigy" who has not ceased to be a prodigy. He went through Harvard in three years and was graduated with honors at seventeen. At 21 he had his LL.B. from Harvard Law School. He worked for a time in the law office of Louis D. Brandeis. During the war his service as an army intelligence officer took him into the Caribbean, and he added the sugar business, Latin-American law, and Caribbean politics and sociology to the subjects on which he was later recognized as an expert. At 24 he went to the Peace Conference as an assistant to Frank Howard Lord, American High Commissioner to Poland, in the redrafting of the eastern frontier of Germany. He thought the solution incorporated in the draft Treaty was indefensible. He resigned and came home to begin the practice of law in New York City. Through his father he had known Lillian Wald since childhood and he began active work at the Henry Street Settlement. He also became interested in the welfare of the Indians and defended their rights in several law suits. His main line of legal work, however, gradually carried him into accepted channels for a respectable and ambitious young corporation lawyer in New York City. He became an active Republican. His marriage relieved him of financial cares. While continuing his law practice he lectured at the Harvard School of Business for a time, then joined the staff of the Columbia Law School.

Professor Berle's short and slender figure is a concentrate of nervous and intellectual energy. Among the original membership of the brains trust, he was the brilliant lawyer, the most thorough analytical economist, a master of prose, and a bit of a moralist. He is not lacking in self-assurance but at times he listens with every appearance of respectful attention to the long dissertations of economists, business men, and lawyers who have not a fraction of his ability. At other times, he is annoyed, and he shows it. During Mr. Roosevelt's presidential campaign he made himself an expert on federal finances, railroad rehabilitation, banking, and control of corporations. He contributed "industrial cannon fodder" and other striking phrases and was the chief draftsman of the manifesto of the New Deal, the Commonwealth Club speech. At the short Congressional session of the winter of 1932–33, he helped to write the Bankruptcy Act.

Professor Berle could have had an important official post in the new Administration, but he preferred to be free to continue his teaching and the practice of law. Nevertheless, he spent two or three days a week in Washington during the first phase of the revolution. His presence was distressing to many of the Democratic lawyers, who, having helped to elect Mr. Roosevelt, had arrived in Washington to reap their reward in handsome legal fees as representatives of banks, corporations, and other business interests. Professor Berle seemed to have some of the clients best able to pay. The legal fraternity could not quite believe that one of their own would consider it unethical to take advantage of his standing in high places by accepting fat retainers. It developed, however, that Mr. Berle's work with the railroad executives and in helping a few large banks to reopen was as a representative of the Administration and that he received no fee.

Mr. Roosevelt made Mr. Berle special adviser to the Reconstruction Finance Corporation. There Mr. Berle tried to make sense out of prodigal loans to railroads to pay off their bankers and meet interest payments on over-capitalized corporate structures. He endeavored to use the government's position as a creditor to hasten the essential co-ordination of the railroad industry. Some of the railroad executives and financiers were flabbergasted —or pretended to be—by his suggestions. The mentality of many railroad executives is not geared to the New Deal, and reorganizations and mergers without huge profits to private bankers violate the fundamental code of Wall Street, even though they may benefit security owners.

The Agricultural Adjustment Administration sought Mr. Berle as its legal counsel during hearings on a sugar agreement. Mr. Berle's finicky sense of ethics led him to refuse on the ground that he was counsel to the American

Molasses Company, which had relations with the sugar business. The NRA was already staffed with business men and labor leaders who felt no hesitation in serving because of their special interests. Excepting Mr. Berle, all the lawyers with knowledge of sugar appeared to be employed by the big producing interests, the refineries, or the Wall Street sugar banks. Mr. Berle was finally persuaded that the AAA had no qualms about his ability to ignore the minor interests of his private client. The sugar producers and refiners found him as exacting as the railroads had. He threw their first proposals out the window. The refiners accused him of prejudice in favor of Cuban refining interests. The inclusion of Cuba in an American closed sugar area was the basic point in the Administration's program for the rehabilitation of Cuba. Early in September Mr. Roosevelt sent Mr. Berle on a temporary mission to Cuba as financial adviser to the U.S. Embassy. He arrived just as the second revolution broke out, spent a few futile days there, and returned to Washington.

During the hundred-day session of Congress, Mr. Berle had a hand in such varied pieces of legislation as the Banking Act, the new Securities Act, and the National Recovery Act. When the banks were on the operating table during the moratorium, he would have done a thorough job of surgery. He was overruled. The Glass-Steagall Banking Act and the Securities Act were both disappointments to him, and he at once went to work to draft amendments or substitute bills to be presented to the 1934 session of Congress. In the summer of 1933, he helped to sift the various schemes for a commodity dollar. Mr. Berle clings doggedly to his hope that bankers and business men and lawyers will realize that restraint, higher standards of conduct, and a social point of view are imperative if the capitalistic régime is to survive, even in a modified form. In speeches to bankers he reminds them that in England it is supposed to be a high social offense for a banker to make a large personal fortune.

When Mr. Berle inserts his mind in a problem he pushes through until he has located the last isolated detail and put it in its proper place. He is able to draw back and get a bird's-eye view. His book with Mr. Means, *The Modern Corporation and Private Property*,[1] is based on the most elaborate studies that have been made of the growth of American corporations, but the masses of detail rise steadily to well-formed conclusions. In summing up, Messrs. Berle and Means wrote: "The rise of the modern corporation has brought a concentration of economic power which can compete on equal terms with the modern state—economic power versus political power, each strong in its own field. The state seeks in some aspects to regulate the corporation, while the corporation, steadily becoming more powerful, makes every effort to avoid such regulation. Where its own interests are concerned, it even attempts to dominate the state. The future may see the economic organism, now typified by the corporation, not only on an equal plane with the state, but possibly even superseding it as the dominant form of social organization. The law of corporations, accordingly, might well be considered as a potential constitutional law for the new economic state, while business practice is increasingly assuming the aspects of economic statesmanship."

These men—Moley, Tugwell, and Berle—are inseparable from the Roosevelt Revolution. No list of the six or eight most important architects and builders of the

---

[1] The Macmillan Company, 1933.

new régime would be valid without them. Next to Mr.
Roosevelt, Mr. Moley was the most important, in or
out of the Cabinet. With Messrs. Tugwell and Berle
would have to be ranked Mr. Douglas, chiefly because of
his restraining influence on certain occasions during the
first months; Louis Howe, in devious and indefinable
ways; Frances Perkins, Hugh S. Johnson, Harold L.
Ickes, and probably Henry A. Wallace and George N.
Peek. A line arbitrarily drawn there excludes many like
James A. Farley, who were important in the political
management, and others who, though farther removed
from the center of action, clearly understood the significance of the experiment.

Specialists and social scientists of liberal thought are
still being drawn into the government. Subsidiary brains
trusts have sprung up around every important experiment of the New Deal.

In the agricultural brains trust one finds: M. L. Wilson, who helped to show the world how to produce wheat
on a large scale and then had to invent a plan for reducing the wheat output; Mordecai Ezekiel, the brilliant
young economist and part author of the revolutionary
farm bill, who can demonstrate by logarithms how to
raise hogs; William I. Myers, former Professor of Farm
Finance at Cornell, the chief author of the Farm Mortgage Act, now Deputy Governor of the Farm Credit Administration; Herman Oliphant, former Professor of Law
at Johns Hopkins; Gardiner C. Means, Mr. Berle's associate at Columbia; Louis Bean and the staff of the Bureau
of Agricultural Economics; Howard E. Babcock, former
Professor of Marketing at Cornell; Dr. Frederic H.
Howe.

In the monetary brains trust may be found: O. M. W.

Sprague, former Professor of Banking and Finance at Harvard, whom Mr. Roosevelt took away from the Bank of England and installed as Special Assistant to the Secretary of the Treasury; Professor Warren of Cornell, one of the leading authorities on the commodity dollar; James H. Rogers, Professor of Political Economy at Yale, another currency specialist.

The National Recovery Administration brought together such men as: Alexander Sachs, who made a reputation by his accuracy in forecasting the course of the depression and then began charting the recovery; Leo Wolman, a member of the faculty of the New School for Social Research, and authority on labor problems; Earle Dean Howard, Professor of Economics at Northwestern.

Among the former academic men scattered here and there are: John Dickinson, former Professor of Law at the University of Pennsylvania, in the post of Assistant Secretary of Commerce; Isador Lubin, former Professor of Economics at the University of Missouri, installed as chief of the statistical division of the Department of Labor; W. M. W. Splawn, former Professor of Economics at the University of Texas, as adviser to the House Committee on Interstate Commerce and one of the leading assistants to Joseph B. Eastman in handling the railroad problem; Arthur E. Morgan, former President of Antioch College, as Chairman of the Board of the Tennessee Valley Authority; Harcourt A. Morgan, former Dean of the School of Agriculture of the University of Tennessee, as another member of the board of the Tennessee Valley Authority.

One could name twenty or more liberal lawyers in the Administration: Donald Richberg, Counsel to the NRA; Jerome Frank, Counsel to AAA; and many of Felix

Frankfurter's protégés. Mr. Frankfurter refused to accept the post of Solicitor General but he responded heartily to the invitation to suggest men to fill many of the legal posts. Mr. Roosevelt appointed a dozen or more men wholly or chiefly on Mr. Frankfurter's recommendation. Of these the most prominent are Dean G. Acheson, Under-Secretary of the Treasury, and David E. Lilienthal, the third member of the Tennessee Valley Authority, and Professor James Landis, former Professor at Harvard Law School, member of the Federal Trade Commission.

The men of the diffused brains trust represent many shades of thought and many specialities. In most of them two characteristics stand out: enthusiasm for the American experiment and unabating criticism of the course of its development. None of the easy optimism or pessimism of men accustomed to gauging the world by the stock market or the momentary profits or losses of their business is to be found in this group. Free competition in ideas and frank criticism are basic characteristics of the Roosevelt Administration. Probably never before in its history has the Federal Government found important rôles for so many men of fertile and courageous minds.

XI

The Next Phase

THE end of the first phase of the Roosevelt Revolution found the United States in rapid transition. The sense of national unity, forged from fright and bewilderment at near catastrophe, was beginning to weaken a little. The nation had moved far enough in new directions for different classes and groups to begin to form opinions about the effect, actual or probable, on their own interests. Impatience was asserting itself on every side. Various vested interests centering in high finance had seen enough to be sure that they wanted to turn back. The farmers were asserting their demand for higher prices in a way which was inimical to the immediate welfare of wage and salary earners. Wage earners, small business men, pensioners—all groups—were beginning to demand more vigorously that prompt and efficacious attention be given to their particular plights.

The command of the conservatives to "go back" began to manifest itself as soon as the upturn came in the spring of 1933. By autumn they began to prepare themselves for the Congressional campaign of 1934 with the cry: "Back to the Constitution." More philosophical conservatives strove to find reassurance in the emergency clauses in the laws authorizing the new experiments in economic relationships.

Most of the legislation passed at the special session of 1933 probably will prove to be temporary. It was hastily put together, and it was incomplete. The first trials of the new experiments brought out rather emphatically the need for enlargement and revision. The emergency clauses were no clue, however, to the probable future of any of the new statutes. They were generally recognized as a handy lubricant to ease the passage of novel legislation, first through Congress, but chiefly through the courts. In times of emergency, the courts have shown the greatest latitude in interpreting the Constitution. During the World War they countenanced the most violent departures from established law. The emergency of 1933 was no less real than the emergency of war and it may well continue for several years to come.

The obvious reluctance of the Administration to let its more drastic powers be carried to the Supreme Court in test cases could legitimately be used to support the assertion that the Administration knew these powers were unconstitutional. Probably a more accurate diagnosis would be that some of the best legal minds of the Administration were doubtful that the existing Supreme Court would hold these powers to be constitutional, even with the prefatory emergency clauses. Constitutionality is no hard and fast thing. The legislation of 1933 did not challenge the Constitution; it merely challenged economic practices which had been clothed with more or less constitutional authority by the Supreme Court over a long period of years. If the Supreme Court had been indubitably liberal in 1933, there might well have been fewer eloquent references to the emergency and perhaps less delay in court tests. Under the American political system, as it has worked out, powers to veto and to interpret, which are a final residue of sovereignty, rest in five men forming a majority of one in the Supreme Court. It is unnecessary and perhaps undesirable to assail the Supreme Court's assumed right to overrule Congress in the interpretation of the Federal Constitution. The Supreme Court has frequently sidestepped or reversed itself when the popular will to change has been emphatically registered. Nevertheless, it would be foolhardy to rely on the restraint or political temporizing of men who have shown themselves to be stalwart supporters of the old economic order.

Broadly speaking the American experiment required liberal interpretation of the interstate commerce and due process clauses and enlargement of the idea of a public utility. The Supreme Court has already gone a long way toward broadening the conception of the power of Congress to regulate interstate commerce. If Congress can prohibit or control practices which place a burden on interstate commerce or interfere with it, one important barrier to the stabilizing of the economic life of the country has been torn down. Intrastate commerce can then be brought under the same type of control—whatever it may be—as interstate business, or at least prevented from undermining such mechanisms for industrial stabilization as the nation finds that it needs. In defining a public utility the Supreme Court has been less liberal. And the due process clauses of the Fifth and Fourteenth Amendments are encrusted with hard economic doctrine which favors vested interests. Some of this crust will have to be knocked off if the American economic system is going to function within the framework of the Constitution.

No special training is needed to see that as a result of myriads of delicate interrelationships almost every part of the economic life of the nation is affected with the public interest that, in a simpler economy, was the peculiar attribute of a ferry-boat, or, later, of the railroad system.

The same type of judicial elaboration of the due process clauses which has made them what they are today certainly can sustain changes designed to correct an economic order which proved so singularly successful in depriving citizens of their property, and even of their means of livelihood, without due process of law. All that is needed is liberal and realistic intelligence to make the interpretation. The least that the American experiment has a right to expect of the courts is interpretation and correlation by men whose broad social philosophy is the same as the philosophy behind the experiment.

When Mr. Roosevelt came into office, the Supreme Court was in fairly even balance. The retirement of a couple of the elderly conservative justices would permit the balance in the Court to be swung over to the liberal side. If that should not eventuate, the appointment of two additional justices would accomplish the same purpose.

Possibly some of the young liberal lawyers in the Administration underestimated the common sense of the Supreme Court conservatives. Judicial destruction or gutting of the main experiments of the Roosevelt Revolution would be a hazardous responsibility for any man to assume while society was in a state of flux. When Chief Justice Hughes administered the oath to Mr. Roosevelt during the banking panic, the distinguished members of the Supreme Court had reasonable grounds for wondering whether they would ever get another pay check. The continued existence of the Supreme Court, like the continued existence of the rest of the political system, depends very largely on whether or not the revolutionary process now under way can be guided and kept more or less orderly.

The experimental attitude precludes any arbitrary classification of the ventures of the new régime under the headings, "temporary" and "permanent."

Mr. Roosevelt has used a football analogy to explain his mode of action. (It is characteristic that he turned to the sports field instead of the battleground.) He is the quarterback. He knows where the goal line is. At any given moment he can call the signal for the next play, but he cannot decide what the play after the next will be until he has seen whether the first play has resulted in a gain or a loss. This is the experimental attitude in action. It is a complete repudiation of the doctrinaire faith that a play will work with the beautiful precision and unfailing success which can be charted on the blackboard. It recognizes also that plays must be executed by men, so that even the most perfectly conceived play may fail through imperfect performance. It also implies that the quarterback may err in his judgment.

When Mr. Roosevelt went into action on March 4, he had a great many more plays in his head than the public generally realized. They included well-established tactics and daring innovations. During the plotting of the game, some of the more daring plays had been laid aside. Their quick use was dictated by the fact that when Mr. Roosevelt was thrown into the game the team was staggering and completely demoralized on its own goal line, if not behind it. Some of the plays conceived in advance were not needed or were too feeble for the kind of game that had to be played. Few of those which were used worked exactly as planned. No one could know the order in which the quarterback would call them. As the season wore on, old plays had to be modified in the light of experience and new plays improvised.

The continual invention and revision of tactics is indispensable to orderly change. Revision of legislation is merely part of that process. The 1933 special session of Congress facilitated the process by conferring enormous discretionary powers on the President. "Dictatorship" became a much-used word. Some of the left-wing radicals preferred "Fascist dictatorship" or "Fascism."

The powers delegated to the President were of tremendous scope—beyond peacetime precedent. But there was no seizure of power. Authority was willingly, even eagerly, delegated. While many of the powers were broad, limits were placed on them and the purposes of their uses were defined. Furthermore, they can be taken back by Congress at any time. The kinds of powers conferred on the President fall into two broad classes. One class consists of the uncontested powers of Congress. The powers over the budget and over currency fall into this category. The other class consists of powers which the Federal Government has heretofore not attempted to assert in peacetime. They are found chiefly in the AAA and the NRA. In both cases, the President is acting as an agent of Congress. Congress could delegate the same authorities to independent agencies of the type of the Interstate Commerce Commission.

The Roosevelt Revolution certainly is not "Fascism" nor is it headed toward Fascism; though, if it fails, it might easily be followed by Fascism. Mr. Roosevelt compelled the big-moneyed interests to do an about-face with their propaganda. In 1932 they began to talk cautiously about the need for a dictatorship; something had to be done to save them—and, of course, the country—from Congress, which, as it happened, was reflecting the intense discontent of the country as a whole in an emphatic, if not too intelligent and orderly manner. Hence the widespread propaganda for conferring broad powers on the Executive, beginning with the power to balance the budget. A year later the vested interests had another chant: "Back to the Constitution," with "Back to the Gold Standard" as an encore. The "dictatorial" powers conferred on the President were the wrong kind, or he was using them in the wrong way. At least something was wrong.

The current experiment involves no departure from democratic government. The real essence of democracy, no less than the formalities as prescribed by the Constitution, has been scrupulously preserved. Freedom of assemblage and the right to petition—to wit Mr. Roosevelt's handling of the second bonus army—have been diligently protected. Free expression of opinion has not only been protected, but has been encouraged. The Roosevelt Administration has taken the public into its confidence as few administrations have done before. The doors have been thrown open to all who seek information or who have ideas to present. By his free discussions with the press and his radio addresses, Mr. Roosevelt has converted the nation into a modern version of the Athenian forum. He has revivified and used simple democracy, expressed through public opinion, to bring pressure on the people's chosen representatives in Congress and on their self-appointed guardians in the economic world.

The Roosevelt Revolution is democracy trying to create out of American materials an economic system which will work with reasonable satisfaction to the great majority of citizens. The nomenclature of political science has been ransacked for a suitable name for the economic system which is the apparent goal of the Roosevelt Revolution.

Regulated capitalism, state capitalism, disciplined democracy, a co-operative state, guild socialism—these and
many other names have been suggested. Henry A. Wallace has used "a balanced social state." As good a phrase
as any is Mr. Roosevelt's, "an economic constitutional
order."

The variety of suggested phrases testifies to the in-
adequacy of the terminology of imported radical thought
or of the current experiments abroad to describe the
American experiment. Certain similarities may be seen in
the methods to which other nations have resorted in the
effort to reconstruct their own broken-down social systems. In their most elementary forms the weaknesses of
capitalism universally assert themselves, but the peculiarities of the American problem are of vital importance.

No other nation has reached so advanced a stage of
industrial development and at the same time continued to
produce a generous surplus of nearly all kinds of raw materials, including foodstuffs. No other nation faced the
paradox of poverty in the midst of plenty in so glaring
a form. The other highly industrialized nations have no
such wealth or variety of raw materials and are dependent
for foodstuffs either on imports or the intensive cultivation of their own soil. The other great raw-materials
nations are merely in the early stages of industrial development. In no nation outside the United States have
the ideals of individual initiative and free competition
been so enshrined. The United States slowly began to
realize that individual initiative and free competition,
when given full play, threaten the extinction of both. In
no nation outside the United States could a prodigious
and mounting surplus-producing power and the long-
cultivated belief that it is in the power of every man to

become a millionaire combine to create such a speculative boom as that which preceded the depression. One could go on listing the peculiarities of the American problem. The important point is that there are many of them of very great importance. The first experiments of the Roosevelt administration are American inventions, devised with those peculiarities in mind.

The ultimate objective of the revolution is a stable economic system, and that objective cannot be reached without the creation of the machinery for distributing the vast production of which we are capable. The task is gigantic because the potential surplus which can be produced is so huge. The attack on the problem has hardly begun. A new perspective is revealed in the realization that the farmer must be enabled to buy and in the first steps toward the substitution of labor for capital as the fixed charge against industry. Probably a great many devices will have to be used to prevent the accumulation of capital which cannot be put to work and to achieve the most equitable distribution of the national income. Among the devices which are already at hand is the power of taxation. Higher taxes on profits and large income, especially income from invested capital, and higher inheritance taxes are crude instruments for this redistribution. If the income of labor is adequately protected, competition, itself, can serve in some lines to prevent the piling up of stagnant capital. In all probability, an increasing part of the national income will have to be skimmed off by the government and spent on public works and social improvements.

The money-accumulating motive can still be utilized. The feed-bag can be dangled in front of the capitalistic horse; he may sniff at it and perhaps be allowed an occasional appetizing mouthful, but he must never be permitted to get his head sunk deep in the bag. The poor animal only knows that when he was a young and lusty colt the contents of the feed-bag made him grow. He isn't aware that if he persists in his coltish habits the only result will be an acute case of indigestion leading to his early death.

The difficulties of regulating the capitalistic system of distribution so that it will work adequately are so formidable that it may prove necessary to seek a partial escape in the return of some of the population of the country to a simpler form of economy. Several states have encouraged the placement of unemployed workers on subsistence homesteads, and the Federal Government is undertaking an experiment in the same line. The subsistence homestead is a slightly artificial reopening of the frontier. Carried a little farther, by the decentralization of industry, so that the homesteader can earn at least a small cash crop in the form of wages, this remedy becomes more attractive. It may not result in the maximum production of wealth of which the country is capable, but it is one road to greater stability and perhaps to a pleasant form of living.

The far-reaching readjustments which have to be made in the United States cannot be completed quickly. A great many people must necessarily be badly hurt in the process. High finance, vested wealth—whatever one wishes to call it—will have to surrender more than it may be expected to surrender without a fight. The export farmer is confronted with the unpleasant fact that for all practical purposes there is a large overproduction of several basic crops. Labor has to face the facts of technological advance. It has been estimated that at the 1929 production level the nation would now have 7,000,000 unemployed, due to technological improvements during the depression years.

The revolutionary process probably will continue until a crude state of equilibrium is reached which satisfies the groups which are best able to assert their power. Or, it will fly apart, leaving the field open for a free-for-all fight. Someone has said that the American experiment is a revolution with shock absorbers. The danger is that the shock absorbers will be knocked off. It would be hazardous to venture a forecast. Various forces may lead us to return to the easy solution of the problem of distributing our surplus—by scattering it as largesse over the world. That might postpone some of our problems for a few years. A good-sized European war might be helpful. We would probably find ourselves unable to resist the temptation to furnish the materials for it. Barring these eventualities, it seems unlikely that the impelling forces of change in the nation will soon subside.

In fact, the bulk of the evidence at the close of the first phase of the Roosevelt Revolution indicates that the pace of the change will be accelerated. Far more radical and more drastic measures may have to be used to reach the joint objective of recovery and reconstruction. Recovery without reconstruction of the economic system is probably impossible (barring the eventualities mentioned above, or the sudden development of a new "ladder" industry) and even if it were possible it would be evanescent. Mr. Roosevelt probably will have to use greater force to drive those facts into the heads of the vested interests of the old régime. By doing so, he would do a kindness. There may be a few individuals in the big property-owning and property-controlling classes who would rather gamble for their heads in a general debacle. For each one of this type there are probably hundreds who would prefer to have a measure of peace and security for themselves and their descendants. Like their forerunners in many old régimes that have crashed into the abyss, most of these people are well-meaning but unintelligent.

Mr. Roosevelt took office at the very moment that the old system was crumbling to the ground. He propped it up and began remodeling operations. The useful portions of the old structure have to be kept propped up while the remodeling is being done. There is bound to be the sharpest divergence of opinion concerning the proper form for the new structure. Some of our capitalists are insisting that either they must have the penthouse all to themselves or they will go back to the old hotel, which their nearsighted vision deludes them into thinking is still in existence. The farmers want accommodations for all their grain and cotton and livestock, and there isn't enough room.

The choices before the nation when Mr. Roosevelt came into office were chaotic social upheaval, a big business dictatorship along Fascist lines, or an orderly readjustment within the framework of democratic institutions. As the Roosevelt Revolution reached the end of its first phase, the choices remained unaltered. Orderly readjustment by democratic methods may turn out to be impossible of achievement; Mr. Roosevelt may turn out to be the Kerensky of the Revolution. However, Mr. Roosevelt is a far abler man than most of the figures who have been thrown up in the transitional periods of history. His extraordinary accomplishments in seven months support the belief that orderly revolution is feasible. His success depends very largely on keeping the middle classes, espe-

cially the farmers, and labor moving down the road together. If the Roosevelt Revolution fails, it will go down
in history as a magnificent failure. If it succeeds, it will
be a remarkable manifestation of the capacity of democratic government to solve the problems of the new industrial age.